House of MYSTERY

ROOM & BOREDOM

MATTHEW STURGES & BILL WILLINGHAM WRITERS

LUCA RÓSSI ARTIST

LEE LOUGHRIDGE COLORIST   TODD KLEIN LETTERER

SAM WEBER   BERNIE WRIGHTSON

ESAO ANDREWS ORIGINAL SERIES COVERS

ROSS CAMPBELL   JILL THOMPSON   ZACHARY BALDUS
STEVE ROLSTON   SEAN MURPHY SHORT STORY ARTISTS
DAVE MCCAIG SHORT STORY COLORIST

KAREN BERGER • SENIOR VP-EXECUTIVE EDITOR

SHELLY BOND & ANGELA RUFINO • CO-EDITORS-ORIGINAL SERIES

SCOTT NYBAKKEN • EDITOR-COLLECTED EDITION

ROBBIN BROSTERMAN • SENIOR ART DIRECTOR

PAUL LEVITZ • PRESIDENT & PUBLISHER

GEORG BREWER • VP-DESIGN & DC DIRECT CREATIVE

RICHARD BRUNING • SENIOR VP-CREATIVE DIRECTOR

PATRICK CALDON • EXECUTIVE VP-FINANCE & OPERATIONS

CHRIS CARAMALIS • VP-FINANCE

JOHN CUNNINGHAM • VP-MARKETING

TERRI CUNNINGHAM • VP-MANAGING EDITOR

AMY GENKINS • SENIOR VP-BUSINESS & LEGAL AFFAIRS

ALISON GILL • VP-MANUFACTURING

DAVID HYDE • VP-PUBLICITY

HANK KANALZ • VP-GENERAL MANAGER, WILDSTORM

JIM LEE • EDITORIAL DIRECTOR-WILDSTORM

GREGORY NOVECK • SENIOR VP-CREATIVE AFFAIRS

SUE POHJA • VP-BOOK TRADE SALES

STEVE ROTTERDAM • SENIOR VP-SALES & MARKETING

CHERYL RUBIN • SENIOR VP-BRAND MANAGEMENT

ALYSSE SOLL • VP-ADVERTISING & CUSTOM PUBLISHING

JEFF TROJAN • VP-BUSINESS DEVELOPMENT, DC DIRECT

BOB WAYNE • VP-SALES

COVER ILLUSTRATION BY SAM WEBER.
PUBLICATION DESIGN BY AMELIA GROHMAN.

HOUSE OF MYSTERY: ROOM AND BOREDOM

DC COMICS, 1700 BROADWAY, NEW YORK, NY 10019
A WARNER BROS. ENTERTAINMENT COMPANY.
PRINTED IN THE USA. 5-19-10. SECOND PRINTING. ISBN: 978-1-4012-2079-2

SUSTAINABLE FORESTRY INITIATIVE

Certified Fiber Sourcing

www.sfiprogram.org

Fiber used in this product line meets the sourcing requireme
of the SFI program. www.sfiprogram.org PWC-SFICOC-260

Issue #1 cover art by Sam Weber.

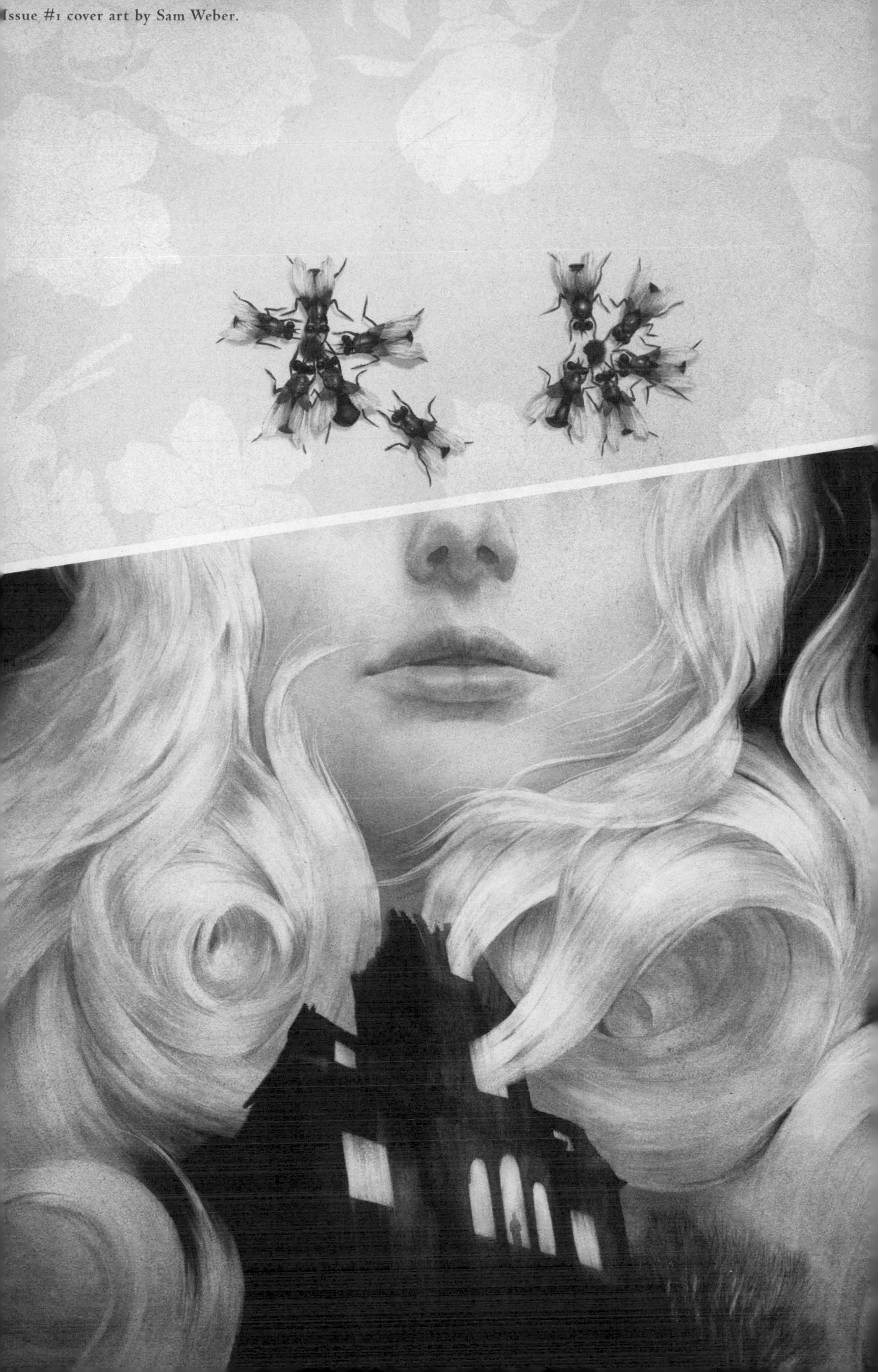

Issue #1 variant cover art by Bernie Wrightson.

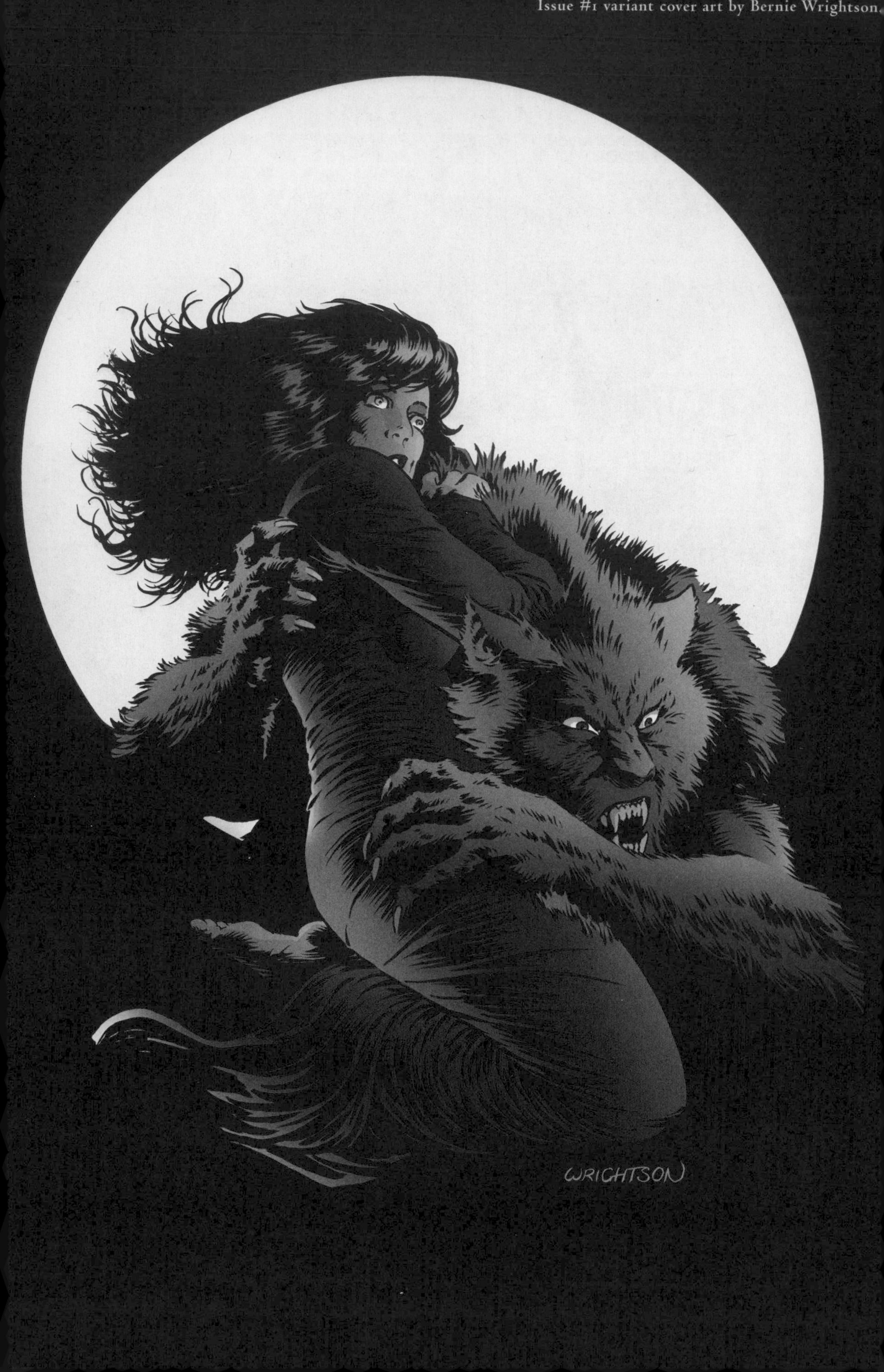
WRIGHTSON

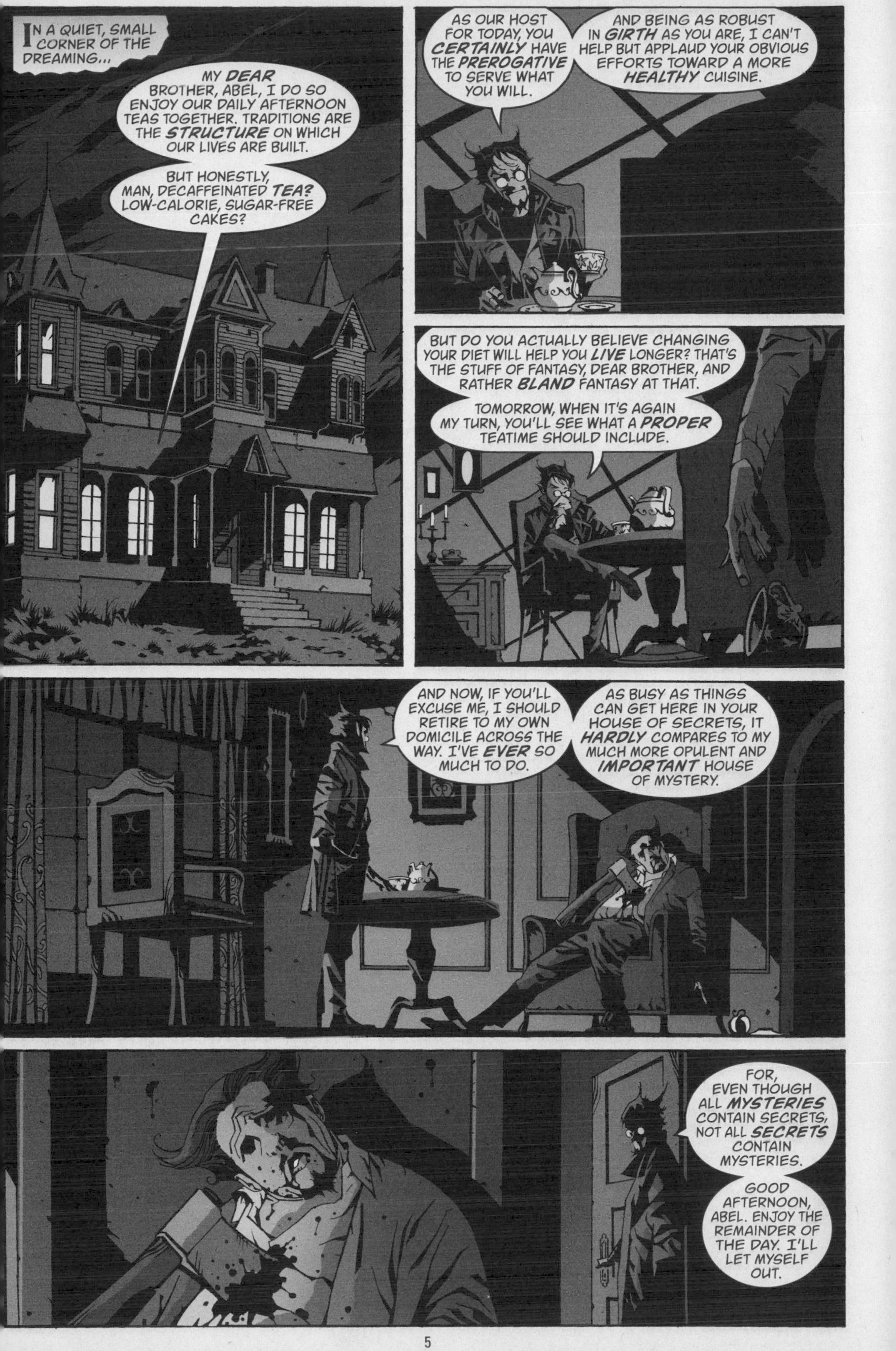
IN A QUIET, SMALL CORNER OF THE DREAMING...
MY DEAR BROTHER, ABEL, I DO SO ENJOY OUR DAILY AFTERNOON TEAS TOGETHER. TRADITIONS ARE THE STRUCTURE ON WHICH OUR LIVES ARE BUILT.
BUT HONESTLY, MAN, DECAFFEINATED TEA? LOW-CALORIE, SUGAR-FREE CAKES?
AS OUR HOST FOR TODAY, YOU CERTAINLY HAVE THE PREROGATIVE TO SERVE WHAT YOU WILL.
AND BEING AS ROBUST IN GIRTH AS YOU ARE, I CAN'T HELP BUT APPLAUD YOUR OBVIOUS EFFORTS TOWARD A MORE HEALTHY CUISINE.
BUT DO YOU ACTUALLY BELIEVE CHANGING YOUR DIET WILL HELP YOU LIVE LONGER? THAT'S THE STUFF OF FANTASY, DEAR BROTHER, AND RATHER BLAND FANTASY AT THAT.
TOMORROW, WHEN IT'S AGAIN MY TURN, YOU'LL SEE WHAT A PROPER TEATIME SHOULD INCLUDE.
AND NOW, IF YOU'LL EXCUSE ME, I SHOULD RETIRE TO MY OWN DOMICILE ACROSS THE WAY. I'VE EVER SO MUCH TO DO.
AS BUSY AS THINGS CAN GET HERE IN YOUR HOUSE OF SECRETS, IT HARDLY COMPARES TO MY MUCH MORE OPULENT AND IMPORTANT HOUSE OF MYSTERY.
FOR, EVEN THOUGH ALL MYSTERIES CONTAIN SECRETS, NOT ALL SECRETS CONTAIN MYSTERIES.
GOOD AFTERNOON, ABEL. ENJOY THE REMAINDER OF THE DAY. I'LL LET MYSELF OUT.

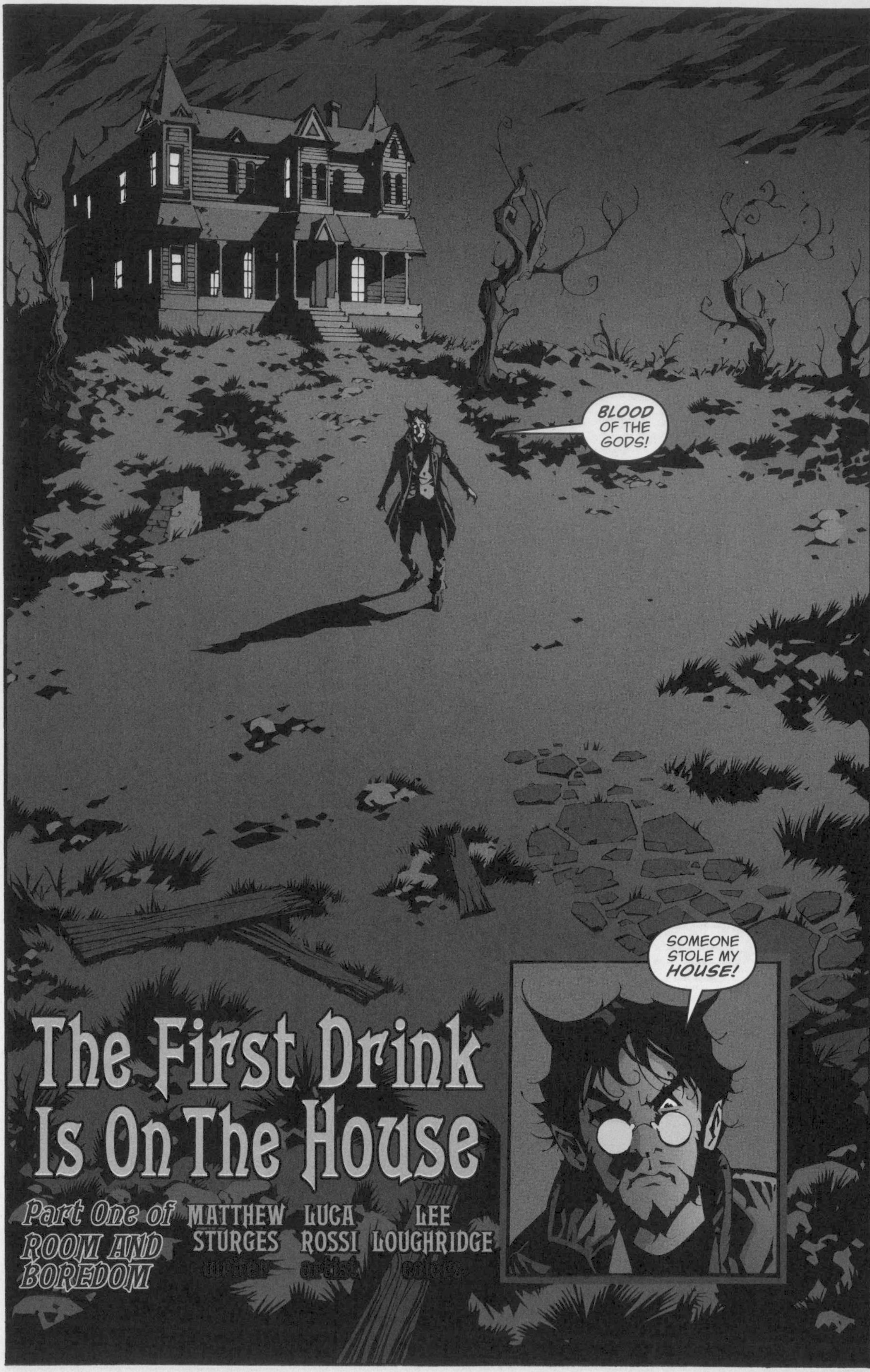
BLOOD OF THE GODS!
SOMEONE STOLE MY HOUSE!
The First Drink Is On The House
Part One of ROOM AND BOREDOM
MATTHEW STURGES
LUCA ROSSI
artist
LEE LOUGHRIDGE

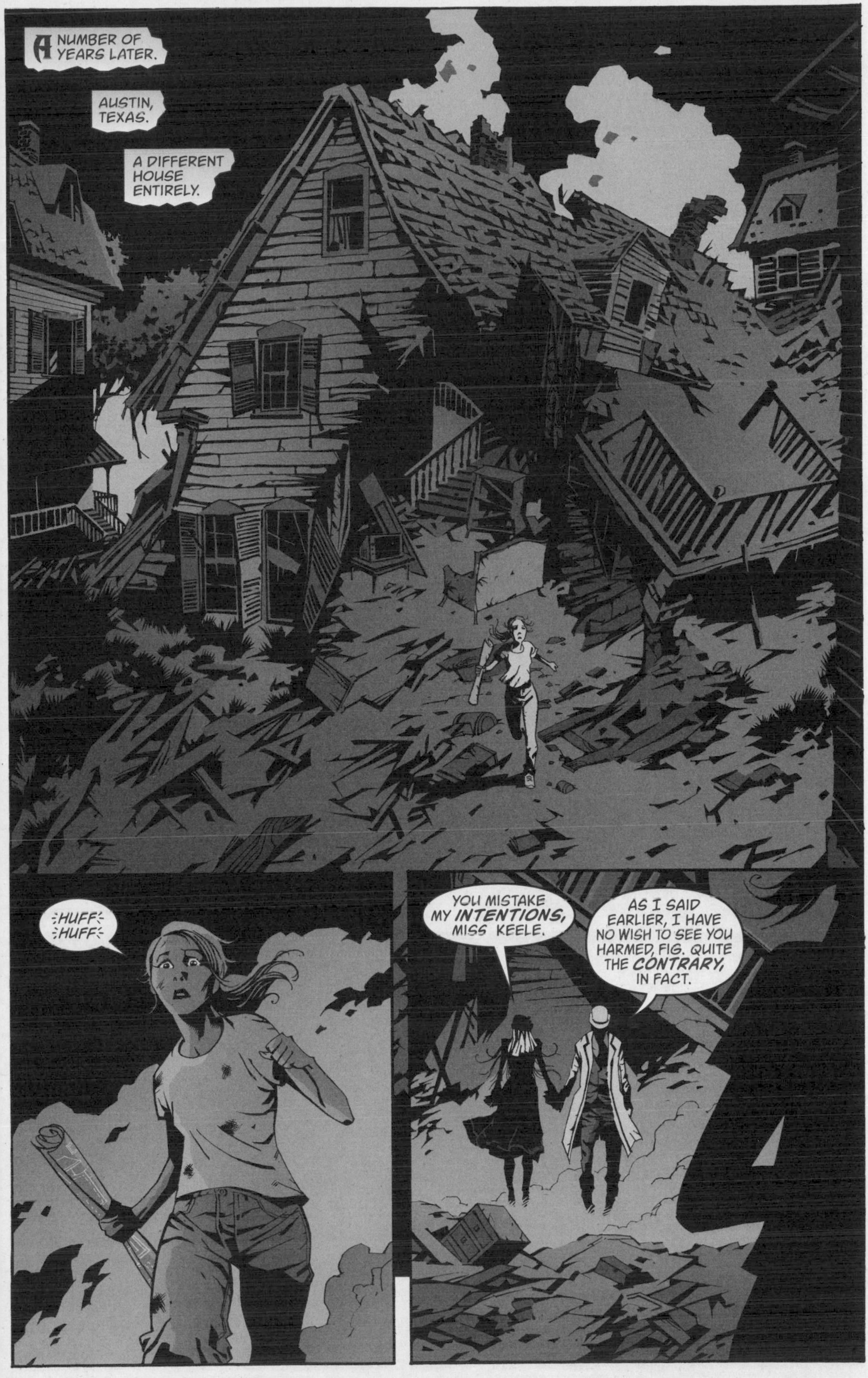
A NUMBER OF YEARS LATER.
AUSTIN, TEXAS.
A DIFFERENT HOUSE ENTIRELY.
HUFF HUFF
YOU MISTAKE MY INTENTIONS, MISS KEELE.
AS I SAID EARLIER, I HAVE NO WISH TO SEE YOU HARMED, FIG. QUITE THE CONTRARY, IN FACT.

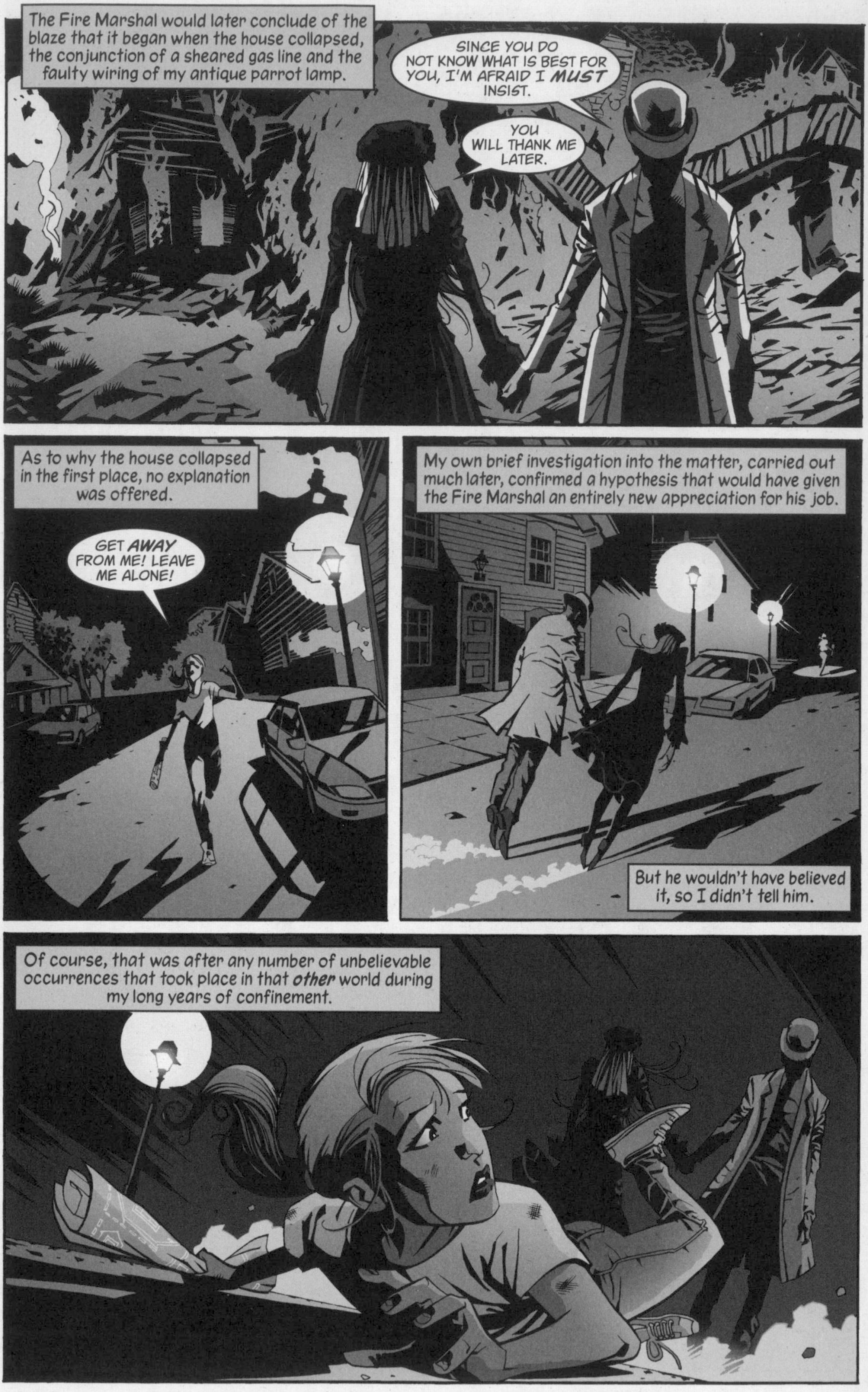
The Fire Marshal would later conclude of the blaze that it began when the house collapsed, the conjunction of a sheared gas line and the faulty wiring of my antique parrot lamp.
SINCE YOU DO NOT KNOW WHAT IS BEST FOR YOU, I'M AFRAID I *MUST* INSIST.
YOU WILL THANK ME LATER.
As to why the house collapsed in the first place, no explanation was offered.
GET *AWAY* FROM ME! LEAVE ME ALONE!
My own brief investigation into the matter, carried out much later, confirmed a hypothesis that would have given the Fire Marshal an entirely new appreciation for his job.
But he wouldn't have believed it, so I didn't tell him.
Of course, that was after any number of unbelievable occurrences that took place in that *other* world during my long years of confinement.

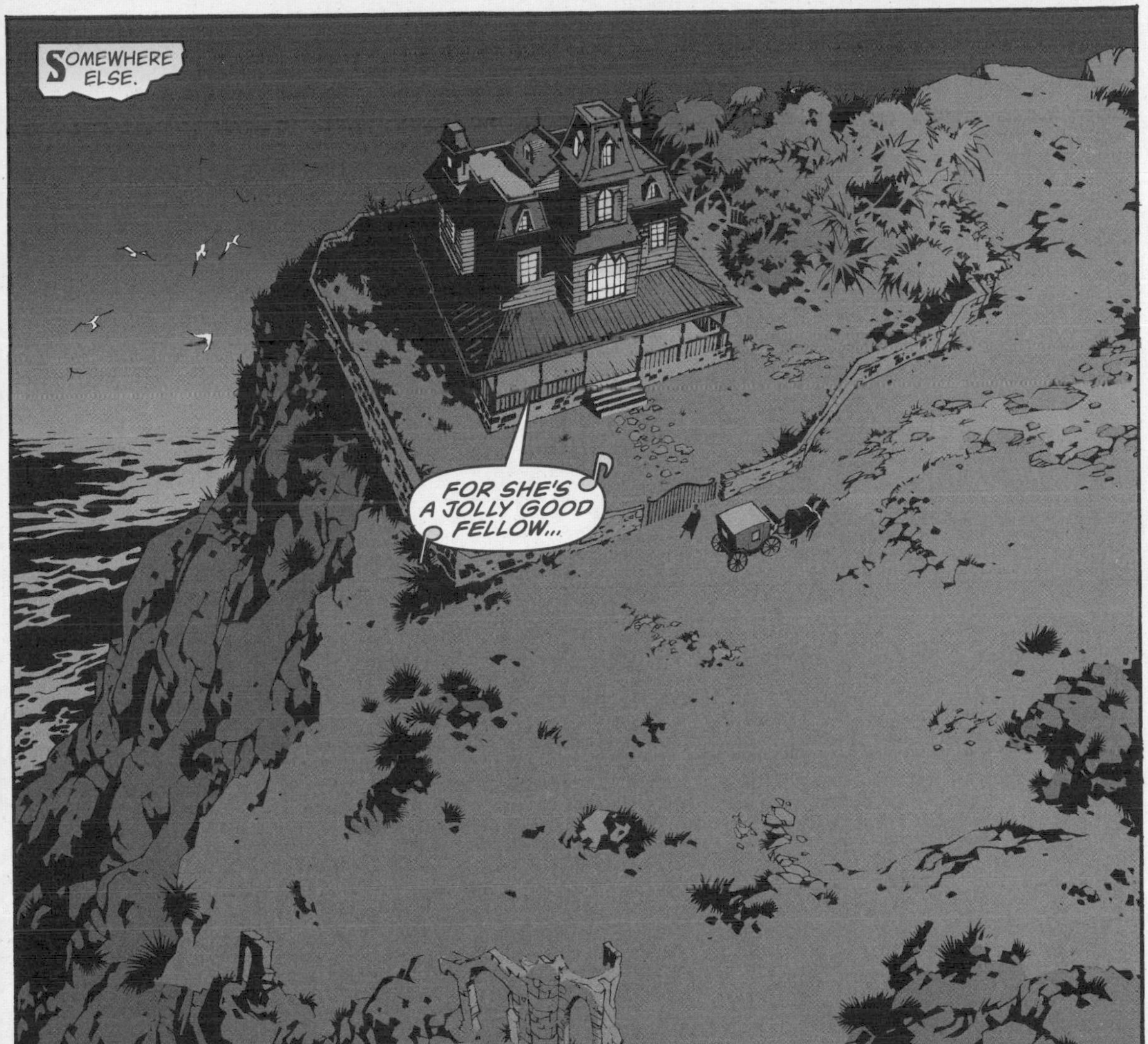
SOMEWHERE ELSE.
FOR SHE'S A JOLLY GOOD FELLOW...

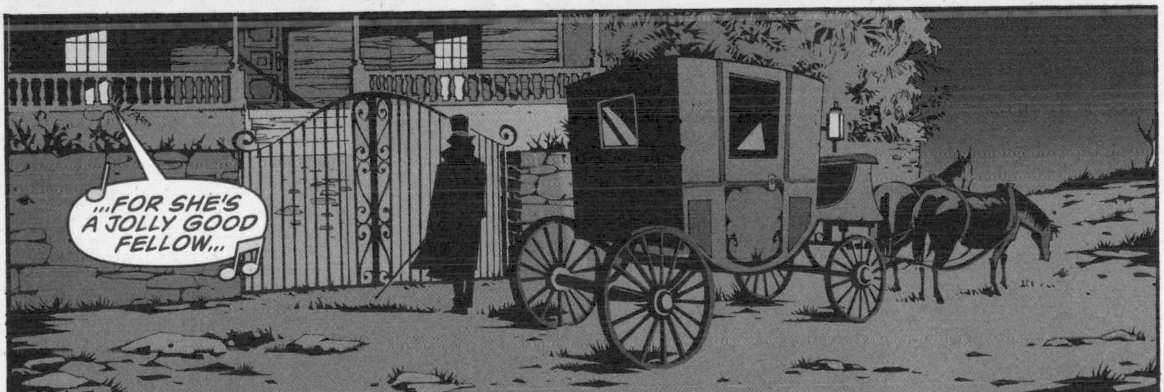
...FOR SHE'S A JOLLY GOOD FELLOW...

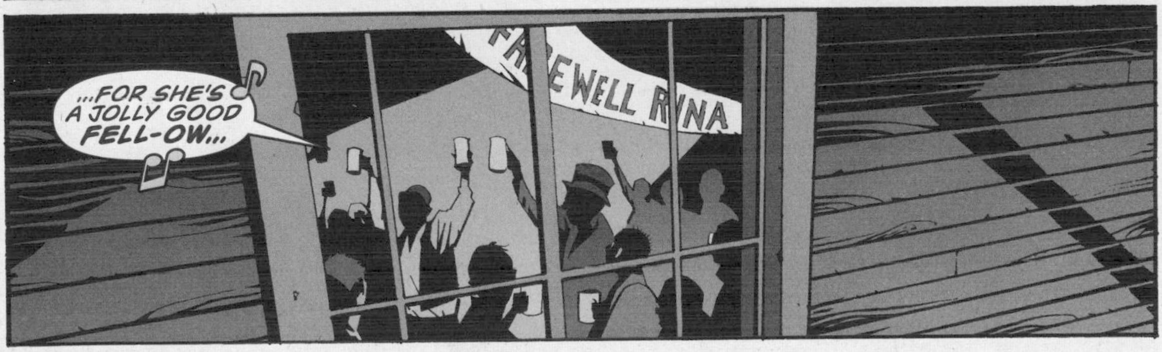
...FOR SHE'S A JOLLY GOOD FELL-OW...
FAREWELL RINA

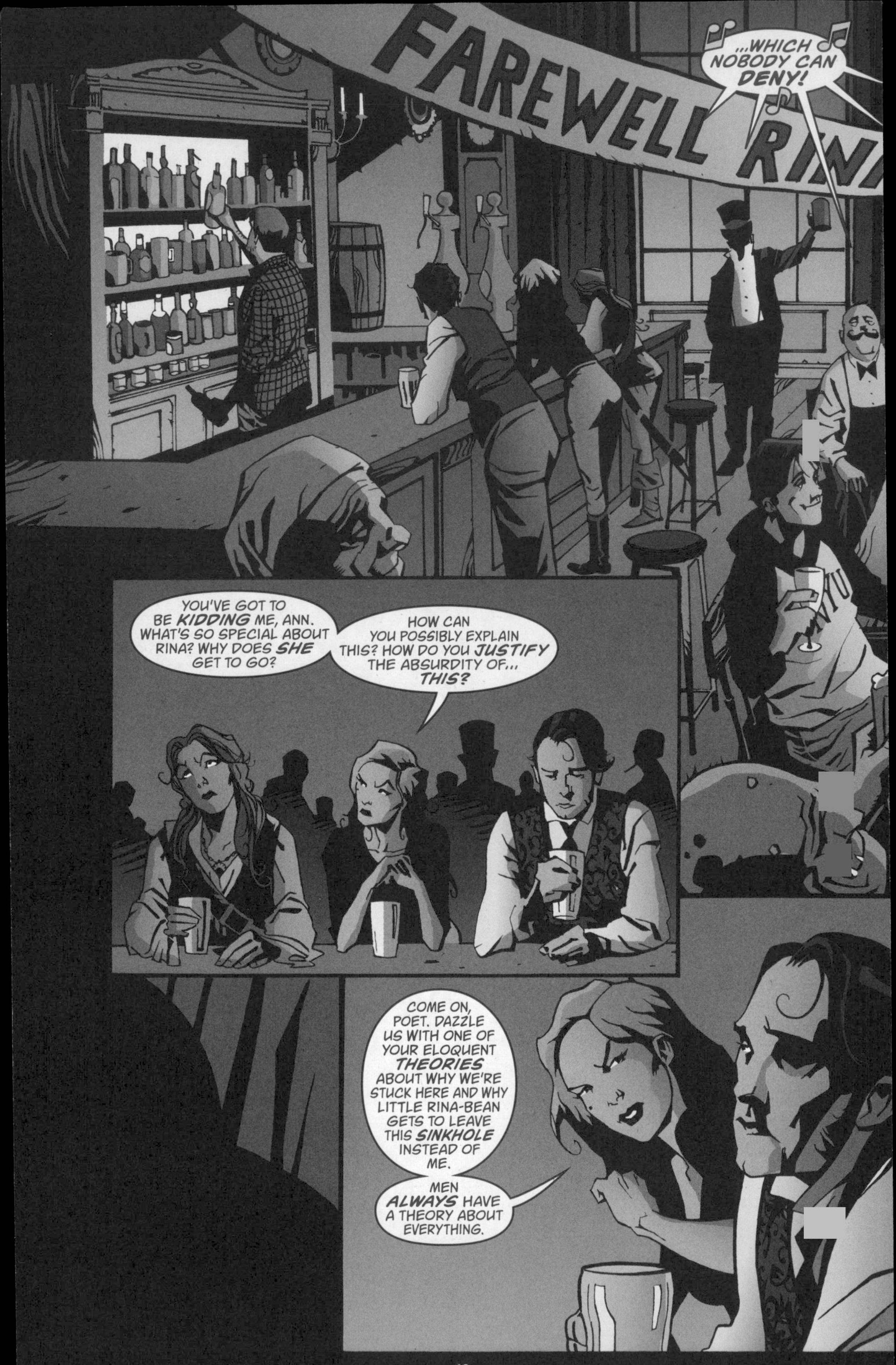
FAREWELL RIN
...WHICH NOBODY CAN DENY!
YOU'VE GOT TO BE KIDDING ME, ANN. WHAT'S SO SPECIAL ABOUT RINA? WHY DOES SHE GET TO GO?
HOW CAN YOU POSSIBLY EXPLAIN THIS? HOW DO YOU JUSTIFY THE ABSURDITY OF... THIS?
COME ON, POET. DAZZLE US WITH ONE OF YOUR ELOQUENT THEORIES ABOUT WHY WE'RE STUCK HERE AND WHY LITTLE RINA-BEAN GETS TO LEAVE THIS SINKHOLE INSTEAD OF ME.
MEN ALWAYS HAVE A THEORY ABOUT EVERYTHING.
NYU

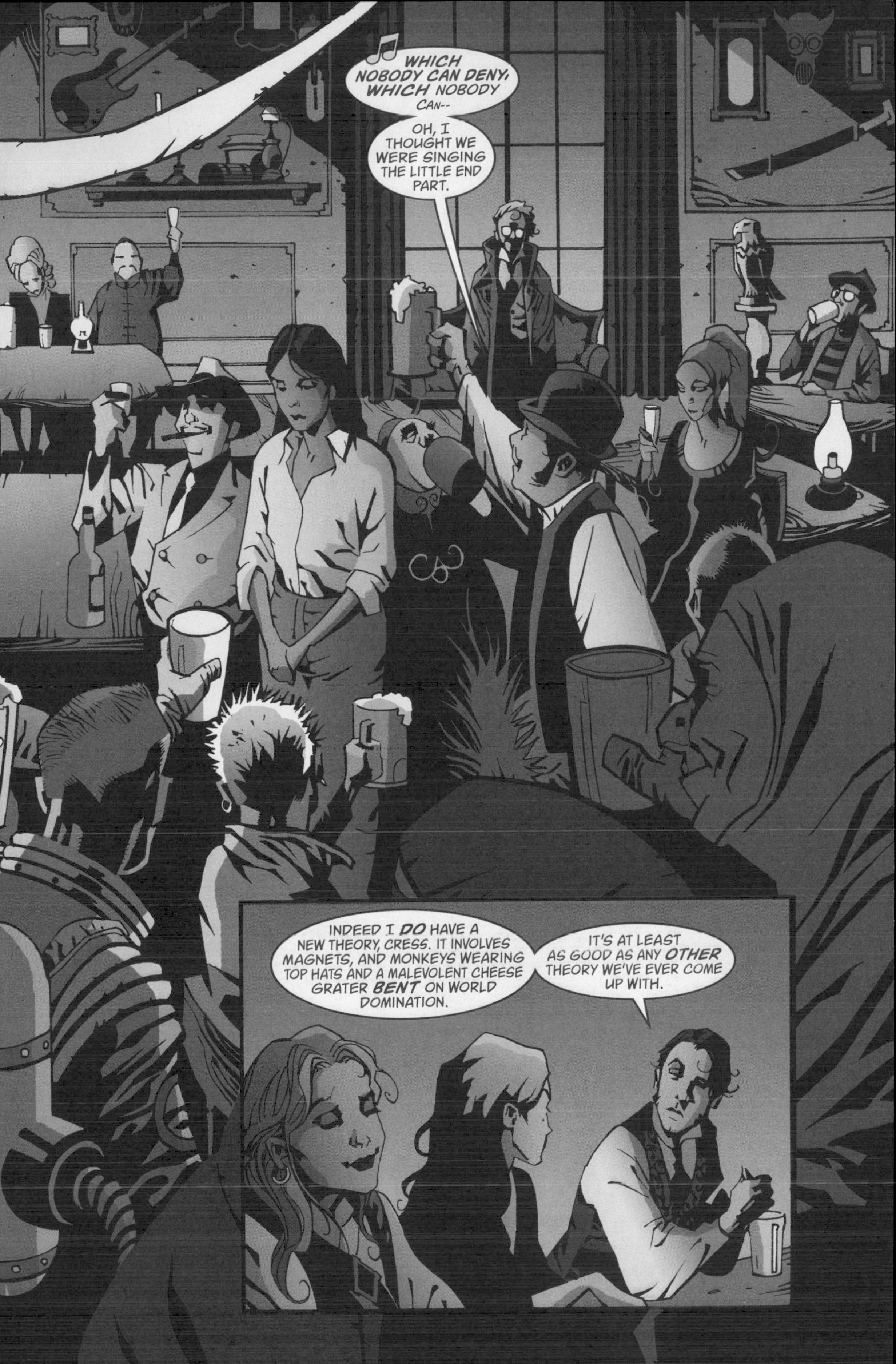

WHICH NOBODY CAN DENY, WHICH NOBODY CAN--
OH, I THOUGHT WE WERE SINGING THE LITTLE END PART.
INDEED I DO HAVE A NEW THEORY, CRESS. IT INVOLVES MAGNETS, AND MONKEYS WEARING TOP HATS AND A MALEVOLENT CHEESE GRATER BENT ON WORLD DOMINATION.
IT'S AT LEAST AS GOOD AS ANY OTHER THEORY WE'VE EVER COME UP WITH.

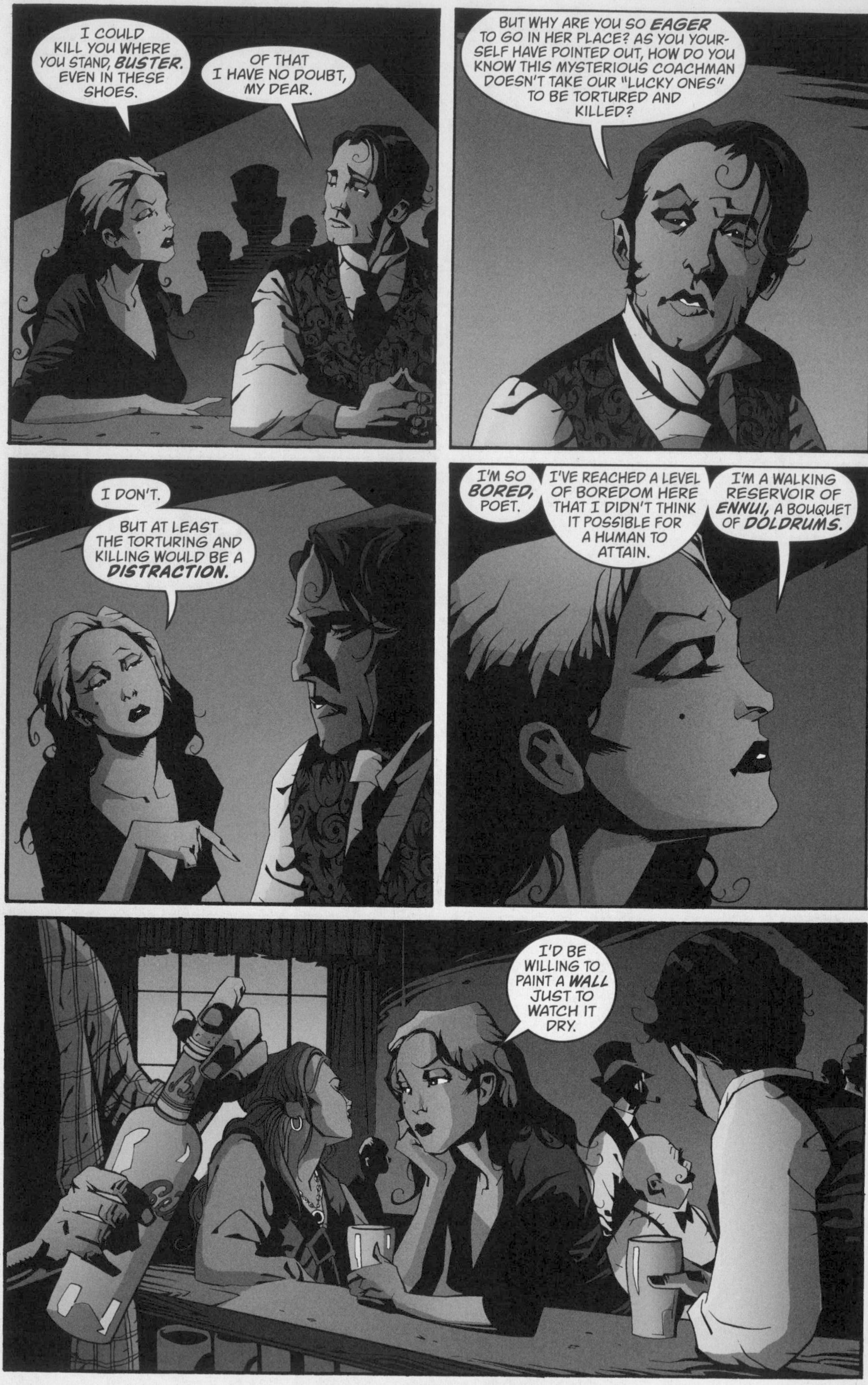
I COULD KILL YOU WHERE YOU STAND, BUSTER. EVEN IN THESE SHOES.
OF THAT I HAVE NO DOUBT, MY DEAR.
BUT WHY ARE YOU SO EAGER TO GO IN HER PLACE? AS YOU YOURSELF HAVE POINTED OUT, HOW DO YOU KNOW THIS MYSTERIOUS COACHMAN DOESN'T TAKE OUR "LUCKY ONES" TO BE TORTURED AND KILLED?
I DON'T.
BUT AT LEAST THE TORTURING AND KILLING WOULD BE A DISTRACTION.
I'M SO BORED, POET.
I'VE REACHED A LEVEL OF BOREDOM HERE THAT I DIDN'T THINK IT POSSIBLE FOR A HUMAN TO ATTAIN.
I'M A WALKING RESERVOIR OF ENNUI, A BOUQUET OF DOLDRUMS.
I'D BE WILLING TO PAINT A WALL JUST TO WATCH IT DRY.

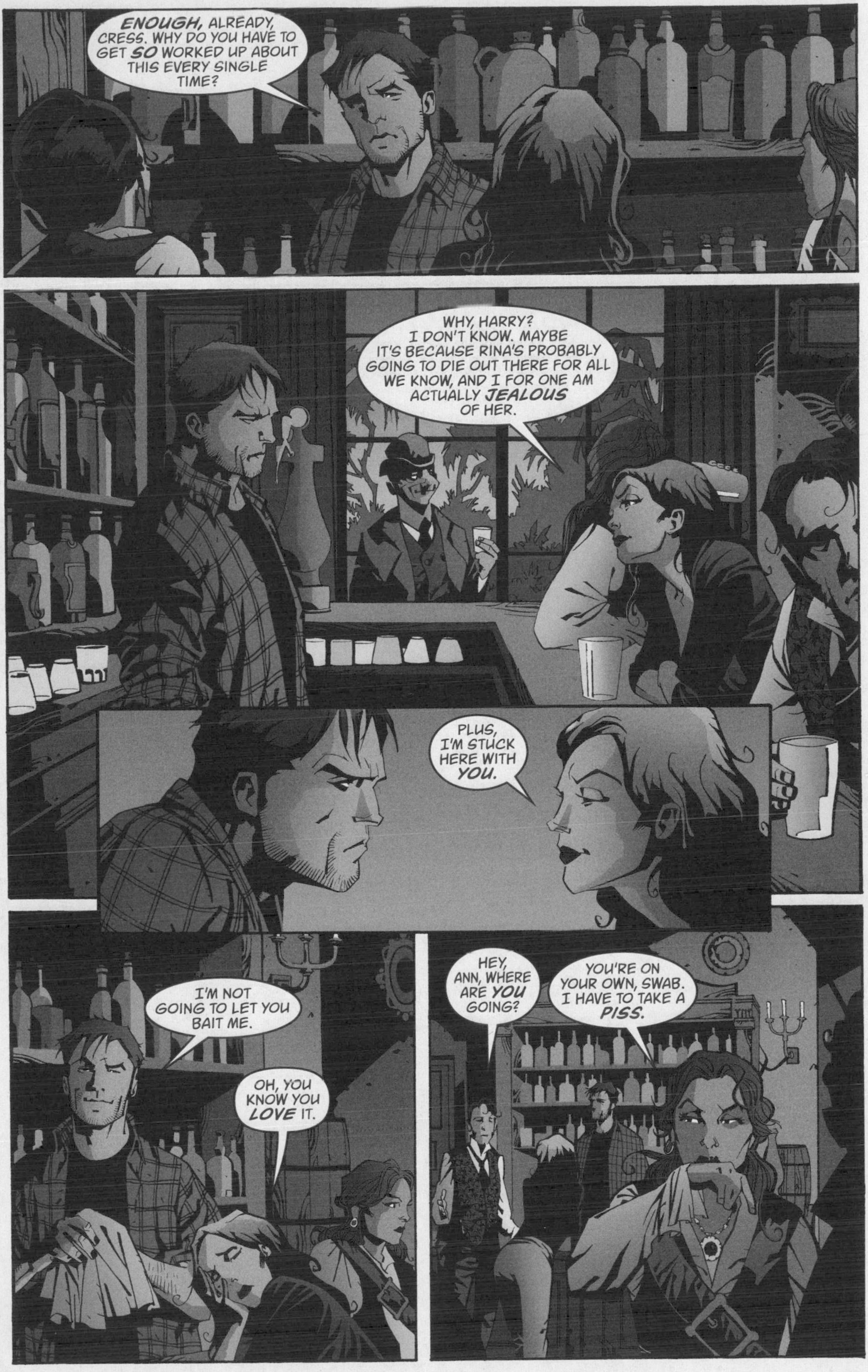
ENOUGH, ALREADY, CRESS. WHY DO YOU HAVE TO GET SO WORKED UP ABOUT THIS EVERY SINGLE TIME?
WHY, HARRY? I DON'T KNOW. MAYBE IT'S BECAUSE RINA'S PROBABLY GOING TO DIE OUT THERE FOR ALL WE KNOW, AND I FOR ONE AM ACTUALLY JEALOUS OF HER.
PLUS, I'M STUCK HERE WITH YOU.
I'M NOT GOING TO LET YOU BAIT ME.
OH, YOU KNOW YOU LOVE IT.
HEY, ANN, WHERE ARE YOU GOING?
YOU'RE ON YOUR OWN, SWAB. I HAVE TO TAKE A PISS.

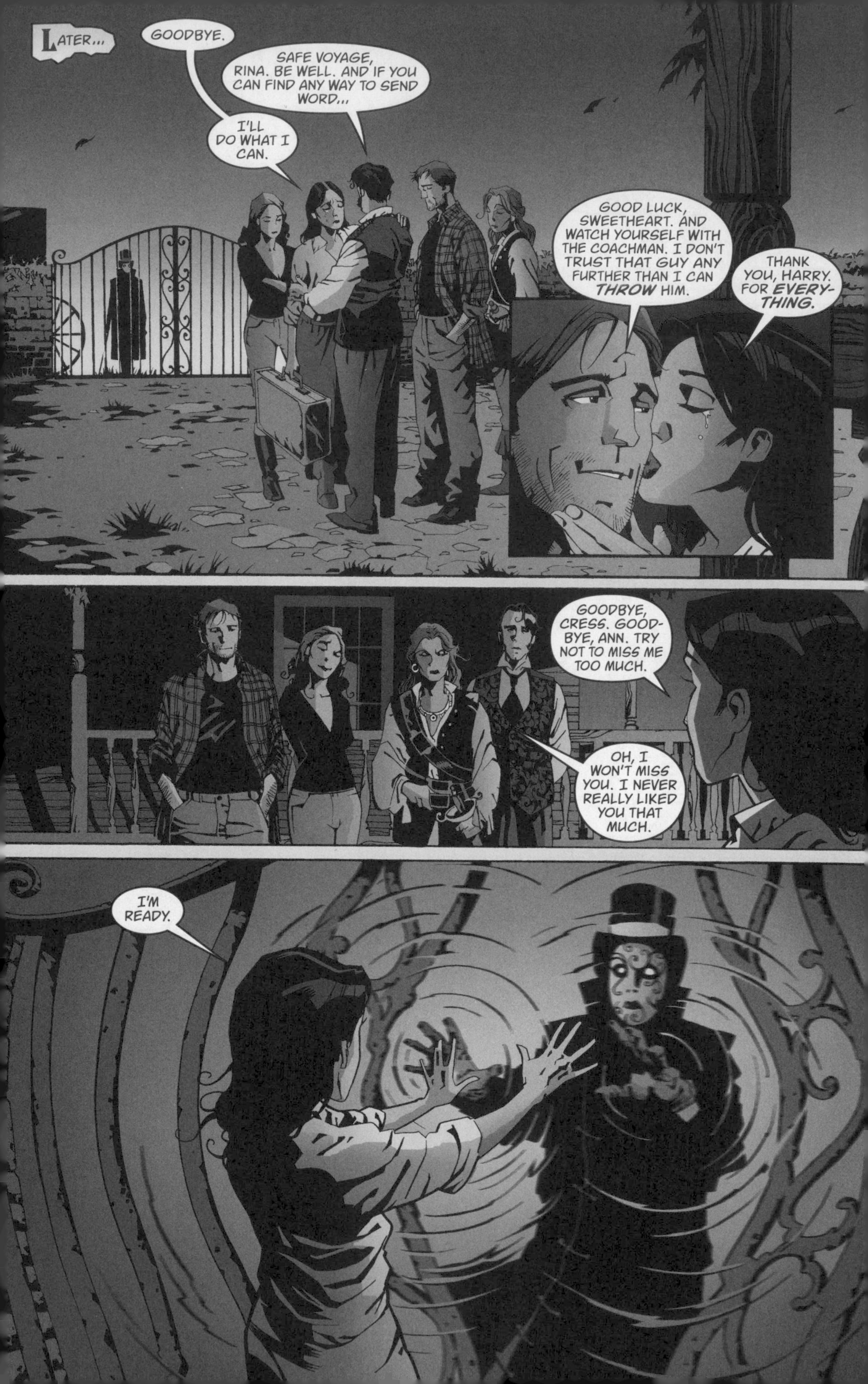
LATER...
GOODBYE.
SAFE VOYAGE, RINA. BE WELL. AND IF YOU CAN FIND ANY WAY TO SEND WORD...
I'LL DO WHAT I CAN.
GOOD LUCK, SWEETHEART. AND WATCH YOURSELF WITH THE COACHMAN. I DON'T TRUST THAT GUY ANY FURTHER THAN I CAN THROW HIM.
THANK YOU, HARRY. FOR EVERYTHING.
GOODBYE, CRESS. GOODBYE, ANN. TRY NOT TO MISS ME TOO MUCH.
OH, I WON'T MISS YOU. I NEVER REALLY LIKED YOU THAT MUCH.
I'M READY.

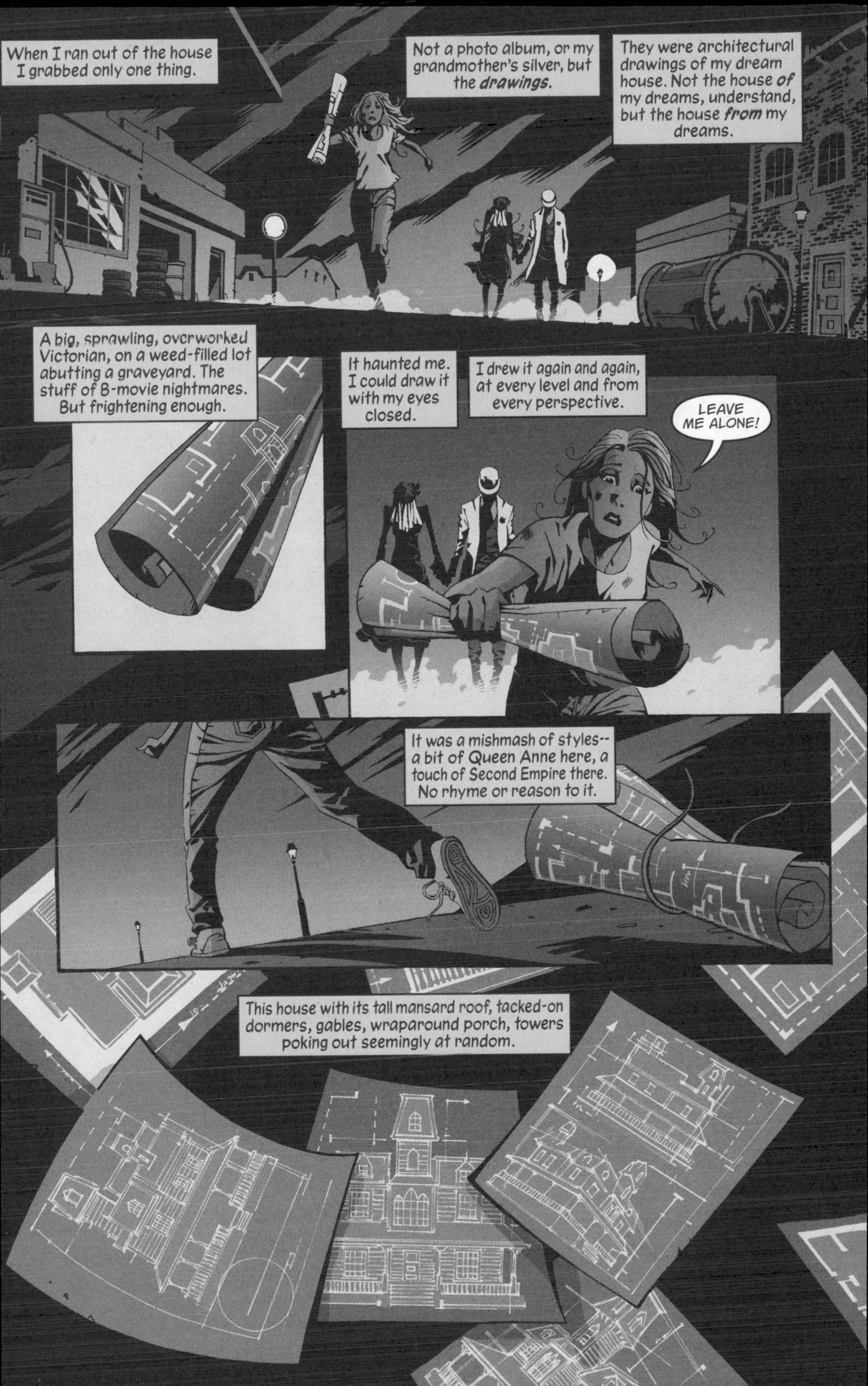
When I ran out of the house I grabbed only one thing.
Not a photo album, or my grandmother's silver, but the *drawings*.
They were architectural drawings of my dream house. Not the house *of* my dreams, understand, but the house *from* my dreams.
A big, sprawling, overworked Victorian, on a weed-filled lot abutting a graveyard. The stuff of B-movie nightmares. But frightening enough.
It haunted me. I could draw it with my eyes closed.
I drew it again and again, at every level and from every perspective.
LEAVE ME ALONE!
It was a mishmash of styles-- a bit of Queen Anne here, a touch of Second Empire there. No rhyme or reason to it.
This house with its tall mansard roof, tacked-on dormers, gables, wraparound porch, towers poking out seemingly at random.

I showed the drawings to a professor once. He dismissed them as "sentimental crap," and he asked why I was wasting so much time on something so pointless.

I didn't have an answer for that. Five years as an architecture student and apparently I hadn't learned much.

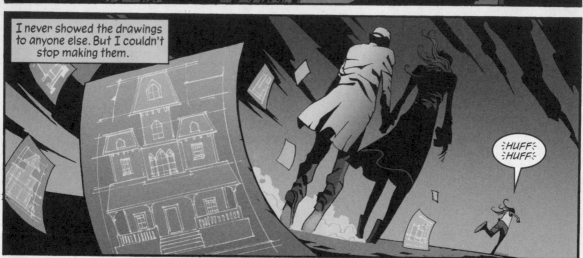

I never showed the drawings to anyone else. But I couldn't stop making them.

:HUFF:
:HUFF:

I thought that if I could just get it down on paper, it would be exorcised from my mind.

Looking back on that sentiment now, all I can do is *laugh*.

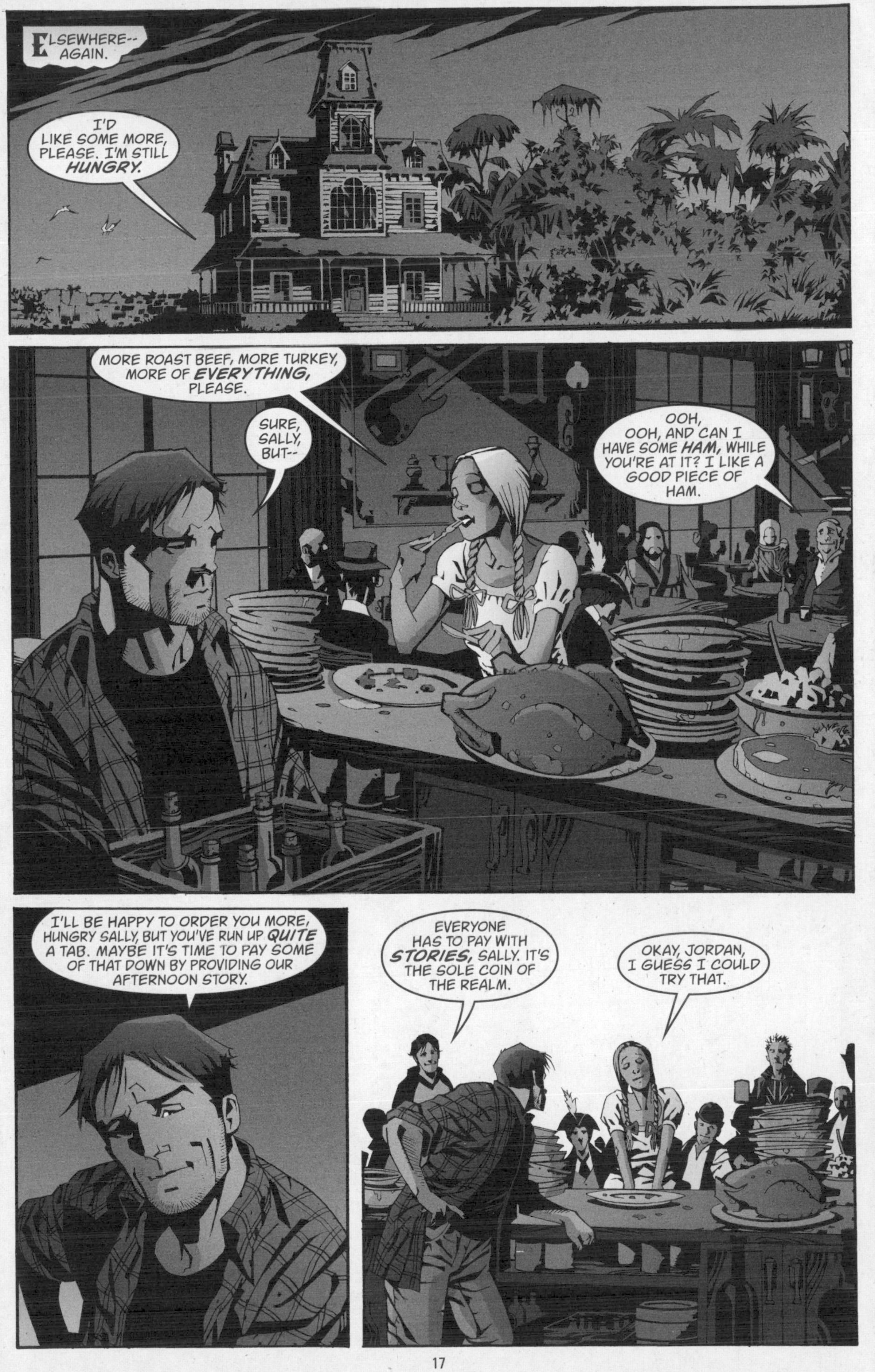
ELSEWHERE--AGAIN.
I'D LIKE SOME MORE, PLEASE. I'M STILL HUNGRY.
MORE ROAST BEEF, MORE TURKEY, MORE OF EVERYTHING, PLEASE.
SURE, SALLY, BUT--
OOH, OOH, AND CAN I HAVE SOME HAM, WHILE YOU'RE AT IT? I LIKE A GOOD PIECE OF HAM.
I'LL BE HAPPY TO ORDER YOU MORE, HUNGRY SALLY, BUT YOU'VE RUN UP QUITE A TAB. MAYBE IT'S TIME TO PAY SOME OF THAT DOWN BY PROVIDING OUR AFTERNOON STORY.
EVERYONE HAS TO PAY WITH STORIES, SALLY. IT'S THE SOLE COIN OF THE REALM.
OKAY, JORDAN, I GUESS I COULD TRY THAT.

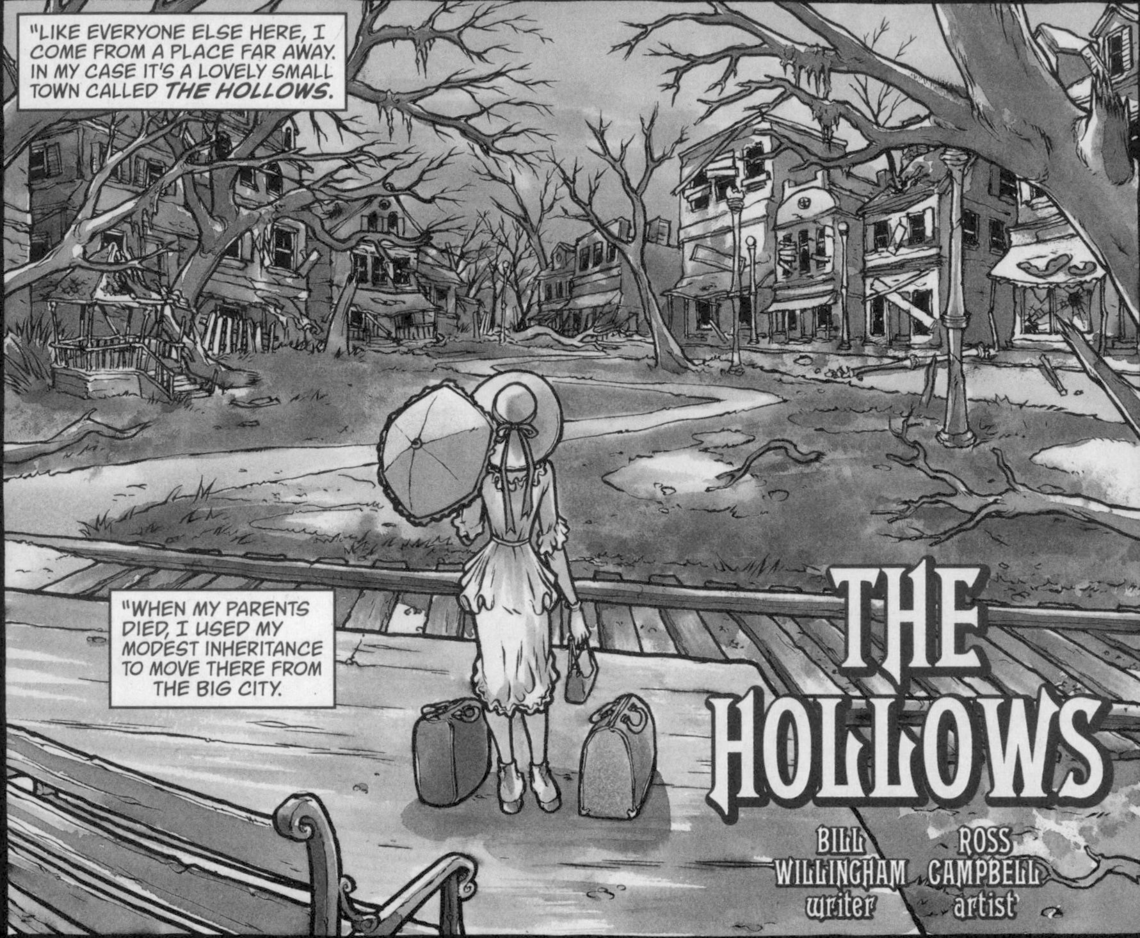
"LIKE EVERYONE ELSE HERE, I COME FROM A PLACE FAR AWAY. IN MY CASE IT'S A LOVELY SMALL TOWN CALLED ***THE HOLLOWS.***
"WHEN MY PARENTS DIED, I USED MY MODEST INHERITANCE TO MOVE THERE FROM THE BIG CITY.
THE HOLLOWS
BILL WILLINGHAM writer
ROSS CAMPBELL artist

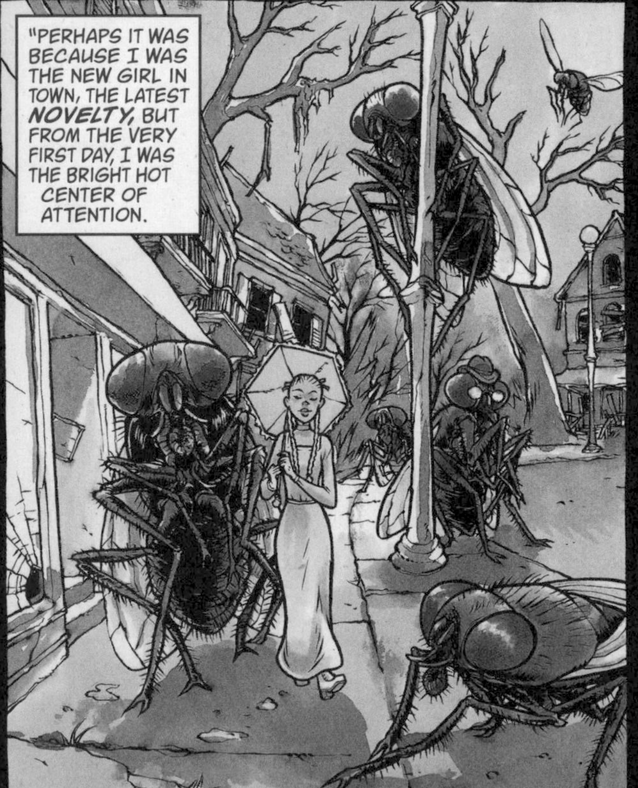
"PERHAPS IT WAS BECAUSE I WAS THE NEW GIRL IN TOWN, THE LATEST ***NOVELTY,*** BUT FROM THE VERY FIRST DAY, I WAS THE BRIGHT HOT CENTER OF ATTENTION.

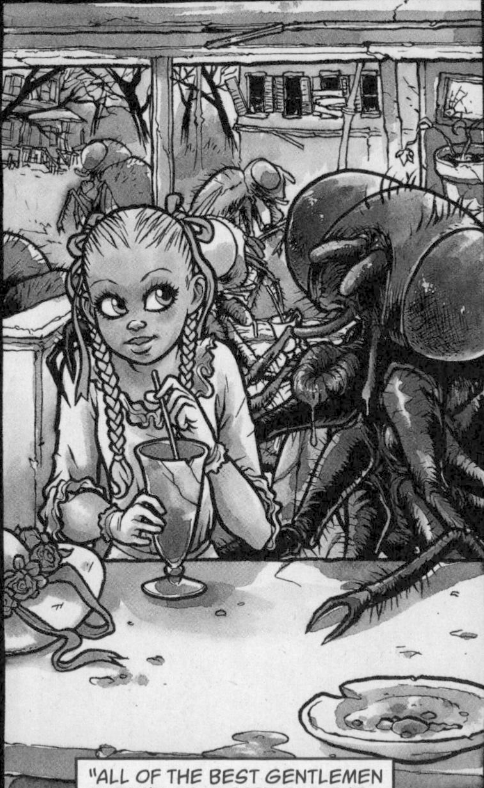
"ALL OF THE BEST GENTLEMEN IN TOWN COMPETED FOR THE PRIVILEGE OF COURTING ME."

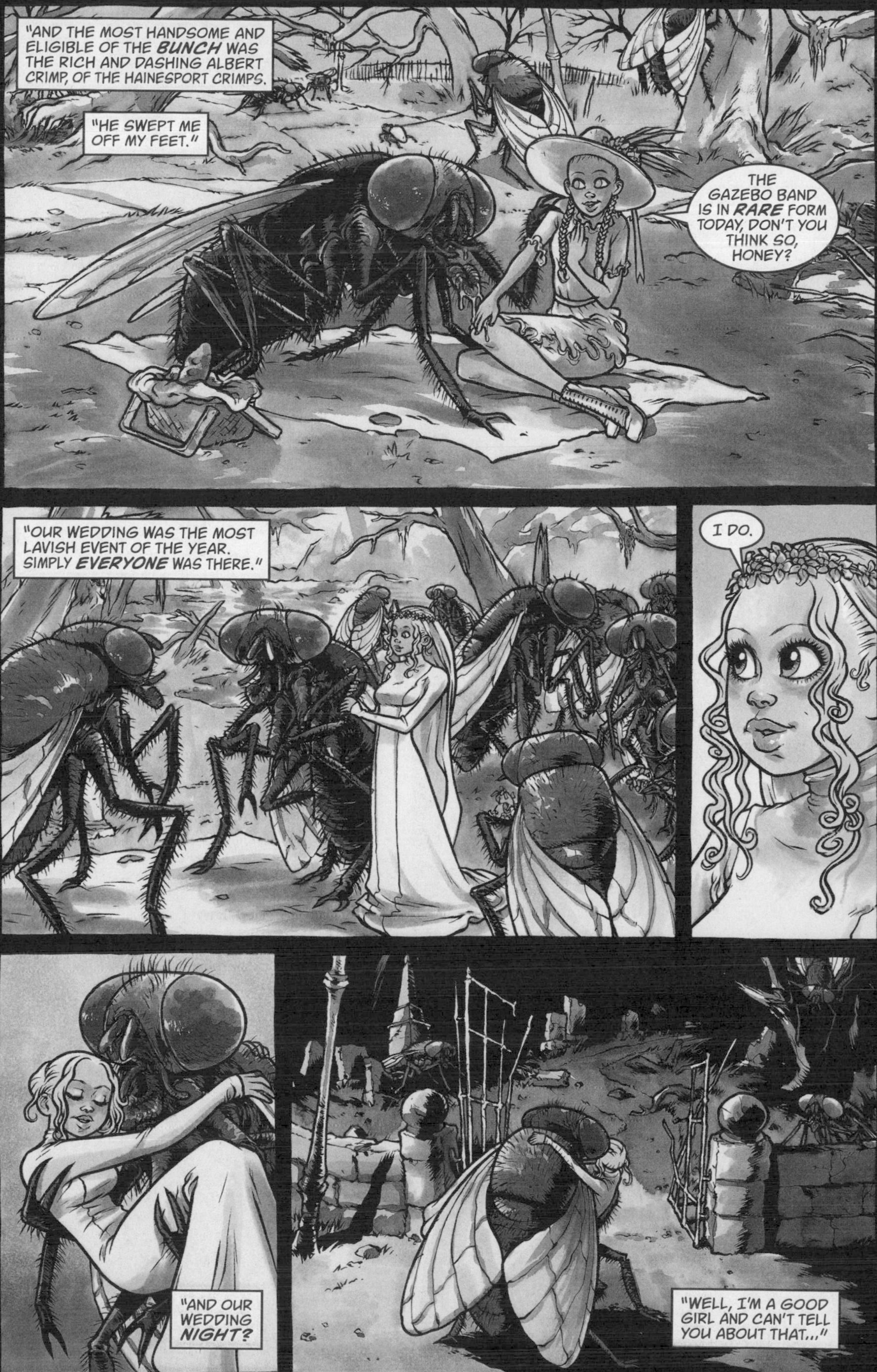
"AND THE MOST HANDSOME AND ELIGIBLE OF THE BUNCH WAS THE RICH AND DASHING ALBERT CRIMP, OF THE HAINESPORT CRIMPS.
"HE SWEPT ME OFF MY FEET."
THE GAZEBO BAND IS IN RARE FORM TODAY, DON'T YOU THINK SO, HONEY?
"OUR WEDDING WAS THE MOST LAVISH EVENT OF THE YEAR. SIMPLY EVERYONE WAS THERE."
I DO.
"AND OUR WEDDING NIGHT?
"WELL, I'M A GOOD GIRL AND CAN'T TELL YOU ABOUT THAT..."

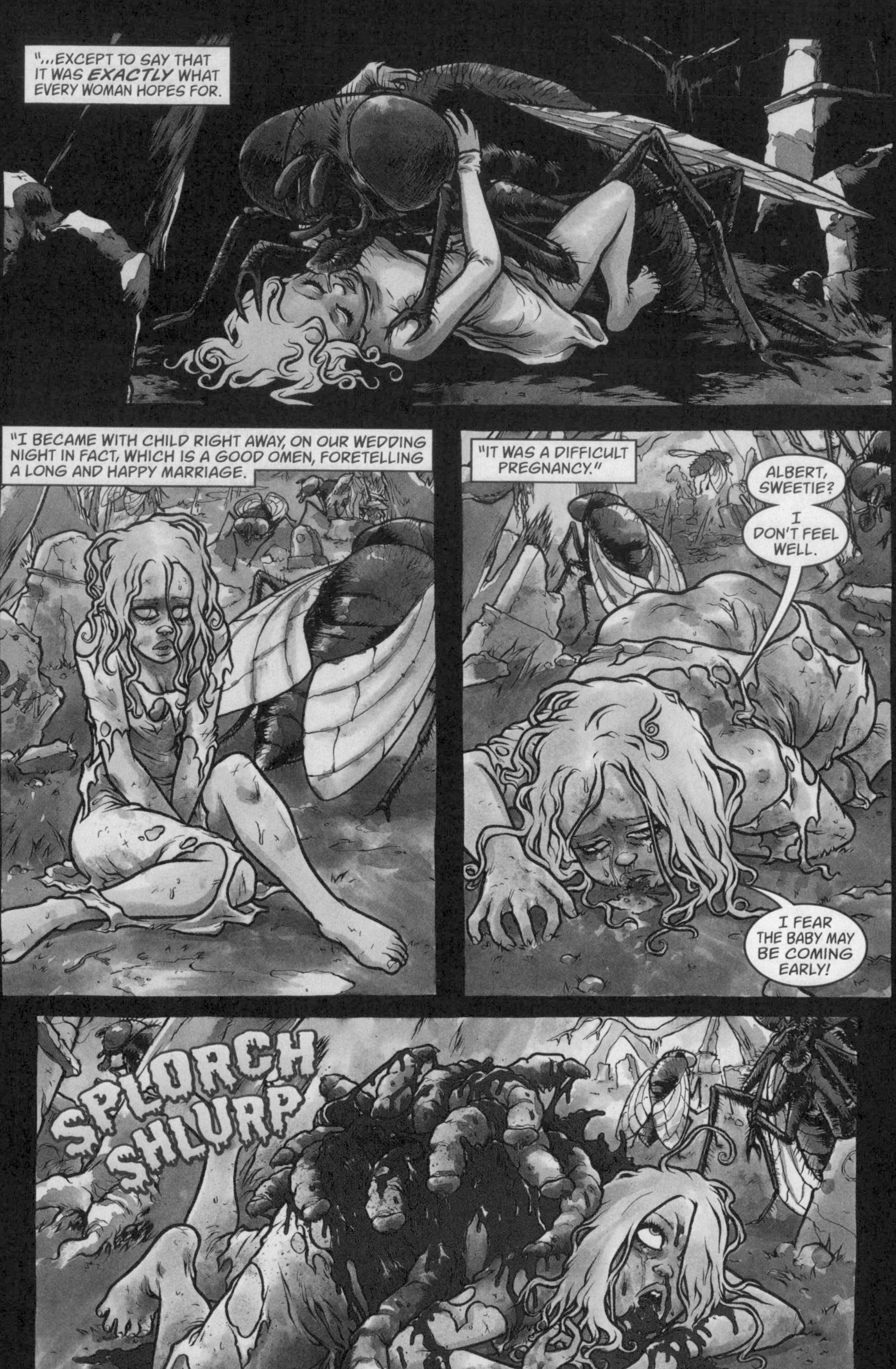
"...EXCEPT TO SAY THAT IT WAS EXACTLY WHAT EVERY WOMAN HOPES FOR.
"I BECAME WITH CHILD RIGHT AWAY, ON OUR WEDDING NIGHT IN FACT, WHICH IS A GOOD OMEN, FORETELLING A LONG AND HAPPY MARRIAGE.
"IT WAS A DIFFICULT PREGNANCY."
ALBERT, SWEETIE?
I DON'T FEEL WELL.
I FEAR THE BABY MAY BE COMING EARLY!
SPLORCH
SHLURP

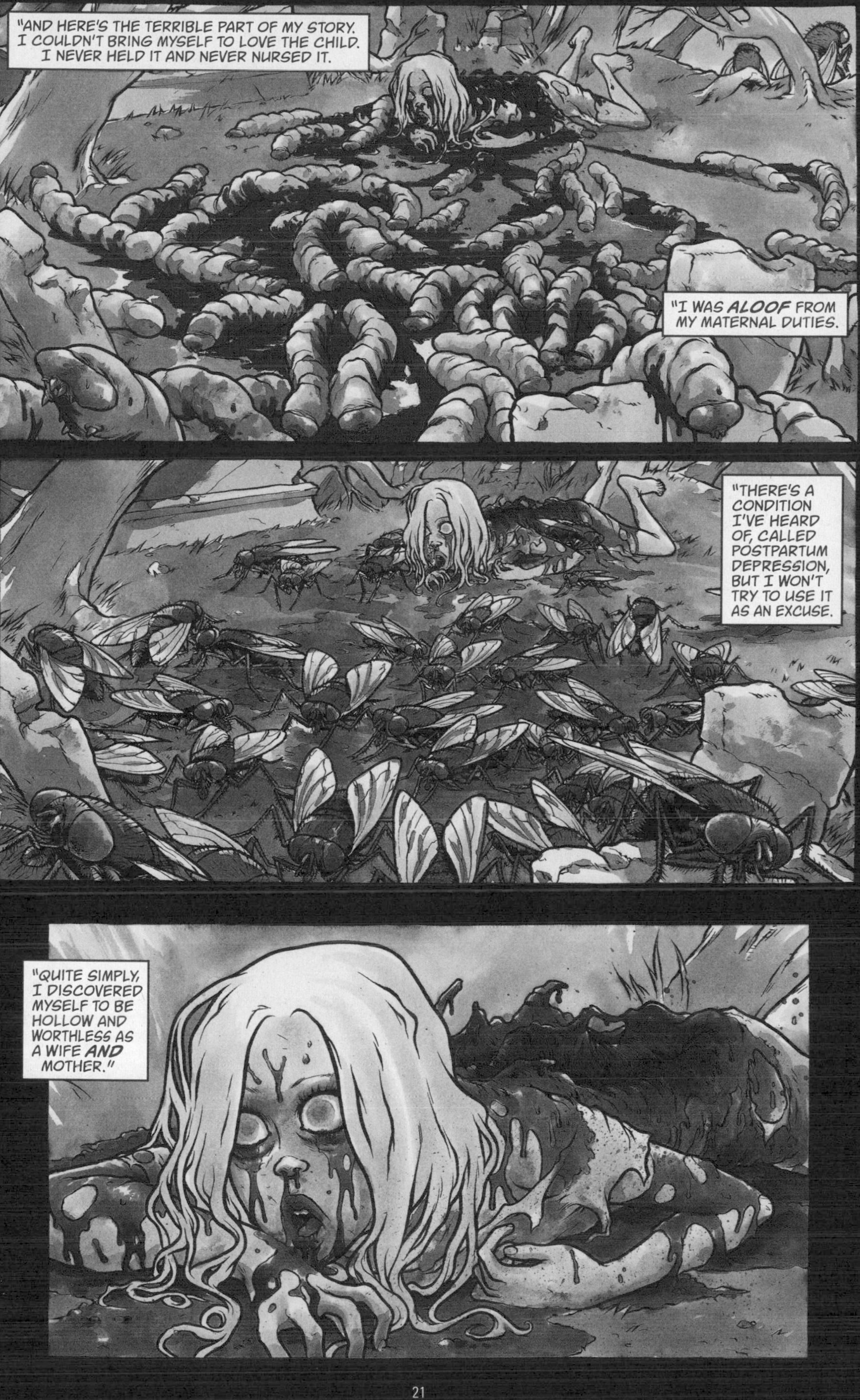
"AND HERE'S THE TERRIBLE PART OF MY STORY. I COULDN'T BRING MYSELF TO LOVE THE CHILD. I NEVER HELD IT AND NEVER NURSED IT.
"I WAS ALOOF FROM MY MATERNAL DUTIES.
"THERE'S A CONDITION I'VE HEARD OF, CALLED POSTPARTUM DEPRESSION, BUT I WON'T TRY TO USE IT AS AN EXCUSE.
"QUITE SIMPLY, I DISCOVERED MYSELF TO BE HOLLOW AND WORTHLESS AS A WIFE AND MOTHER."

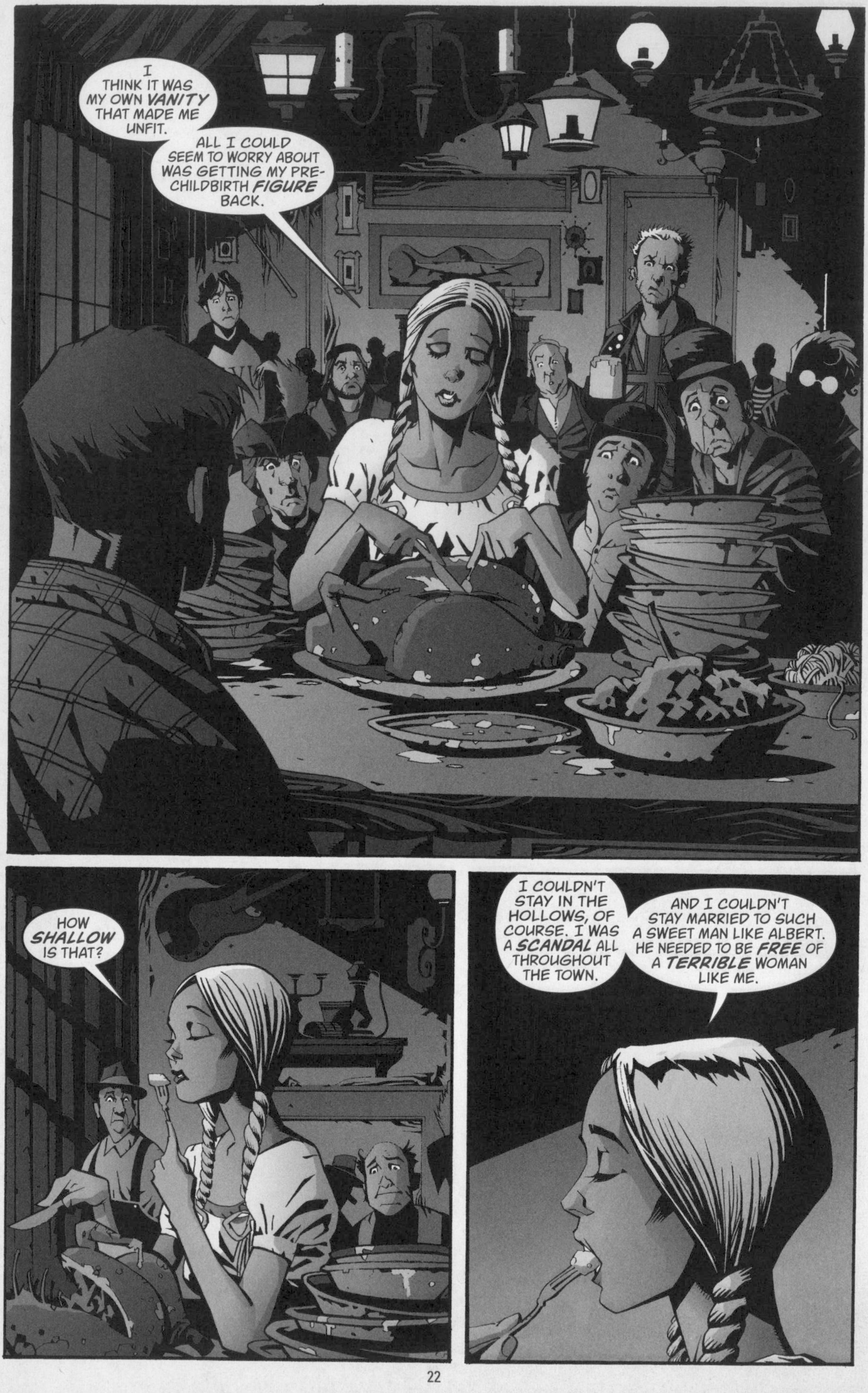

I THINK IT WAS MY OWN VANITY THAT MADE ME UNFIT.
ALL I COULD SEEM TO WORRY ABOUT WAS GETTING MY PRE-CHILDBIRTH FIGURE BACK.
HOW SHALLOW IS THAT?
I COULDN'T STAY IN THE HOLLOWS, OF COURSE. I WAS A SCANDAL ALL THROUGHOUT THE TOWN.
AND I COULDN'T STAY MARRIED TO SUCH A SWEET MAN LIKE ALBERT. HE NEEDED TO BE FREE OF A TERRIBLE WOMAN LIKE ME.

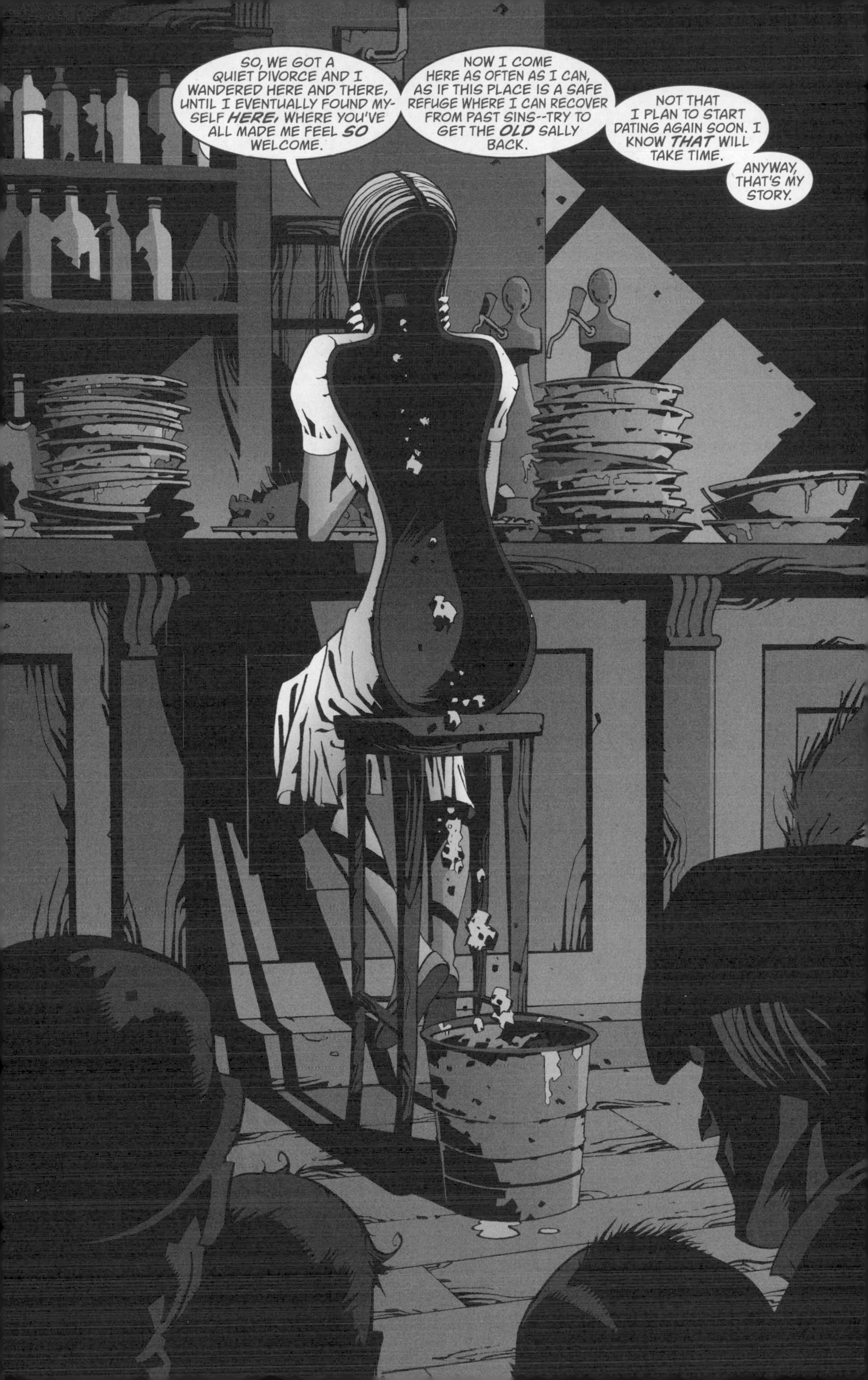
SO, WE GOT A QUIET DIVORCE AND I WANDERED HERE AND THERE, UNTIL I EVENTUALLY FOUND MY-SELF *HERE,* WHERE YOU'VE ALL MADE ME FEEL *SO* WELCOME.
NOW I COME HERE AS OFTEN AS I CAN, AS IF THIS PLACE IS A SAFE REFUGE WHERE I CAN RECOVER FROM PAST SINS--TRY TO GET THE *OLD* SALLY BACK.
NOT THAT I PLAN TO START DATING AGAIN SOON. I KNOW *THAT* WILL TAKE TIME.
ANYWAY, THAT'S MY STORY.

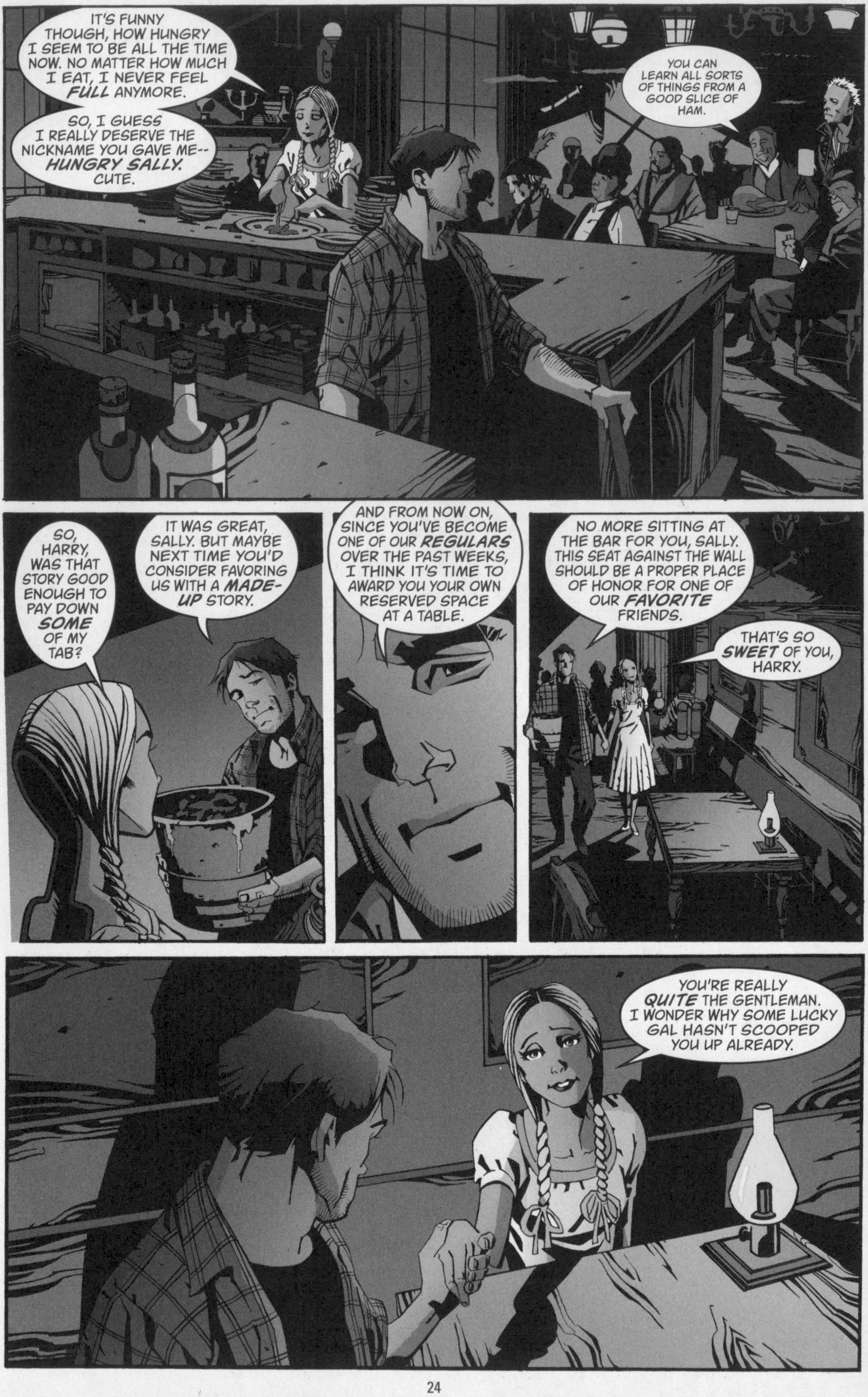
IT'S FUNNY THOUGH, HOW HUNGRY I SEEM TO BE ALL THE TIME NOW. NO MATTER HOW MUCH I EAT, I NEVER FEEL FULL ANYMORE.
SO, I GUESS I REALLY DESERVE THE NICKNAME YOU GAVE ME-- HUNGRY SALLY. CUTE.
YOU CAN LEARN ALL SORTS OF THINGS FROM A GOOD SLICE OF HAM.
SO, HARRY, WAS THAT STORY GOOD ENOUGH TO PAY DOWN SOME OF MY TAB?
IT WAS GREAT, SALLY. BUT MAYBE NEXT TIME YOU'D CONSIDER FAVORING US WITH A MADE-UP STORY.
AND FROM NOW ON, SINCE YOU'VE BECOME ONE OF OUR REGULARS OVER THE PAST WEEKS, I THINK IT'S TIME TO AWARD YOU YOUR OWN RESERVED SPACE AT A TABLE.
NO MORE SITTING AT THE BAR FOR YOU, SALLY. THIS SEAT AGAINST THE WALL SHOULD BE A PROPER PLACE OF HONOR FOR ONE OF OUR FAVORITE FRIENDS.
THAT'S SO SWEET OF YOU, HARRY.
YOU'RE REALLY QUITE THE GENTLEMAN. I WONDER WHY SOME LUCKY GAL HASN'T SCOOPED YOU UP ALREADY.

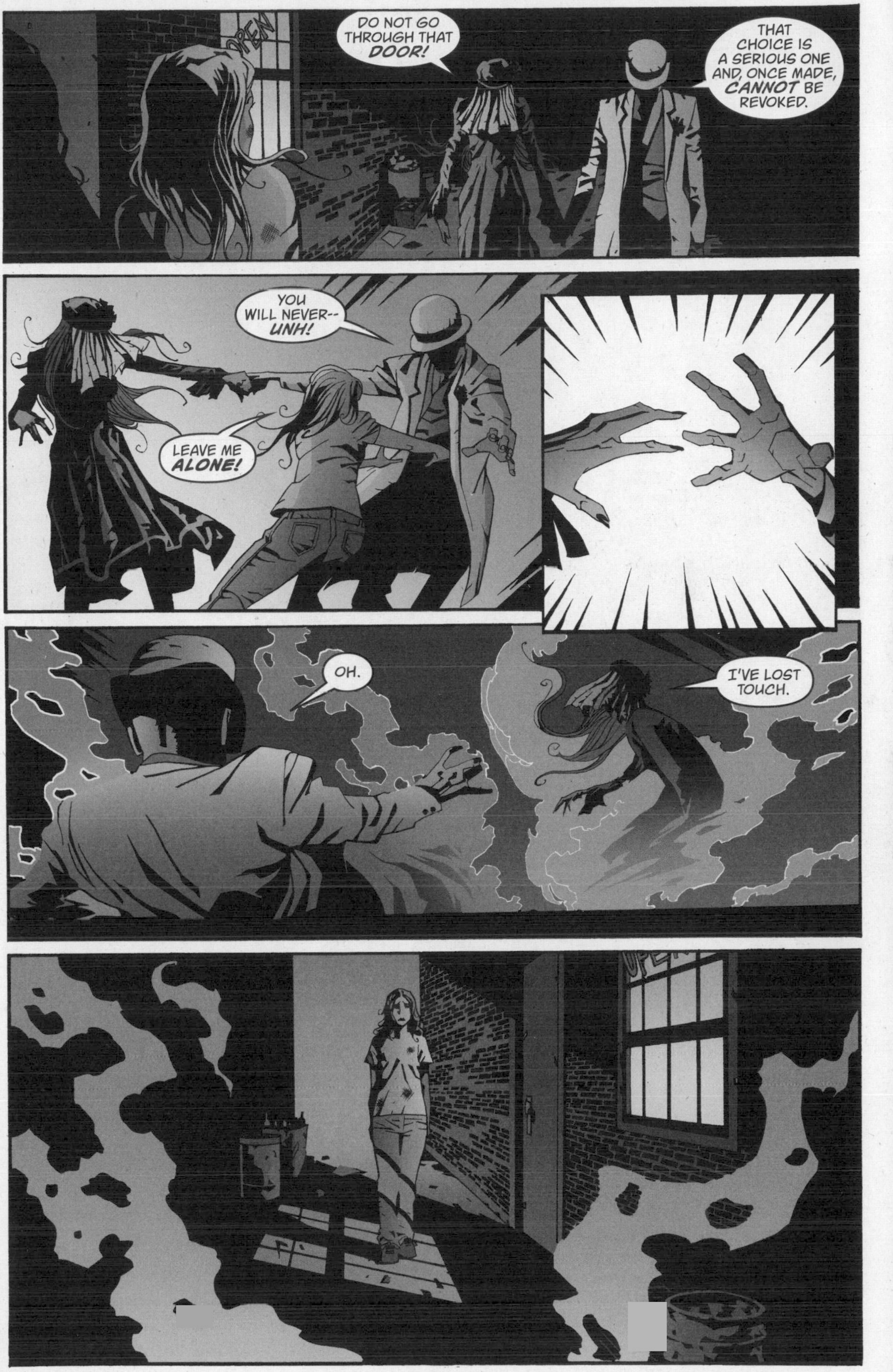
OPEN
DO NOT GO THROUGH THAT DOOR!
THAT CHOICE IS A SERIOUS ONE AND, ONCE MADE, CANNOT BE REVOKED.
YOU WILL NEVER-- UNH!
LEAVE ME ALONE!
OH.
I'VE LOST TOUCH.

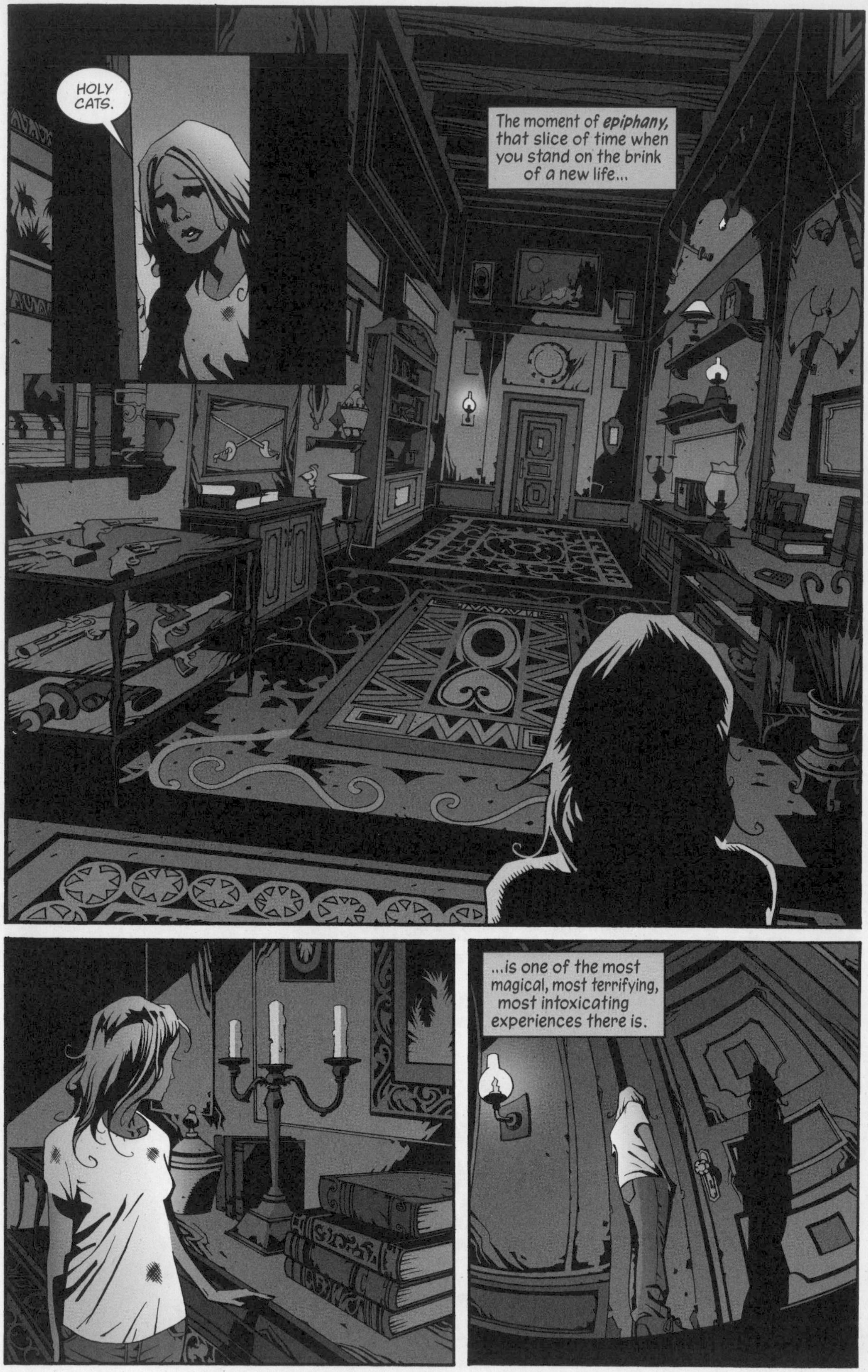
HOLY CATS.
The moment of *epiphany,* that slice of time when you stand on the brink of a new life...
...is one of the most magical, most terrifying, most intoxicating experiences there is.

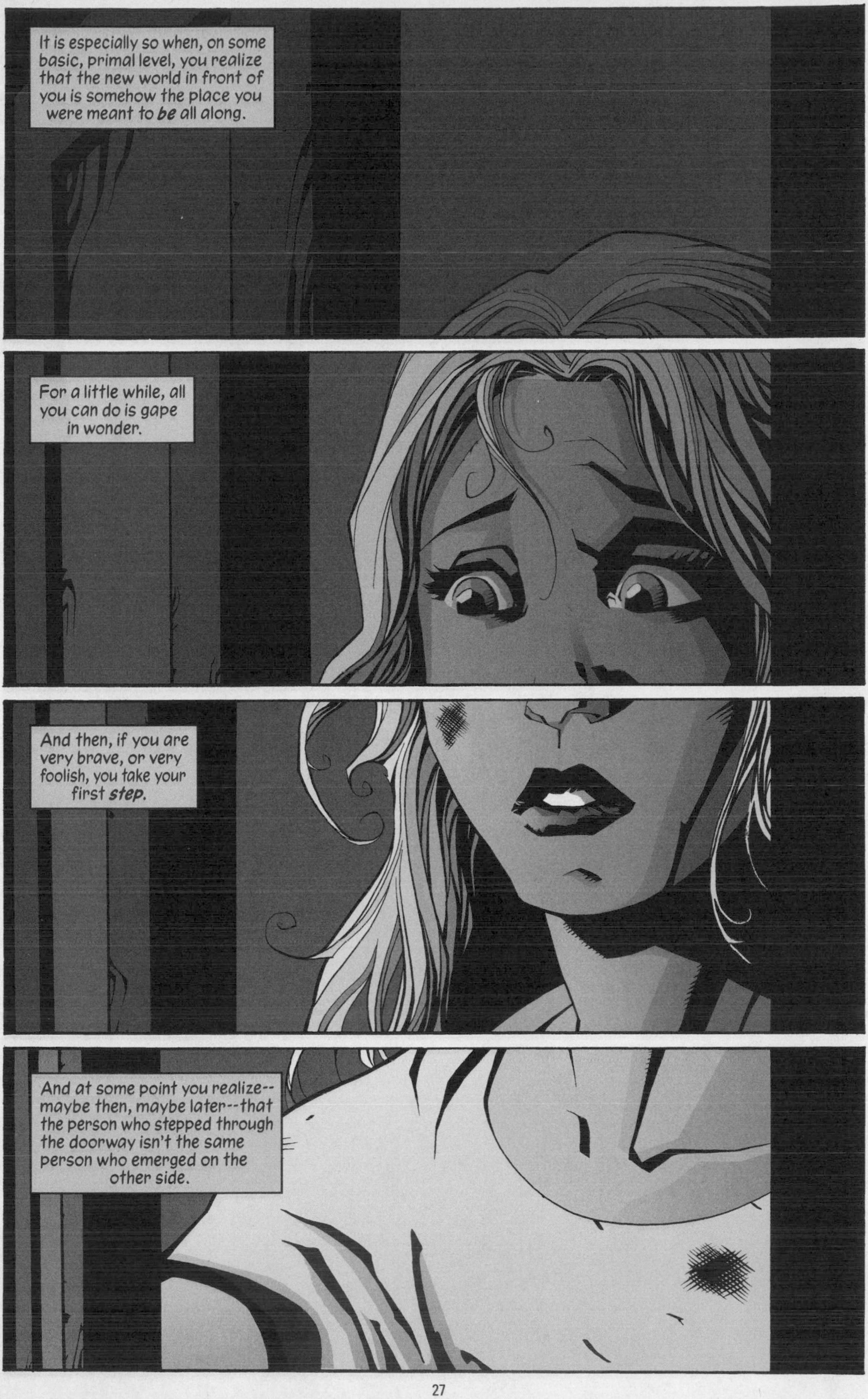
It is especially so when, on some basic, primal level, you realize that the new world in front of you is somehow the place you were meant to *be* all along.
For a little while, all you can do is gape in wonder.
And then, if you are very brave, or very foolish, you take your first *step*.
And at some point you realize-- maybe then, maybe later--that the person who stepped through the doorway isn't the same person who emerged on the other side.

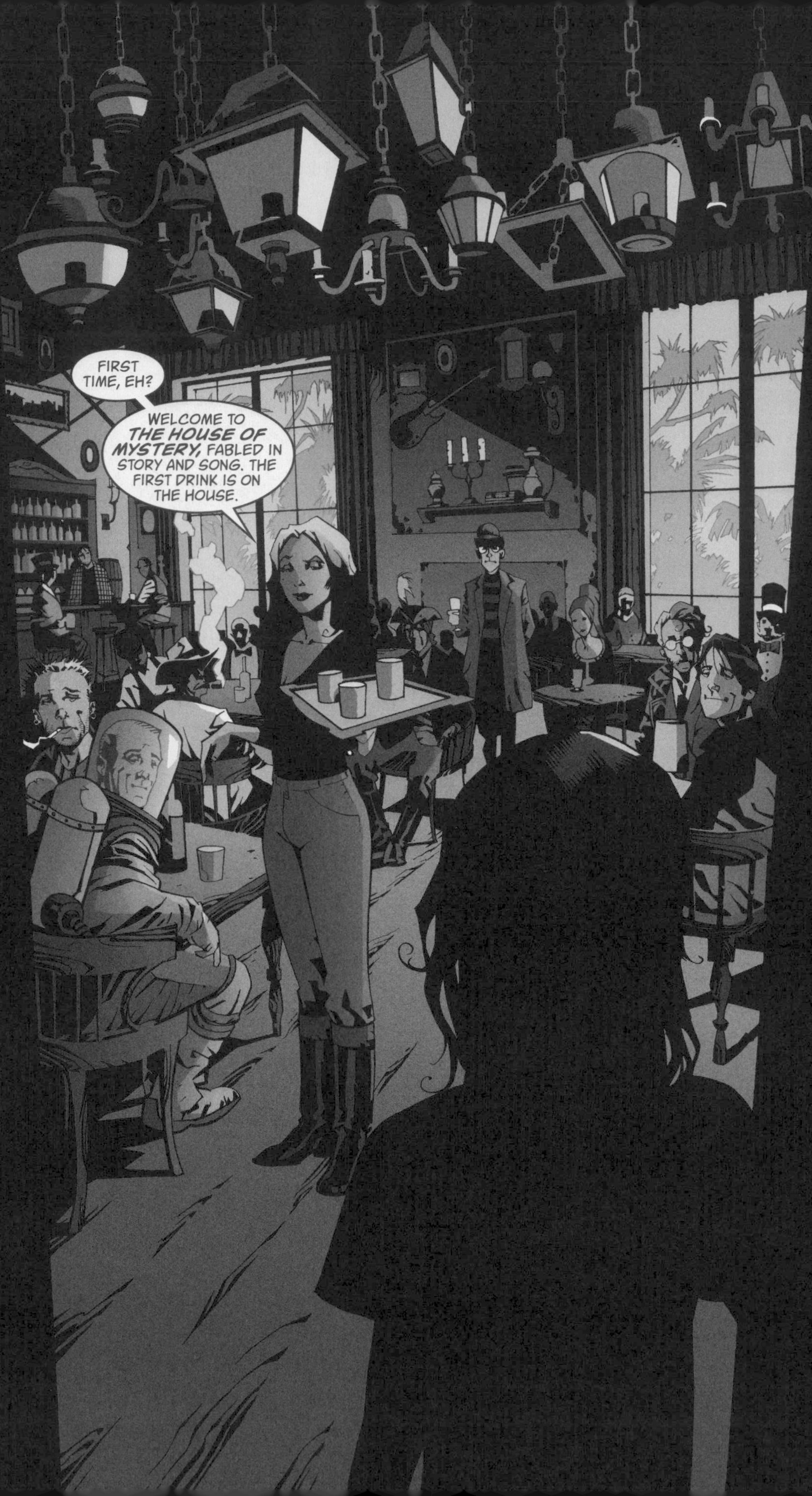
FIRST TIME, EH?
WELCOME TO THE HOUSE OF MYSTERY, FABLED IN STORY AND SONG. THE FIRST DRINK IS ON THE HOUSE.

Issue #2 cover art by Sam Weber.

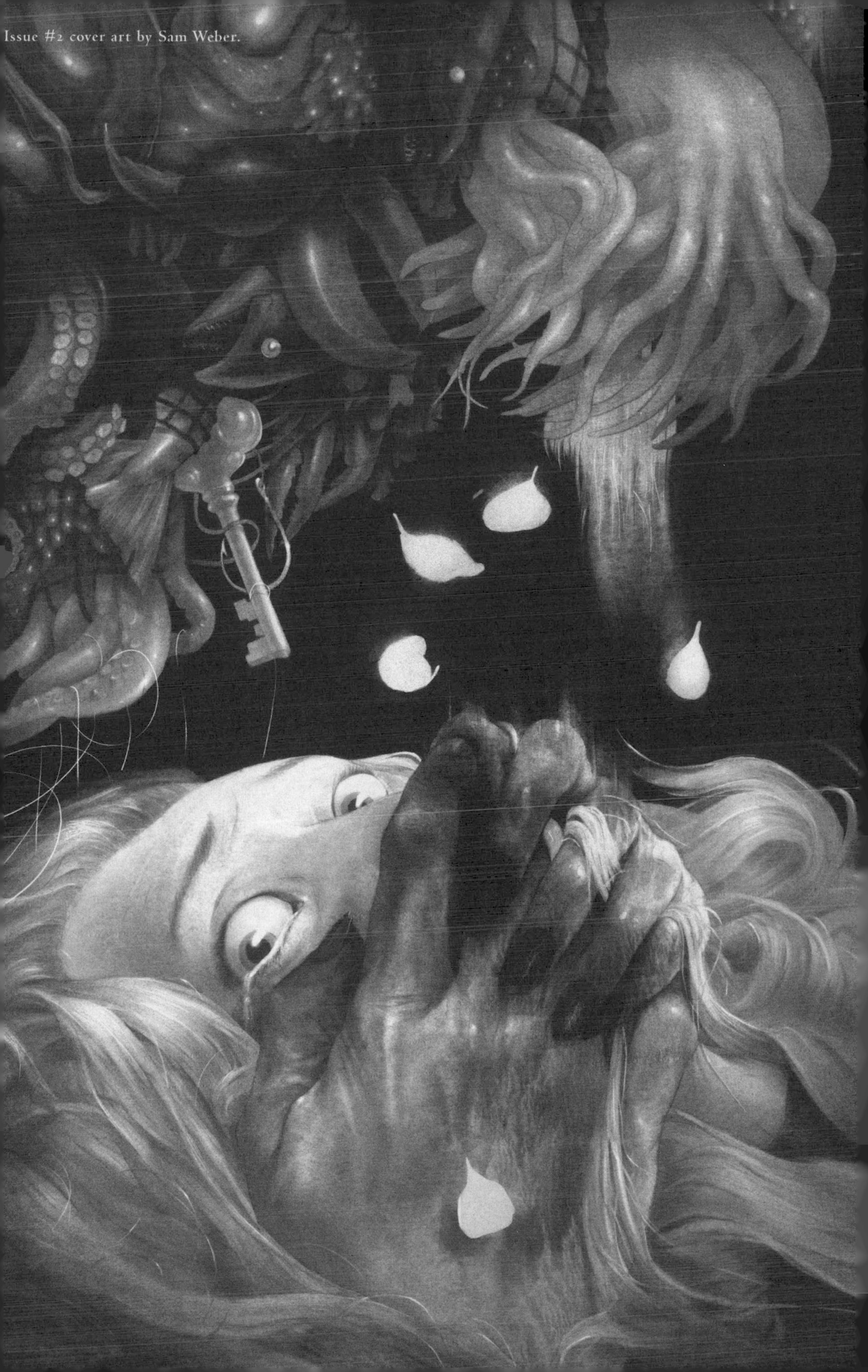

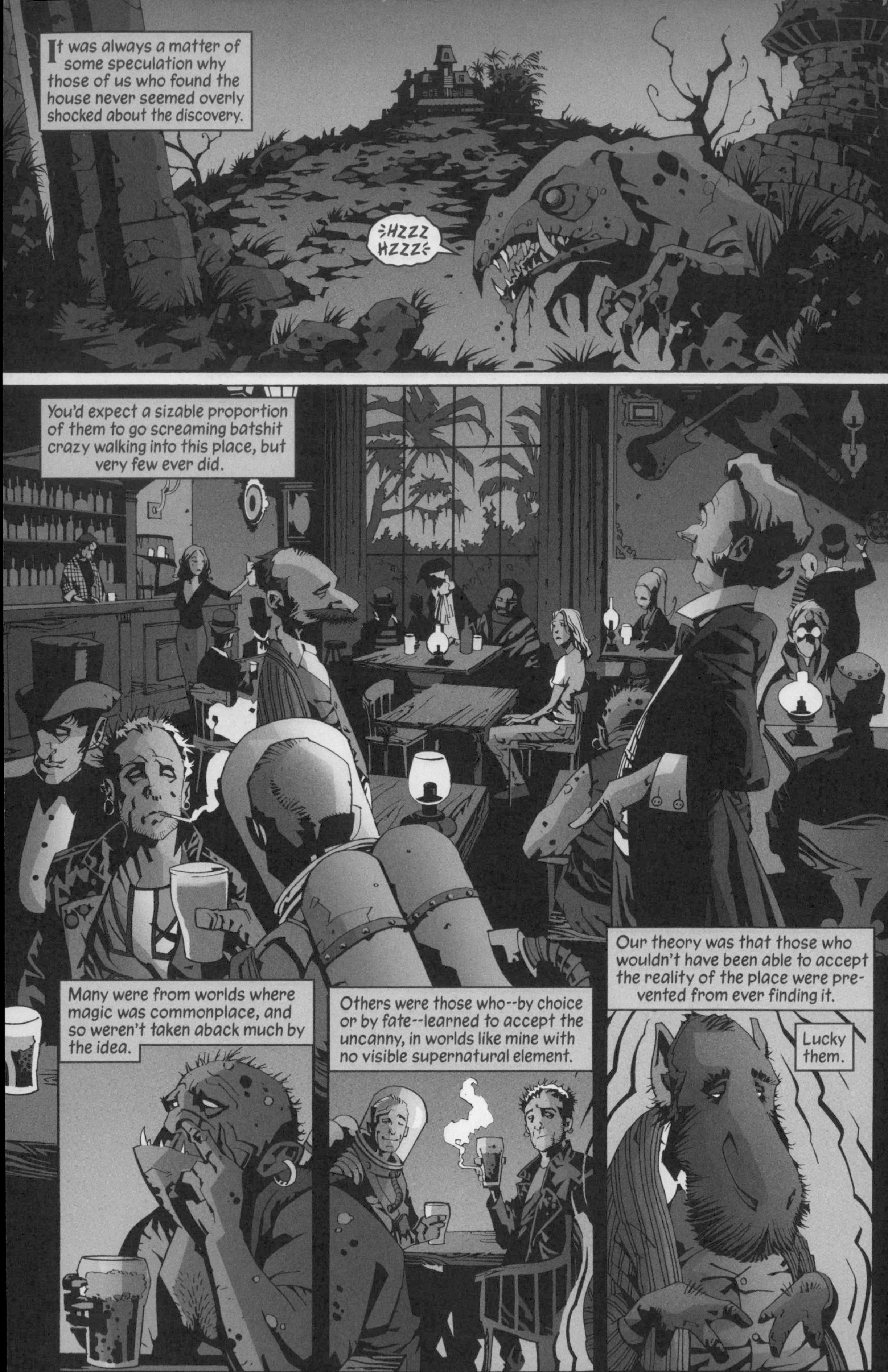
It was always a matter of some speculation why those of us who found the house never seemed overly shocked about the discovery.
HZZZ HZZZ
You'd expect a sizable proportion of them to go screaming batshit crazy walking into this place, but very few ever did.
Many were from worlds where magic was commonplace, and so weren't taken aback much by the idea.
Others were those who--by choice or by fate--learned to accept the uncanny, in worlds like mine with no visible supernatural element.
Our theory was that those who wouldn't have been able to accept the reality of the place were prevented from ever finding it.
Lucky them.

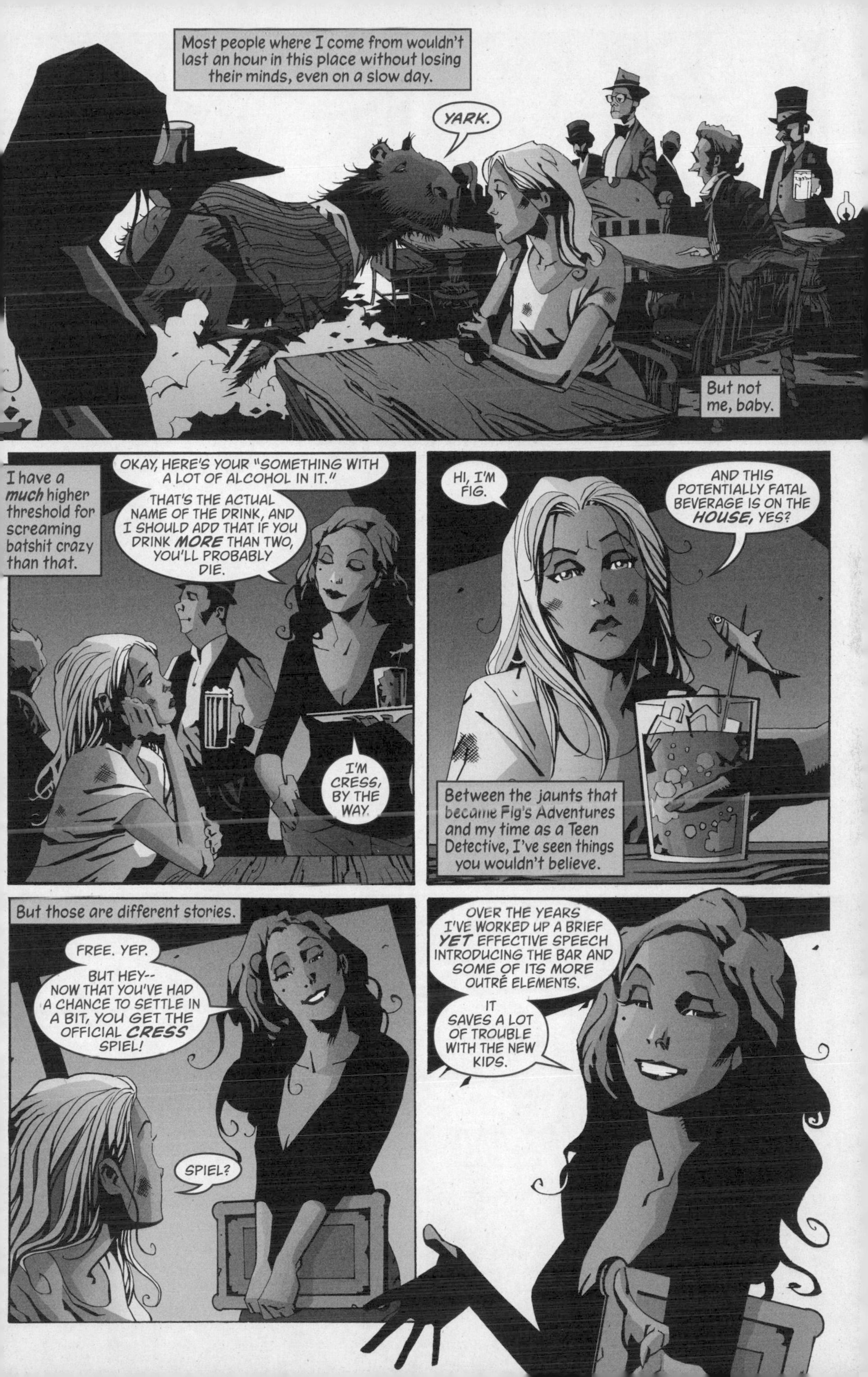

Most people where I come from wouldn't last an hour in this place without losing their minds, even on a slow day.
YARK.
But not me, baby.
I have a much higher threshold for screaming batshit crazy than that.
OKAY, HERE'S YOUR "SOMETHING WITH A LOT OF ALCOHOL IN IT."
THAT'S THE ACTUAL NAME OF THE DRINK, AND I SHOULD ADD THAT IF YOU DRINK MORE THAN TWO, YOU'LL PROBABLY DIE.
I'M CRESS, BY THE WAY.
HI, I'M FIG.
AND THIS POTENTIALLY FATAL BEVERAGE IS ON THE HOUSE, YES?
Between the jaunts that became Fig's Adventures and my time as a Teen Detective, I've seen things you wouldn't believe.
But those are different stories.
FREE. YEP.
BUT HEY-- NOW THAT YOU'VE HAD A CHANCE TO SETTLE IN A BIT, YOU GET THE OFFICIAL CRESS SPIEL!
SPIEL?
OVER THE YEARS I'VE WORKED UP A BRIEF YET EFFECTIVE SPEECH INTRODUCING THE BAR AND SOME OF ITS MORE OUTRÉ ELEMENTS.
IT SAVES A LOT OF TROUBLE WITH THE NEW KIDS.

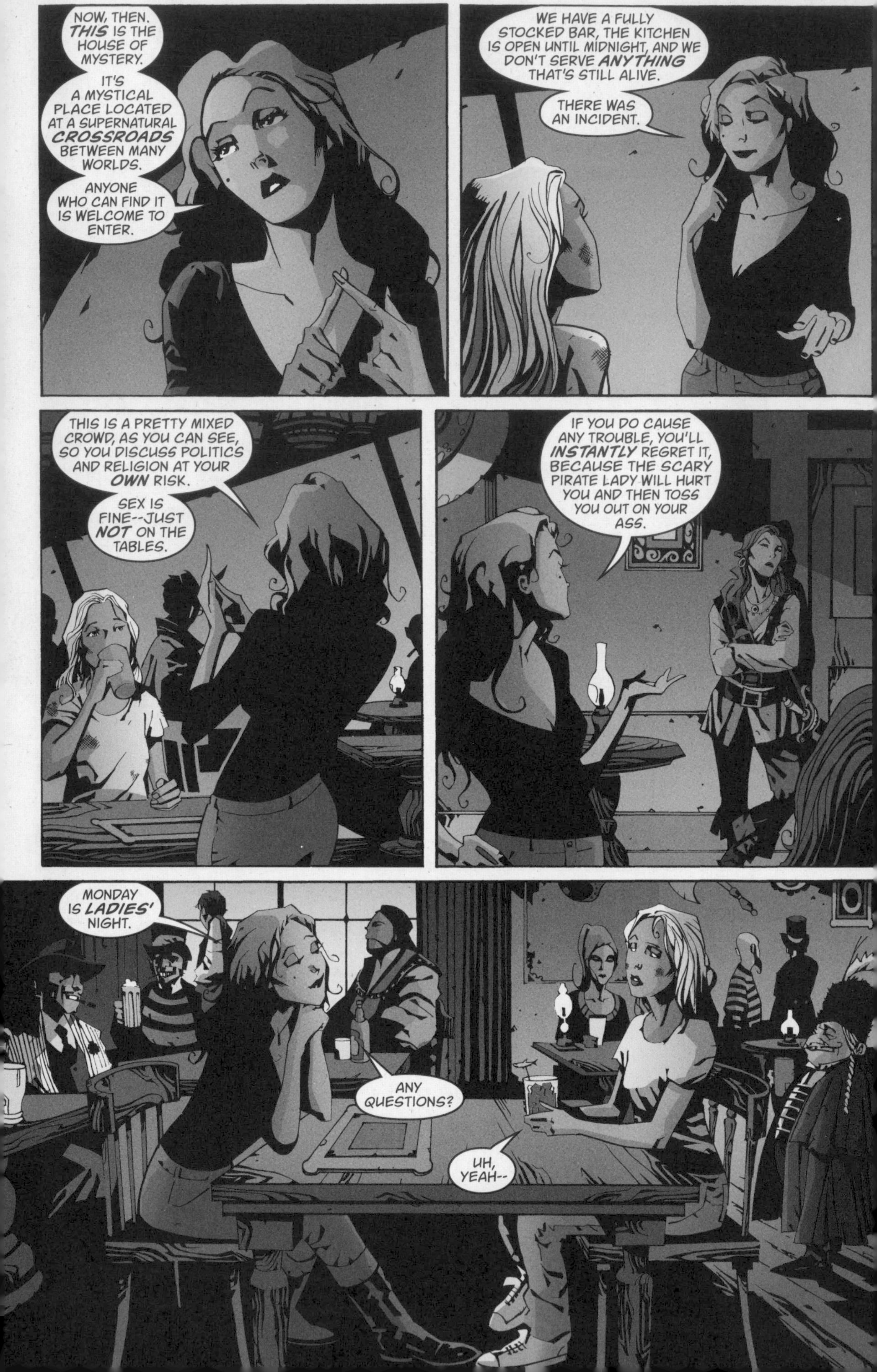
NOW, THEN. THIS IS THE HOUSE OF MYSTERY.
IT'S A MYSTICAL PLACE LOCATED AT A SUPERNATURAL CROSSROADS BETWEEN MANY WORLDS.
ANYONE WHO CAN FIND IT IS WELCOME TO ENTER.
WE HAVE A FULLY STOCKED BAR, THE KITCHEN IS OPEN UNTIL MIDNIGHT, AND WE DON'T SERVE ANYTHING THAT'S STILL ALIVE.
THERE WAS AN INCIDENT.
THIS IS A PRETTY MIXED CROWD, AS YOU CAN SEE, SO YOU DISCUSS POLITICS AND RELIGION AT YOUR OWN RISK.
SEX IS FINE--JUST NOT ON THE TABLES.
IF YOU DO CAUSE ANY TROUBLE, YOU'LL INSTANTLY REGRET IT, BECAUSE THE SCARY PIRATE LADY WILL HURT YOU AND THEN TOSS YOU OUT ON YOUR ASS.
MONDAY IS LADIES' NIGHT.
ANY QUESTIONS?
UH, YEAH--

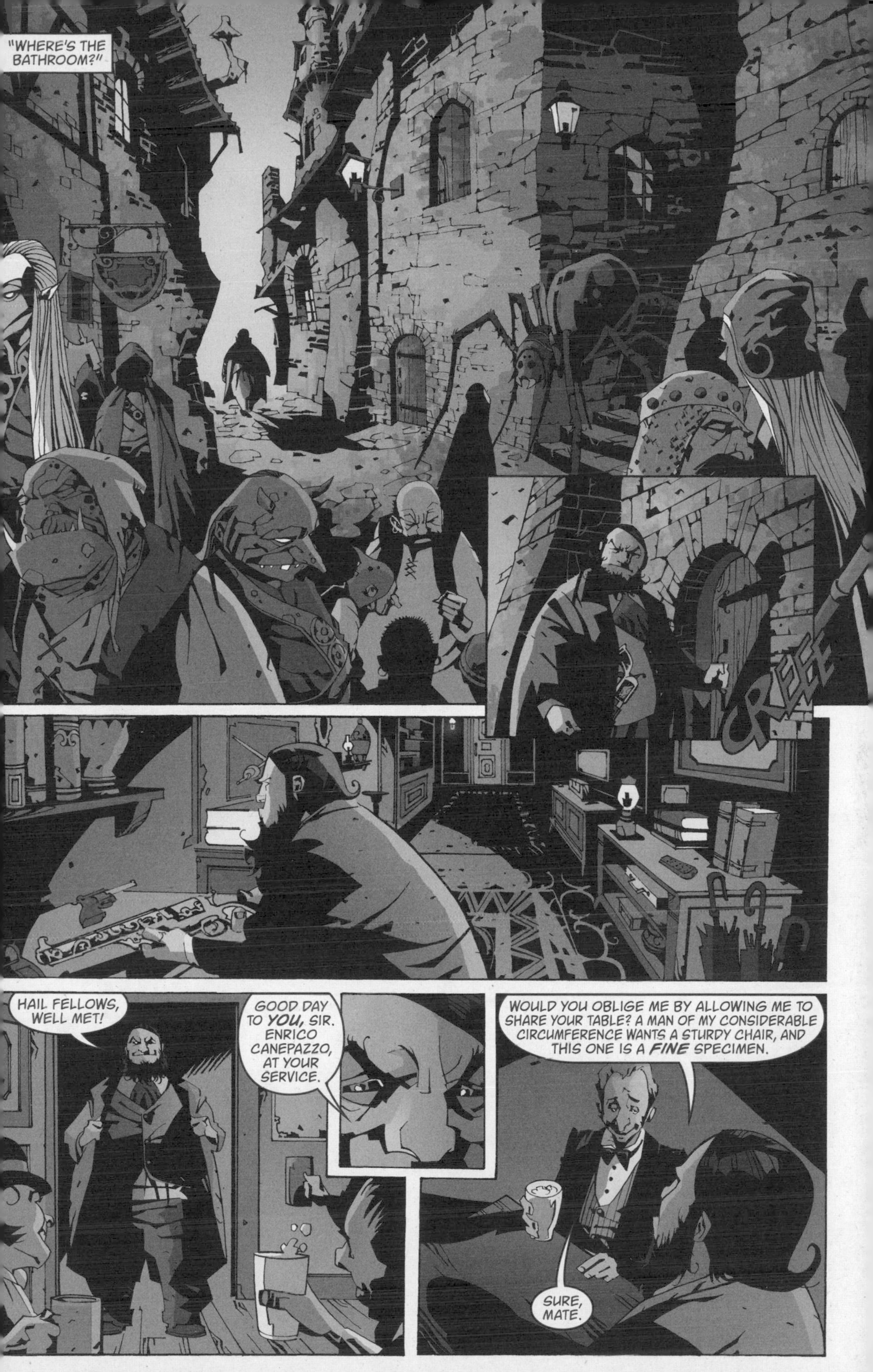
"WHERE'S THE BATHROOM?"
CREEEE
HAIL FELLOWS, WELL MET!
GOOD DAY TO *YOU,* SIR. ENRICO CANEPAZZO, AT YOUR SERVICE.
WOULD YOU OBLIGE ME BY ALLOWING ME TO SHARE YOUR TABLE? A MAN OF MY CONSIDERABLE CIRCUMFERENCE WANTS A STURDY CHAIR, AND THIS ONE IS A *FINE* SPECIMEN.
SURE, MATE.

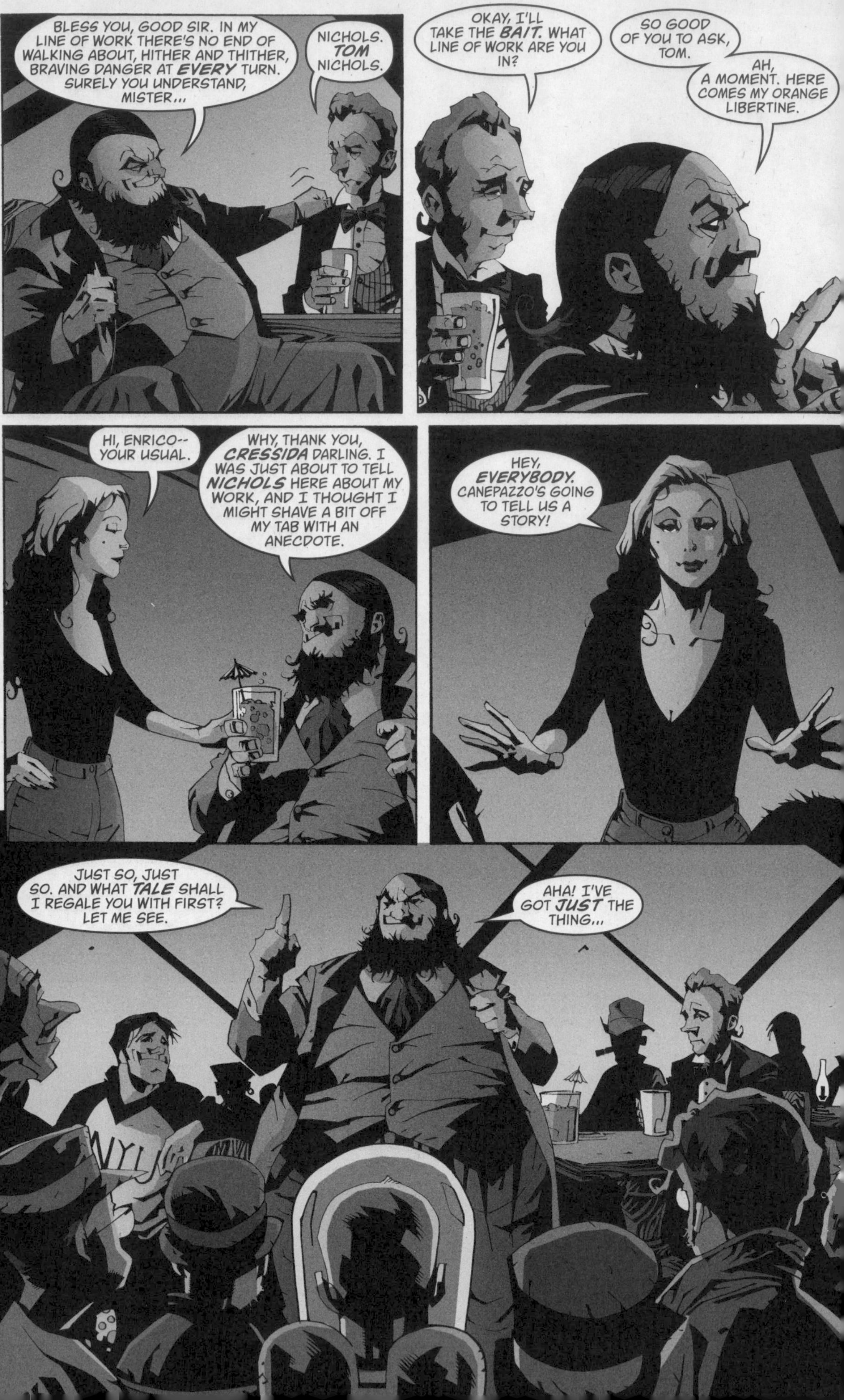
BLESS YOU, GOOD SIR. IN MY LINE OF WORK THERE'S NO END OF WALKING ABOUT, HITHER AND THITHER, BRAVING DANGER AT EVERY TURN. SURELY YOU UNDERSTAND, MISTER...
NICHOLS. TOM NICHOLS.
OKAY, I'LL TAKE THE BAIT. WHAT LINE OF WORK ARE YOU IN?
SO GOOD OF YOU TO ASK, TOM.
AH, A MOMENT. HERE COMES MY ORANGE LIBERTINE.
HI, ENRICO-- YOUR USUAL.
WHY, THANK YOU, CRESSIDA DARLING. I WAS JUST ABOUT TO TELL NICHOLS HERE ABOUT MY WORK, AND I THOUGHT I MIGHT SHAVE A BIT OFF MY TAB WITH AN ANECDOTE.
HEY, EVERYBODY. CANEPAZZO'S GOING TO TELL US A STORY!
JUST SO, JUST SO. AND WHAT TALE SHALL I REGALE YOU WITH FIRST? LET ME SEE.
AHA! I'VE GOT JUST THE THING...
NYU

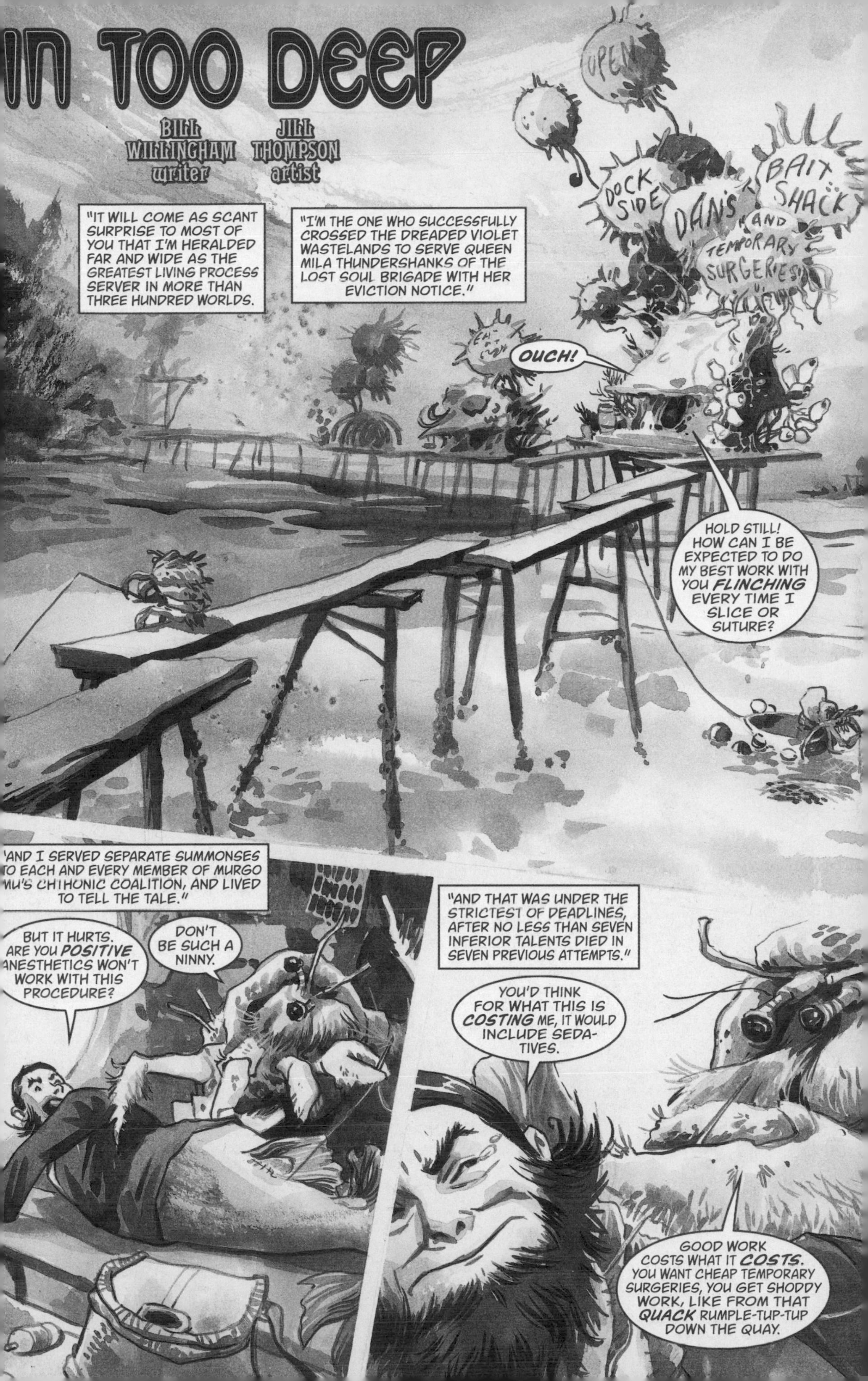

IN TOO DEEP
BILL WILLINGHAM writer
JILL THOMPSON artist
OPEN
DOCK SIDE
DAN'S
BAIT SHACK
AND TEMPORARY SURGERIES
"IT WILL COME AS SCANT SURPRISE TO MOST OF YOU THAT I'M HERALDED FAR AND WIDE AS THE GREATEST LIVING PROCESS SERVER IN MORE THAN THREE HUNDRED WORLDS.
"I'M THE ONE WHO SUCCESSFULLY CROSSED THE DREADED VIOLET WASTELANDS TO SERVE QUEEN MILA THUNDERSHANKS OF THE LOST SOUL BRIGADE WITH HER EVICTION NOTICE."
OUCH!
HOLD STILL! HOW CAN I BE EXPECTED TO DO MY BEST WORK WITH YOU FLINCHING EVERY TIME I SLICE OR SUTURE?
"AND I SERVED SEPARATE SUMMONSES TO EACH AND EVERY MEMBER OF MURGO MU'S CHTHONIC COALITION, AND LIVED TO TELL THE TALE."
BUT IT HURTS. ARE YOU POSITIVE ANESTHETICS WON'T WORK WITH THIS PROCEDURE?
DON'T BE SUCH A NINNY.
"AND THAT WAS UNDER THE STRICTEST OF DEADLINES, AFTER NO LESS THAN SEVEN INFERIOR TALENTS DIED IN SEVEN PREVIOUS ATTEMPTS."
YOU'D THINK FOR WHAT THIS IS COSTING ME, IT WOULD INCLUDE SEDATIVES.
GOOD WORK COSTS WHAT IT COSTS. YOU WANT CHEAP TEMPORARY SURGERIES, YOU GET SHODDY WORK, LIKE FROM THAT QUACK RUMPLE-TUP-TUP DOWN THE QUAY.

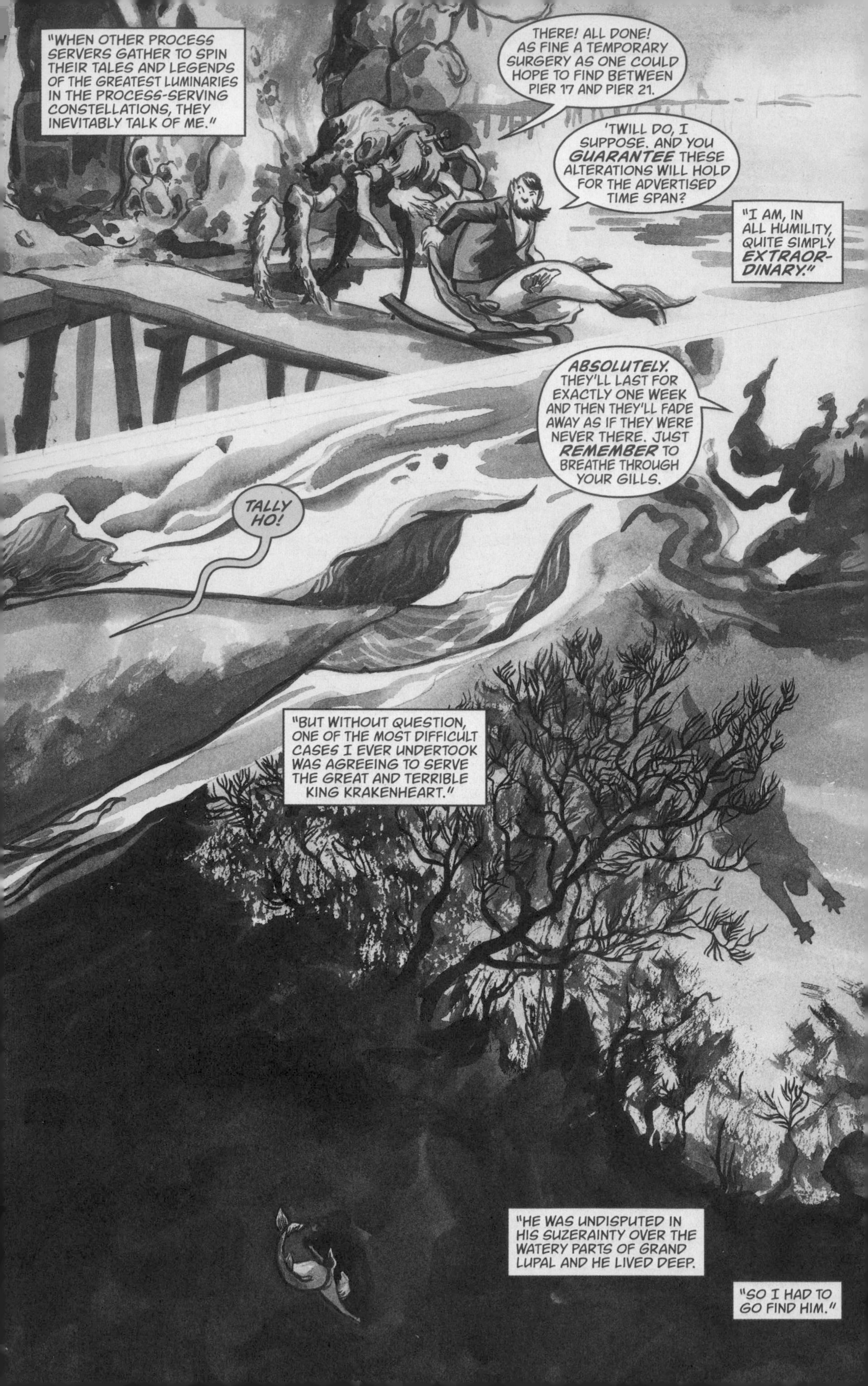
"WHEN OTHER PROCESS SERVERS GATHER TO SPIN THEIR TALES AND LEGENDS OF THE GREATEST LUMINARIES IN THE PROCESS-SERVING CONSTELLATIONS, THEY INEVITABLY TALK OF ME."
THERE! ALL DONE! AS FINE A TEMPORARY SURGERY AS ONE COULD HOPE TO FIND BETWEEN PIER 17 AND PIER 21.
'TWILL DO, I SUPPOSE. AND YOU GUARANTEE THESE ALTERATIONS WILL HOLD FOR THE ADVERTISED TIME SPAN?
"I AM, IN ALL HUMILITY, QUITE SIMPLY EXTRAORDINARY."
ABSOLUTELY. THEY'LL LAST FOR EXACTLY ONE WEEK AND THEN THEY'LL FADE AWAY AS IF THEY WERE NEVER THERE. JUST REMEMBER TO BREATHE THROUGH YOUR GILLS.
TALLY HO!
"BUT WITHOUT QUESTION, ONE OF THE MOST DIFFICULT CASES I EVER UNDERTOOK WAS AGREEING TO SERVE THE GREAT AND TERRIBLE KING KRAKENHEART."
"HE WAS UNDISPUTED IN HIS SUZERAINTY OVER THE WATERY PARTS OF GRAND LUPAL AND HE LIVED DEEP.
"SO I HAD TO GO FIND HIM."

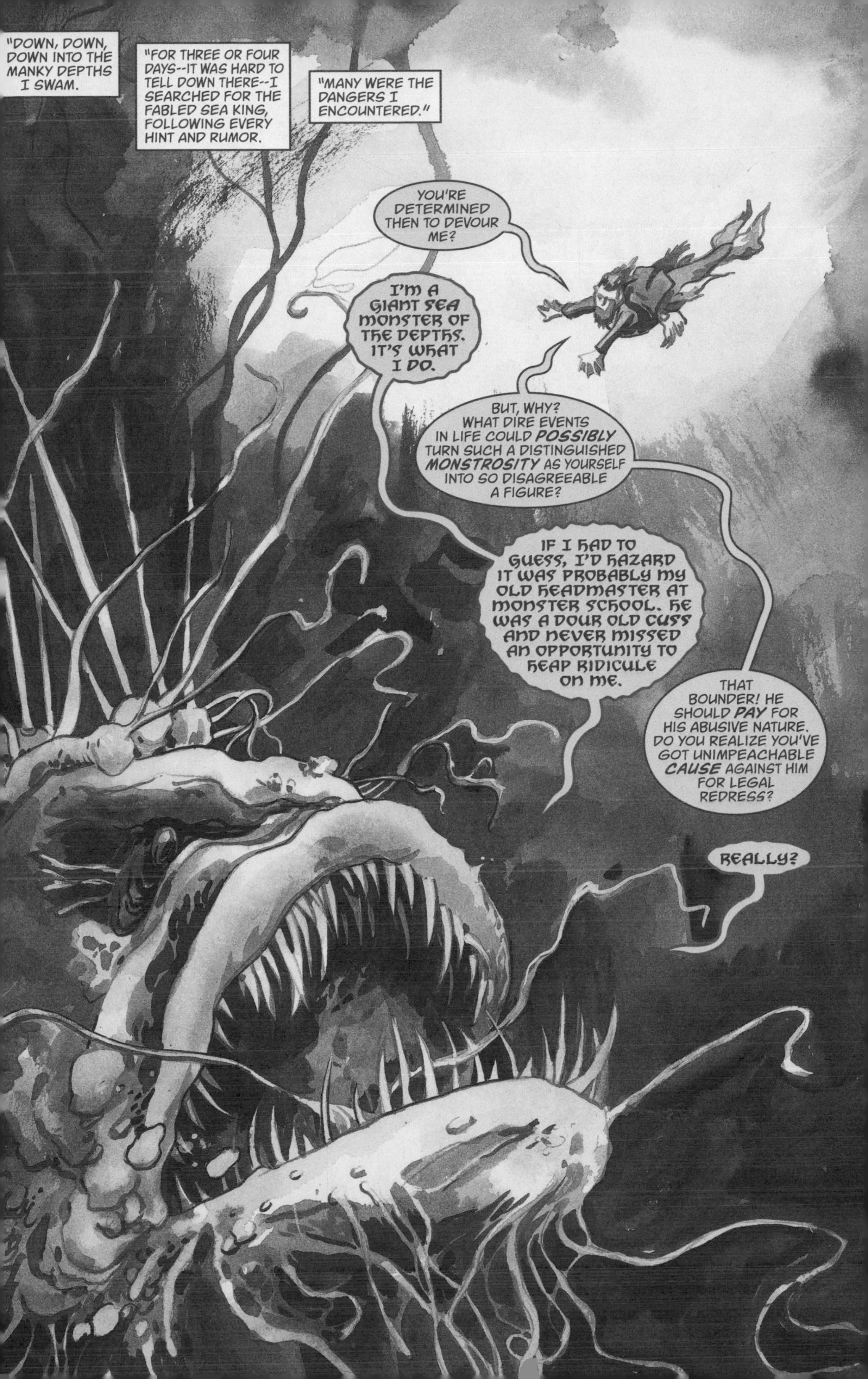
"DOWN, DOWN, DOWN INTO THE MANKY DEPTHS I SWAM.
"FOR THREE OR FOUR DAYS--IT WAS HARD TO TELL DOWN THERE--I SEARCHED FOR THE FABLED SEA KING, FOLLOWING EVERY HINT AND RUMOR.
"MANY WERE THE DANGERS I ENCOUNTERED."
YOU'RE DETERMINED THEN TO DEVOUR ME?
I'M A GIANT *SEA* MONSTER OF THE DEPTHS. IT'S WHAT I *DO*.
BUT, WHY? WHAT DIRE EVENTS IN LIFE COULD *POSSIBLY* TURN SUCH A DISTINGUISHED *MONSTROSITY* AS YOURSELF INTO SO DISAGREEABLE A FIGURE?
IF I HAD TO GUESS, I'D HAZARD IT WAS PROBABLY MY OLD HEADMASTER AT MONSTER SCHOOL. HE WAS A DOUR OLD *CUSS* AND NEVER MISSED AN OPPORTUNITY TO HEAP RIDICULE ON ME.
THAT BOUNDER! HE SHOULD *PAY* FOR HIS ABUSIVE NATURE. DO YOU REALIZE YOU'VE GOT UNIMPEACHABLE *CAUSE* AGAINST HIM FOR LEGAL REDRESS?
REALLY?

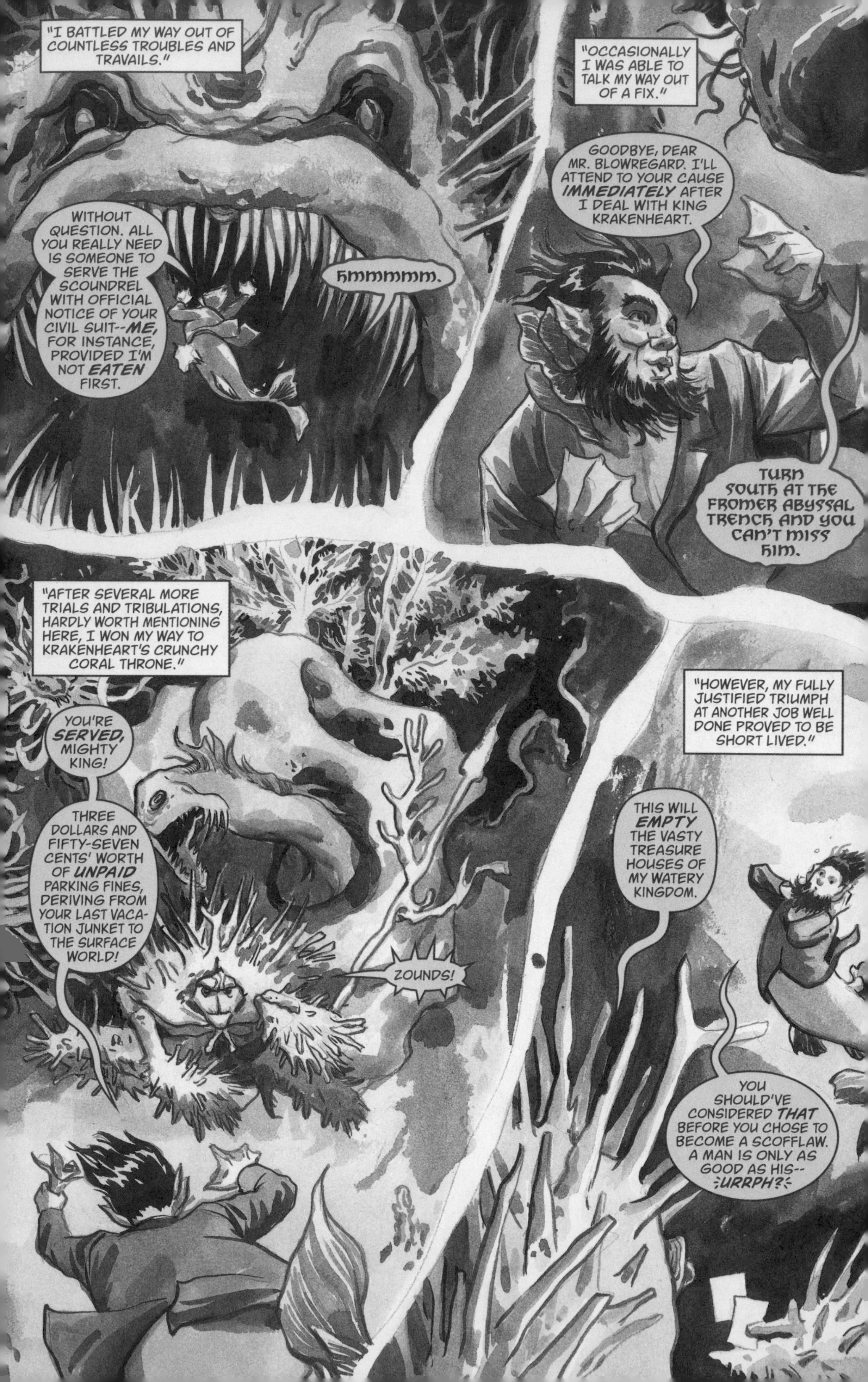
"I BATTLED MY WAY OUT OF COUNTLESS TROUBLES AND TRAVAILS."
WITHOUT QUESTION. ALL YOU REALLY NEED IS SOMEONE TO SERVE THE SCOUNDREL WITH OFFICIAL NOTICE OF YOUR CIVIL SUIT--ME, FOR INSTANCE, PROVIDED I'M NOT EATEN FIRST.
HMMMMM.
"OCCASIONALLY I WAS ABLE TO TALK MY WAY OUT OF A FIX."
GOODBYE, DEAR MR. BLOWREGARD. I'LL ATTEND TO YOUR CAUSE IMMEDIATELY AFTER I DEAL WITH KING KRAKENHEART.
TURN SOUTH AT THE FROMER ABYSSAL TRENCH AND YOU CAN'T MISS HIM.
"AFTER SEVERAL MORE TRIALS AND TRIBULATIONS, HARDLY WORTH MENTIONING HERE, I WON MY WAY TO KRAKENHEART'S CRUNCHY CORAL THRONE."
YOU'RE SERVED, MIGHTY KING!
THREE DOLLARS AND FIFTY-SEVEN CENTS' WORTH OF UNPAID PARKING FINES, DERIVING FROM YOUR LAST VACATION JUNKET TO THE SURFACE WORLD!
ZOUNDS!
"HOWEVER, MY FULLY JUSTIFIED TRIUMPH AT ANOTHER JOB WELL DONE PROVED TO BE SHORT LIVED."
THIS WILL EMPTY THE VASTY TREASURE HOUSES OF MY WATERY KINGDOM.
YOU SHOULD'VE CONSIDERED THAT BEFORE YOU CHOSE TO BECOME A SCOFFLAW. A MAN IS ONLY AS GOOD AS HIS-- URRPH?

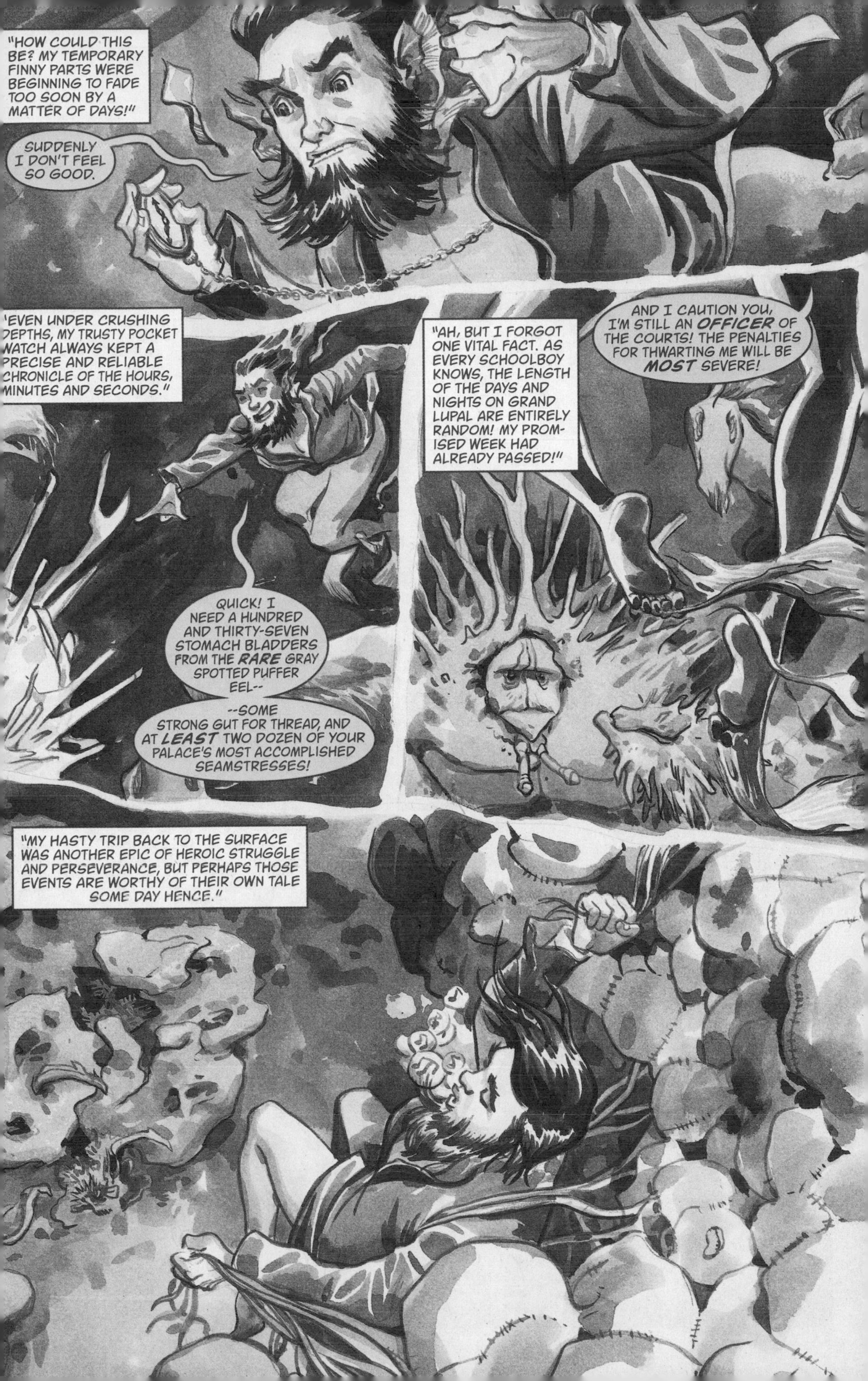
"HOW COULD THIS BE? MY TEMPORARY FINNY PARTS WERE BEGINNING TO FADE TOO SOON BY A MATTER OF DAYS!"
SUDDENLY I DON'T FEEL SO GOOD.
"EVEN UNDER CRUSHING DEPTHS, MY TRUSTY POCKET WATCH ALWAYS KEPT A PRECISE AND RELIABLE CHRONICLE OF THE HOURS, MINUTES AND SECONDS."
QUICK! I NEED A HUNDRED AND THIRTY-SEVEN STOMACH BLADDERS FROM THE RARE GRAY SPOTTED PUFFER EEL--
--SOME STRONG GUT FOR THREAD, AND AT LEAST TWO DOZEN OF YOUR PALACE'S MOST ACCOMPLISHED SEAMSTRESSES!
"AH, BUT I FORGOT ONE VITAL FACT. AS EVERY SCHOOLBOY KNOWS, THE LENGTH OF THE DAYS AND NIGHTS ON GRAND LUPAL ARE ENTIRELY RANDOM! MY PROMISED WEEK HAD ALREADY PASSED!"
AND I CAUTION YOU, I'M STILL AN OFFICER OF THE COURTS! THE PENALTIES FOR THWARTING ME WILL BE MOST SEVERE!
"MY HASTY TRIP BACK TO THE SURFACE WAS ANOTHER EPIC OF HEROIC STRUGGLE AND PERSEVERANCE, BUT PERHAPS THOSE EVENTS ARE WORTHY OF THEIR OWN TALE SOME DAY HENCE."

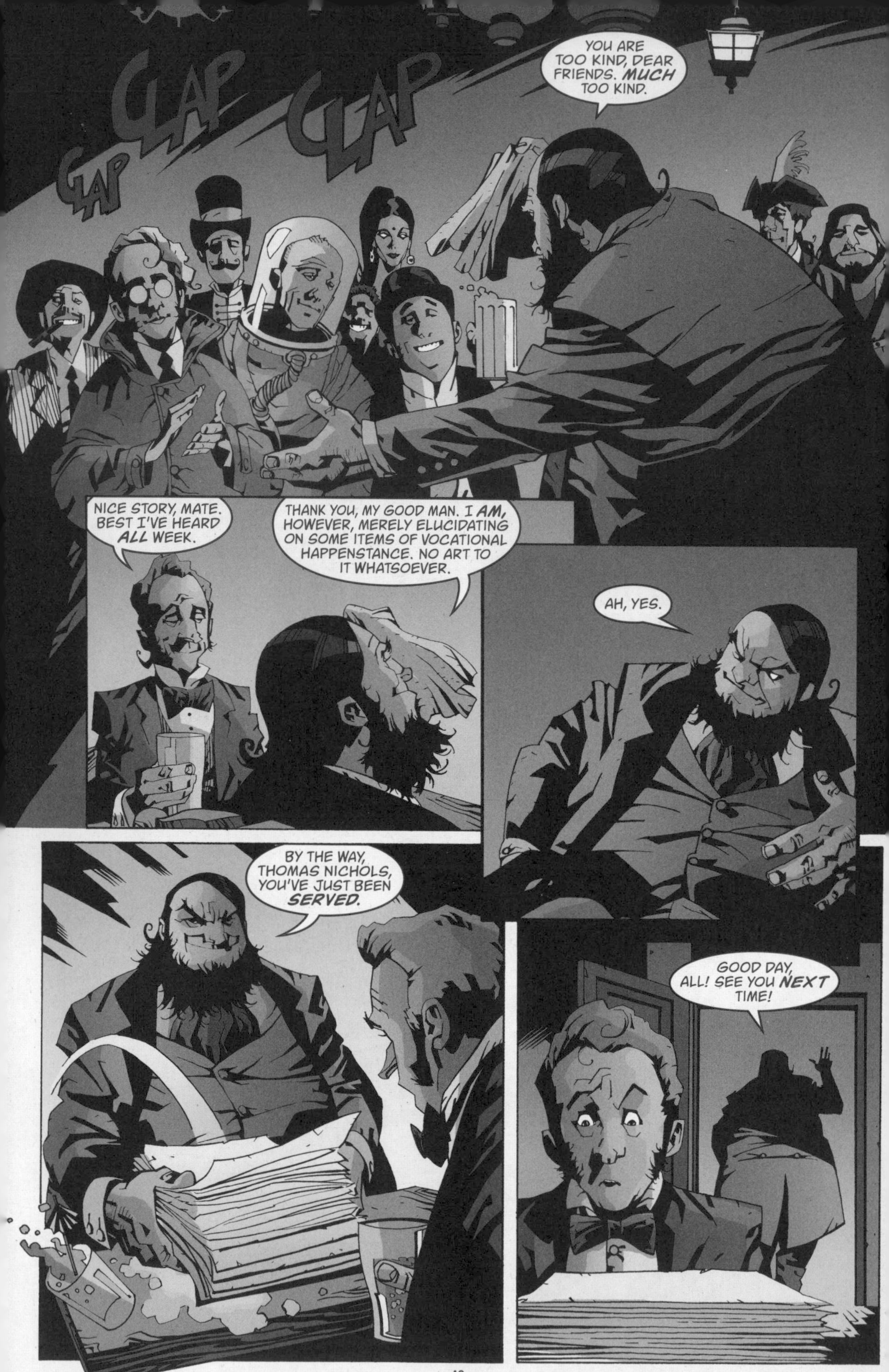
CLAP CLAP CLAP
YOU ARE TOO KIND, DEAR FRIENDS. MUCH TOO KIND.
NICE STORY, MATE. BEST I'VE HEARD ALL WEEK.
THANK YOU, MY GOOD MAN. I AM, HOWEVER, MERELY ELUCIDATING ON SOME ITEMS OF VOCATIONAL HAPPENSTANCE. NO ART TO IT WHATSOEVER.
AH, YES.
BY THE WAY, THOMAS NICHOLS, YOU'VE JUST BEEN SERVED.
GOOD DAY, ALL! SEE YOU NEXT TIME!

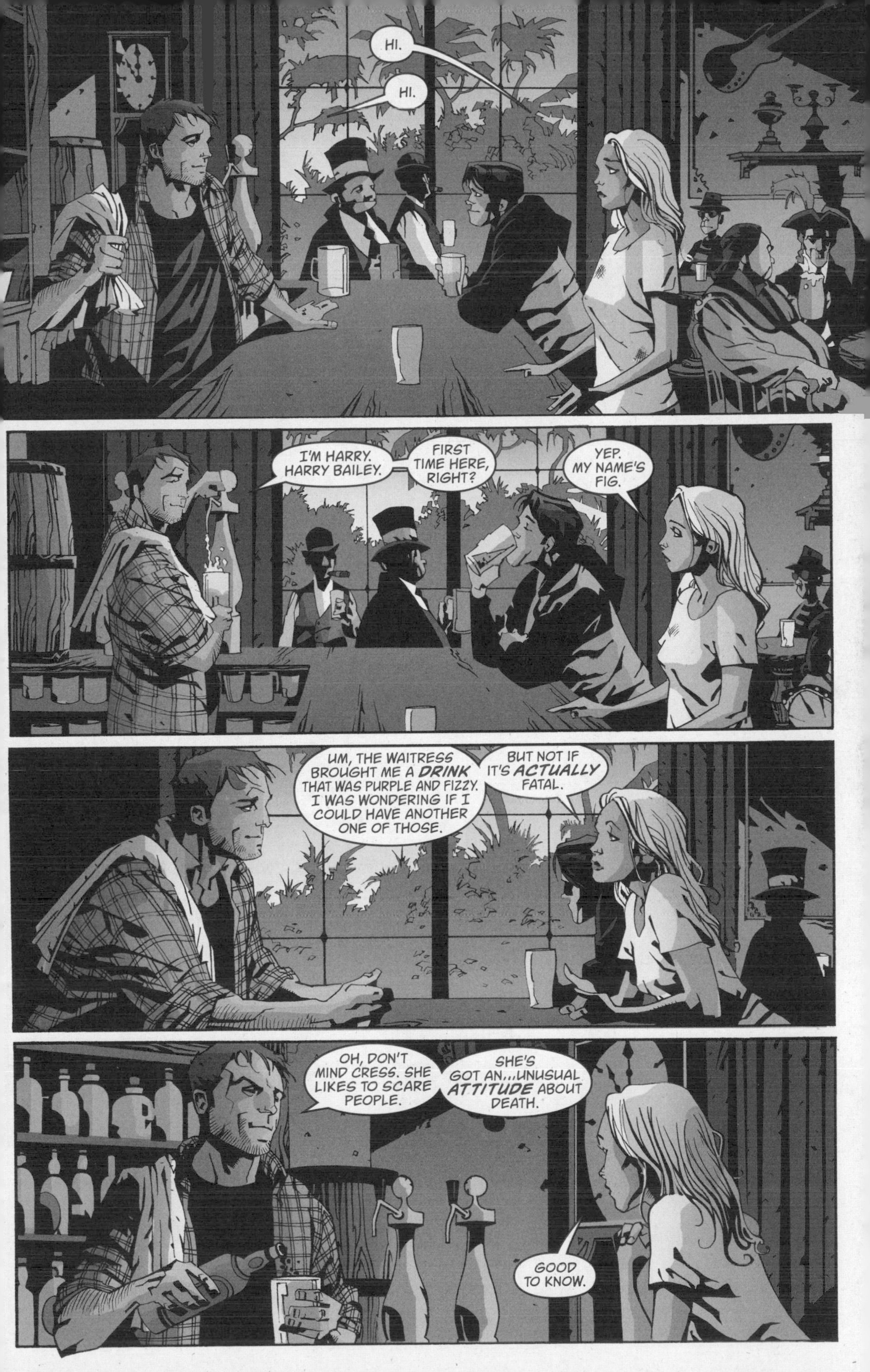
HI.
HI.
I'M HARRY. HARRY BAILEY.
FIRST TIME HERE, RIGHT?
YEP. MY NAME'S FIG.
UM, THE WAITRESS BROUGHT ME A DRINK THAT WAS PURPLE AND FIZZY. I WAS WONDERING IF I COULD HAVE ANOTHER ONE OF THOSE.
BUT NOT IF IT'S ACTUALLY FATAL.
OH, DON'T MIND CRESS. SHE LIKES TO SCARE PEOPLE.
SHE'S GOT AN...UNUSUAL ATTITUDE ABOUT DEATH.
GOOD TO KNOW.

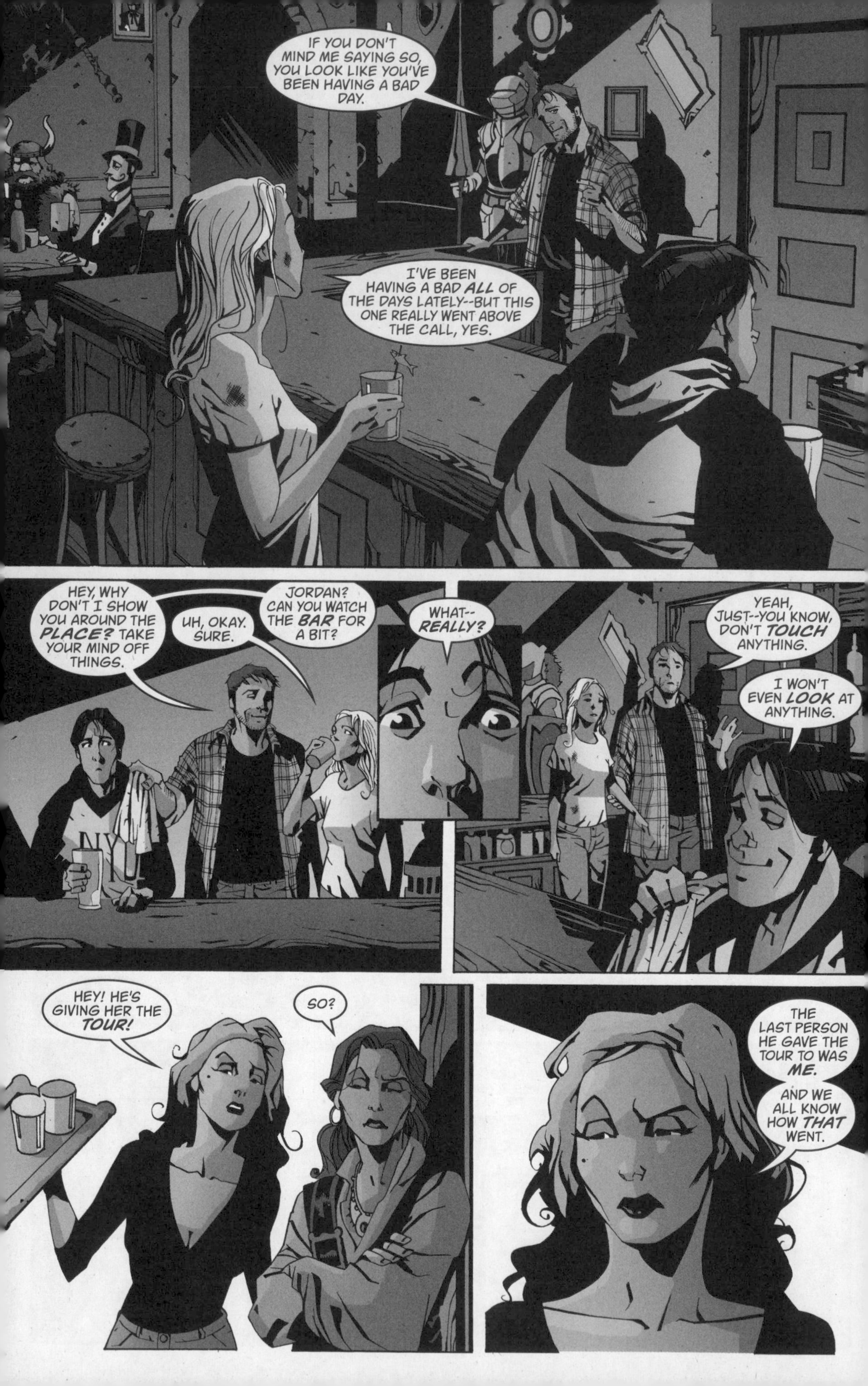
IF YOU DON'T MIND ME SAYING SO, YOU LOOK LIKE YOU'VE BEEN HAVING A BAD DAY.
I'VE BEEN HAVING A BAD ALL OF THE DAYS LATELY--BUT THIS ONE REALLY WENT ABOVE THE CALL, YES.
HEY, WHY DON'T I SHOW YOU AROUND THE PLACE? TAKE YOUR MIND OFF THINGS.
UH, OKAY. SURE.
JORDAN? CAN YOU WATCH THE BAR FOR A BIT?
WHAT-- REALLY?
YEAH, JUST--YOU KNOW, DON'T TOUCH ANYTHING.
I WON'T EVEN LOOK AT ANYTHING.
HEY! HE'S GIVING HER THE TOUR!
SO?
THE LAST PERSON HE GAVE THE TOUR TO WAS ME.
AND WE ALL KNOW HOW THAT WENT.

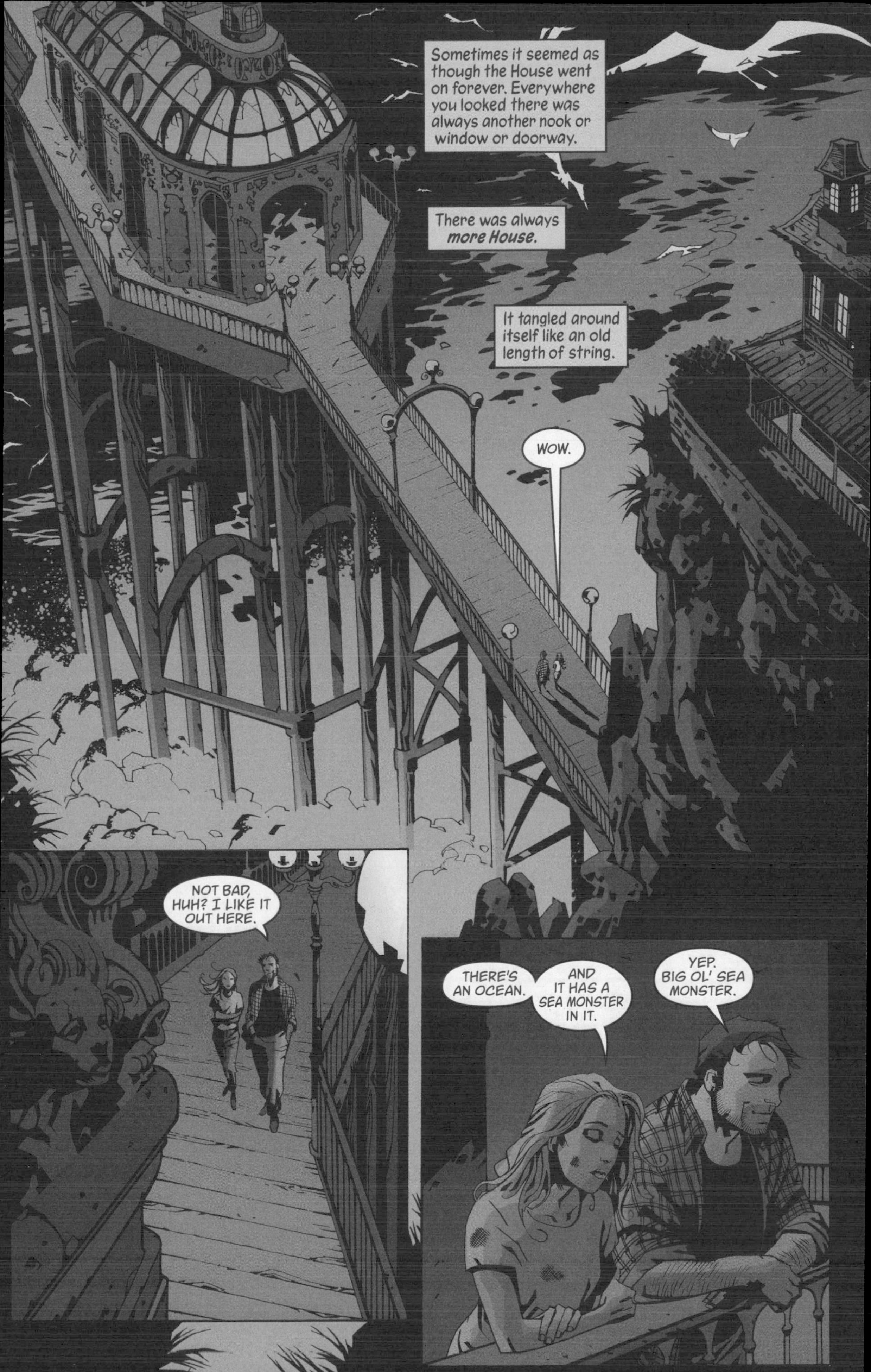
Sometimes it seemed as though the House went on forever. Everywhere you looked there was always another nook or window or doorway.
There was always *more House.*
It tangled around itself like an old length of string.
WOW.
NOT BAD, HUH? I LIKE IT OUT HERE.
THERE'S AN OCEAN.
AND IT HAS A SEA MONSTER IN IT.
YEP. BIG OL' SEA MONSTER.

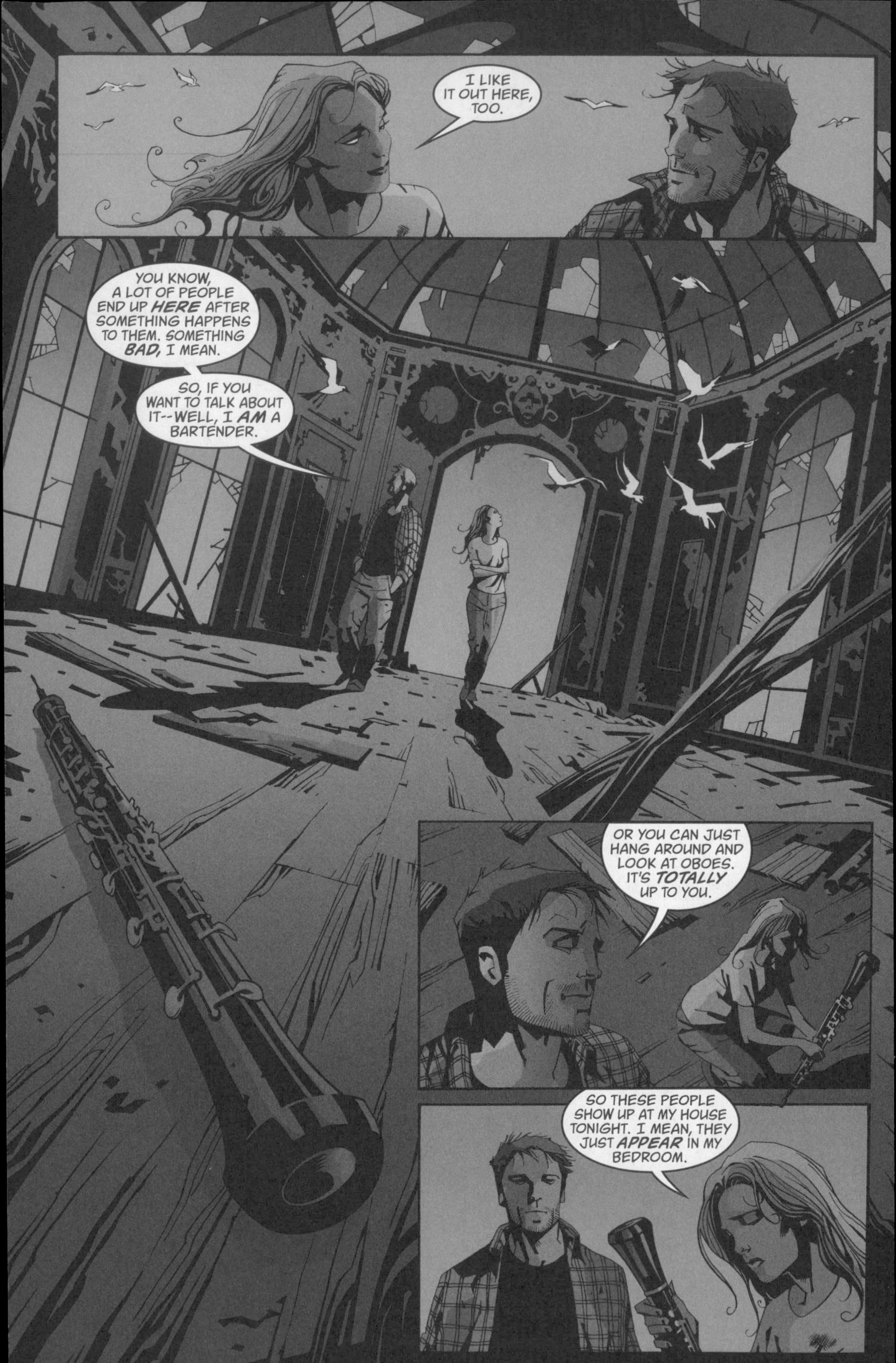

I LIKE IT OUT HERE, TOO.
YOU KNOW, A LOT OF PEOPLE END UP HERE AFTER SOMETHING HAPPENS TO THEM. SOMETHING BAD, I MEAN.
SO, IF YOU WANT TO TALK ABOUT IT--WELL, I AM A BARTENDER.
OR YOU CAN JUST HANG AROUND AND LOOK AT OBOES. IT'S TOTALLY UP TO YOU.
SO THESE PEOPLE SHOW UP AT MY HOUSE TONIGHT. I MEAN, THEY JUST APPEAR IN MY BEDROOM.

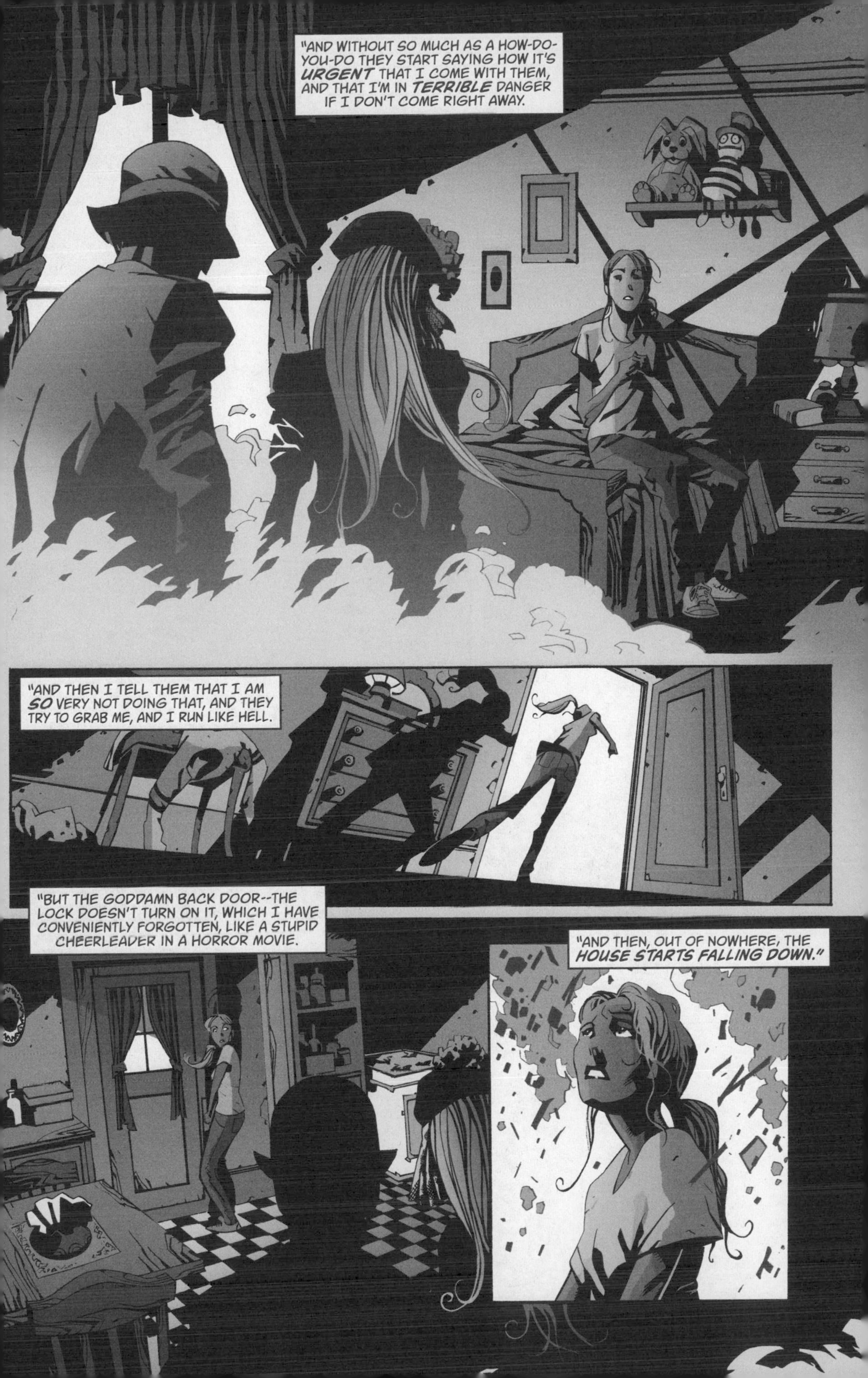
"AND WITHOUT SO MUCH AS A HOW-DO-YOU-DO THEY START SAYING HOW IT'S URGENT THAT I COME WITH THEM, AND THAT I'M IN TERRIBLE DANGER IF I DON'T COME RIGHT AWAY.
"AND THEN I TELL THEM THAT I AM SO VERY NOT DOING THAT, AND THEY TRY TO GRAB ME, AND I RUN LIKE HELL.
"BUT THE GODDAMN BACK DOOR--THE LOCK DOESN'T TURN ON IT, WHICH I HAVE CONVENIENTLY FORGOTTEN, LIKE A STUPID CHEERLEADER IN A HORROR MOVIE.
"AND THEN, OUT OF NOWHERE, THE HOUSE STARTS FALLING DOWN."

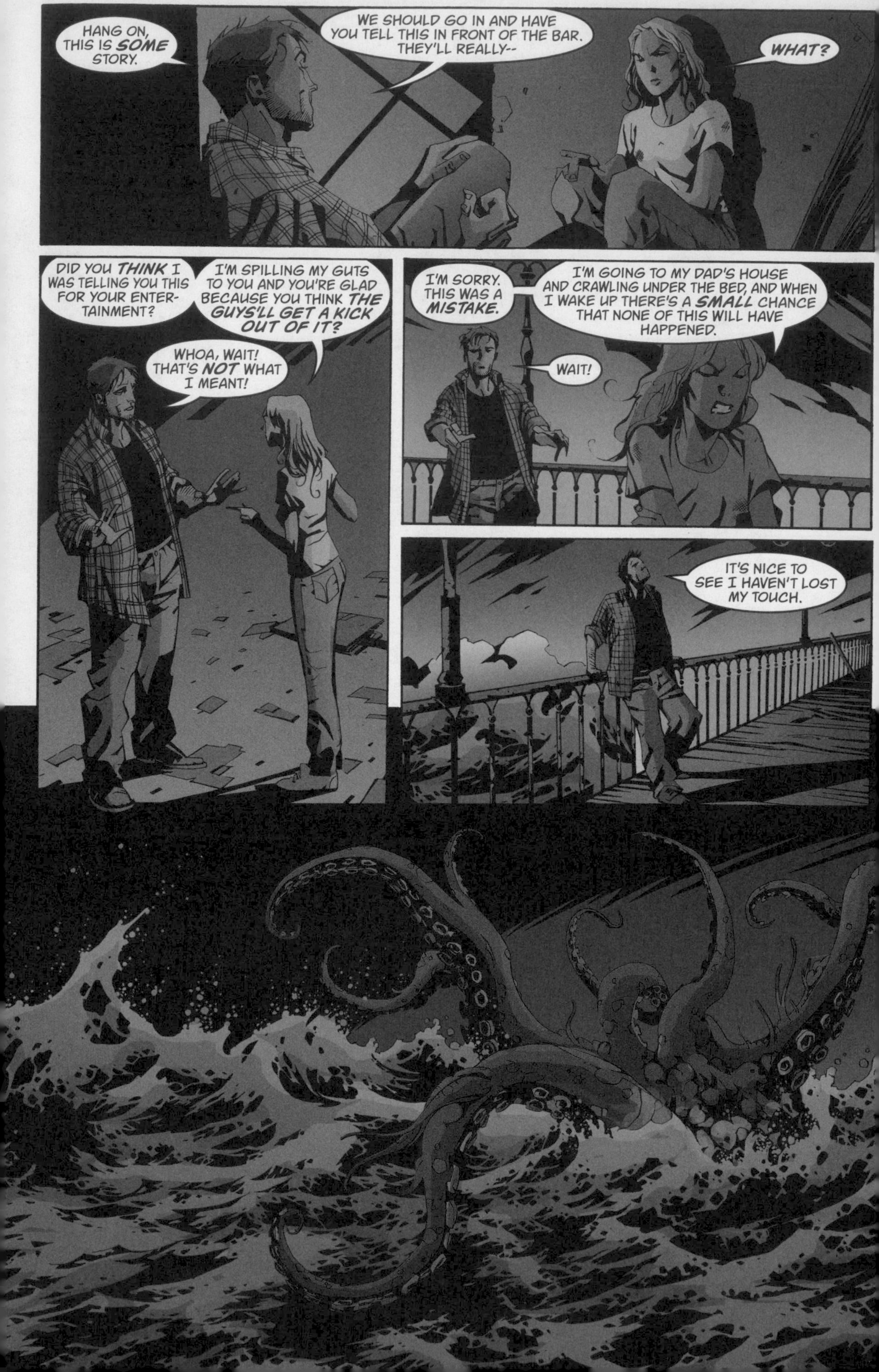
HANG ON, THIS IS SOME STORY.
WE SHOULD GO IN AND HAVE YOU TELL THIS IN FRONT OF THE BAR. THEY'LL REALLY--
WHAT?
DID YOU THINK I WAS TELLING YOU THIS FOR YOUR ENTERTAINMENT?
I'M SPILLING MY GUTS TO YOU AND YOU'RE GLAD BECAUSE YOU THINK THE GUYS'LL GET A KICK OUT OF IT?
WHOA, WAIT! THAT'S NOT WHAT I MEANT!
I'M SORRY. THIS WAS A MISTAKE.
I'M GOING TO MY DAD'S HOUSE AND CRAWLING UNDER THE BED, AND WHEN I WAKE UP THERE'S A SMALL CHANCE THAT NONE OF THIS WILL HAVE HAPPENED.
WAIT!
IT'S NICE TO SEE I HAVEN'T LOST MY TOUCH.

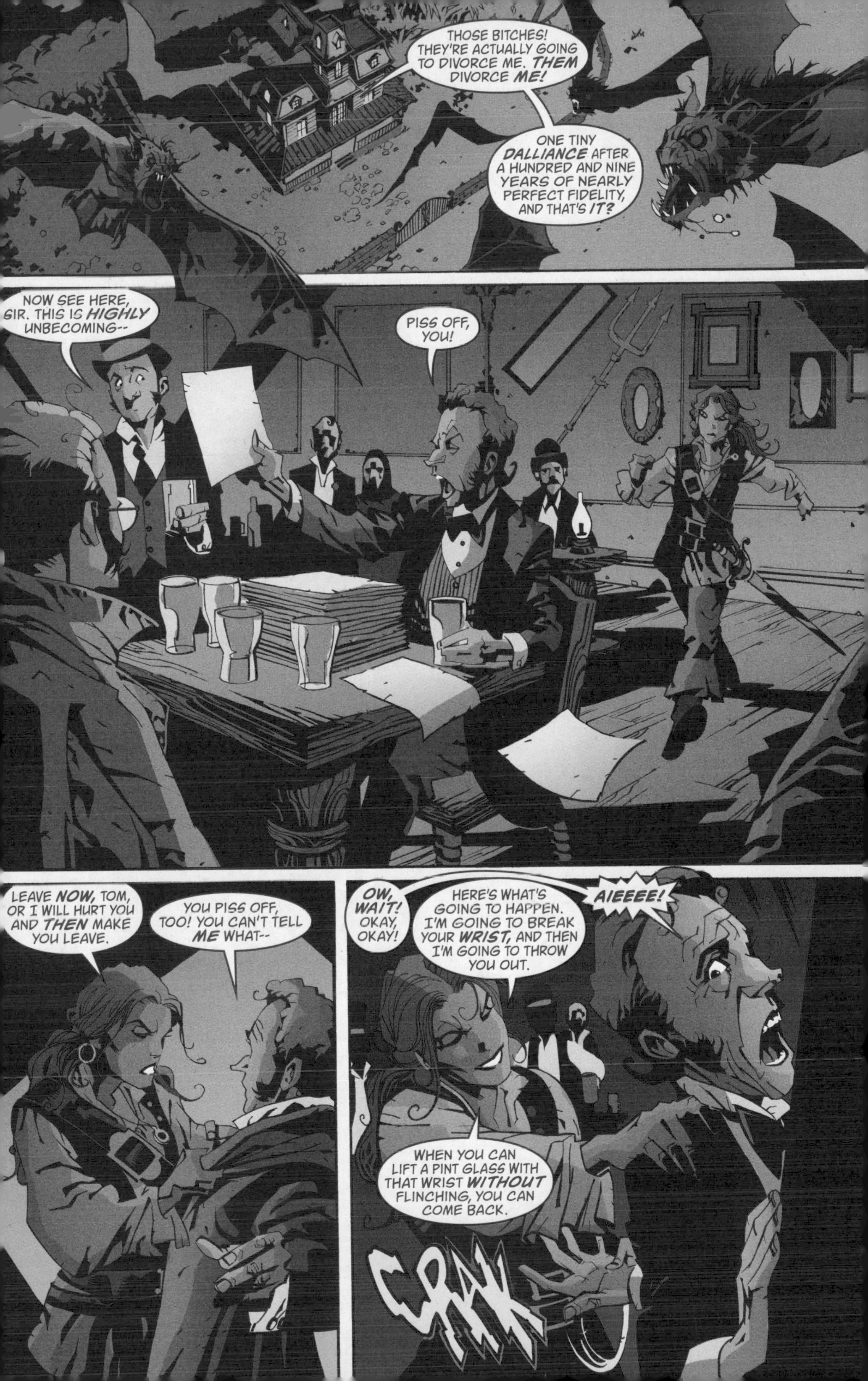
THOSE BITCHES! THEY'RE ACTUALLY GOING TO DIVORCE ME. THEM DIVORCE ME!
ONE TINY DALLIANCE AFTER A HUNDRED AND NINE YEARS OF NEARLY PERFECT FIDELITY, AND THAT'S IT?
NOW SEE HERE, SIR. THIS IS HIGHLY UNBECOMING--
PISS OFF, YOU!
LEAVE NOW, TOM, OR I WILL HURT YOU AND THEN MAKE YOU LEAVE.
YOU PISS OFF, TOO! YOU CAN'T TELL ME WHAT--
HERE'S WHAT'S GOING TO HAPPEN. I'M GOING TO BREAK YOUR WRIST, AND THEN I'M GOING TO THROW YOU OUT.
OW, WAIT! OKAY, OKAY!
AIEEEE!
CRAK
WHEN YOU CAN LIFT A PINT GLASS WITH THAT WRIST WITHOUT FLINCHING, YOU CAN COME BACK.

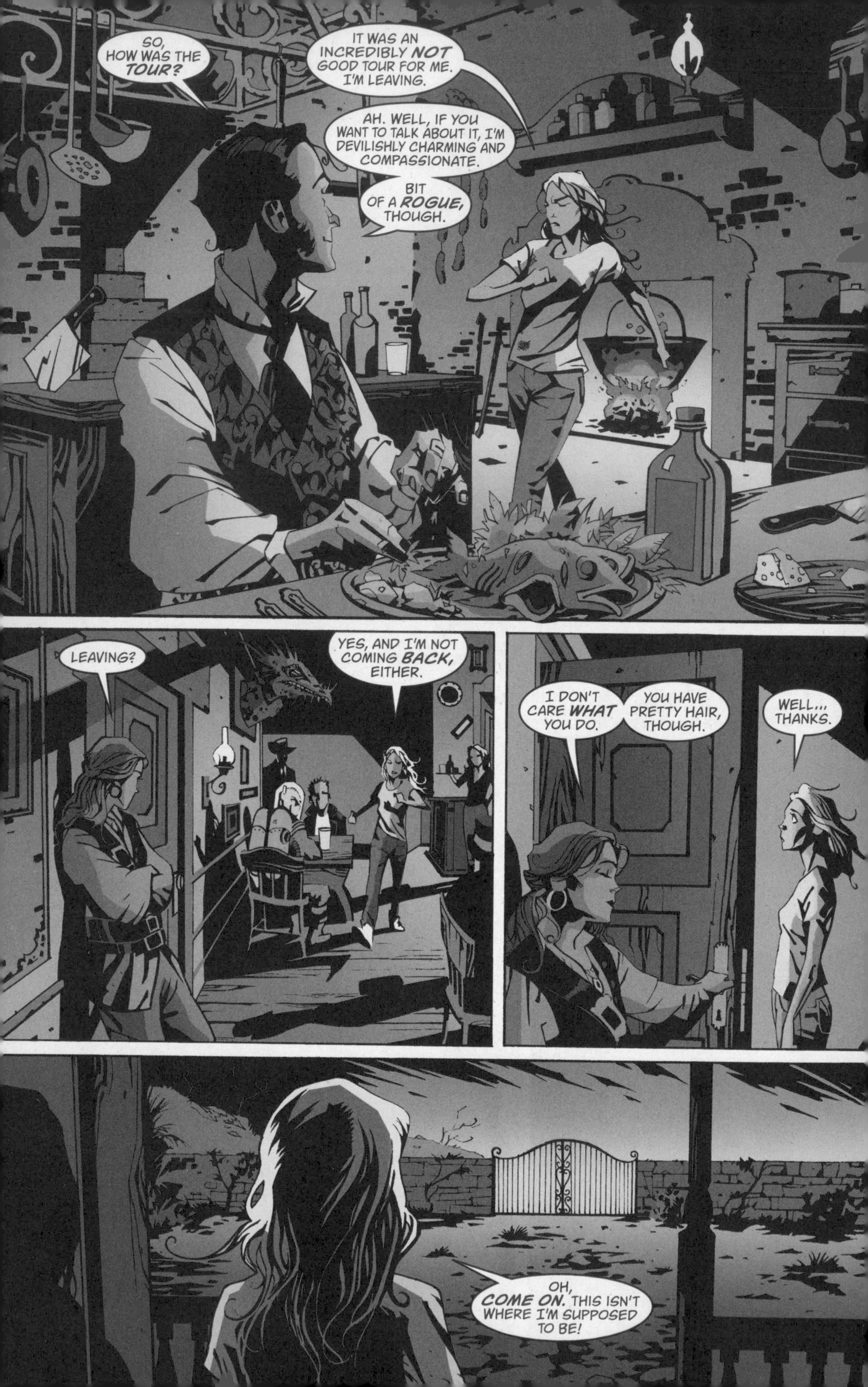
SO, HOW WAS THE TOUR?
IT WAS AN INCREDIBLY NOT GOOD TOUR FOR ME. I'M LEAVING.
AH. WELL, IF YOU WANT TO TALK ABOUT IT, I'M DEVILISHLY CHARMING AND COMPASSIONATE.
BIT OF A ROGUE, THOUGH.
LEAVING?
YES, AND I'M NOT COMING BACK, EITHER.
I DON'T CARE WHAT YOU DO.
YOU HAVE PRETTY HAIR, THOUGH.
WELL... THANKS.
OH, COME ON. THIS ISN'T WHERE I'M SUPPOSED TO BE!

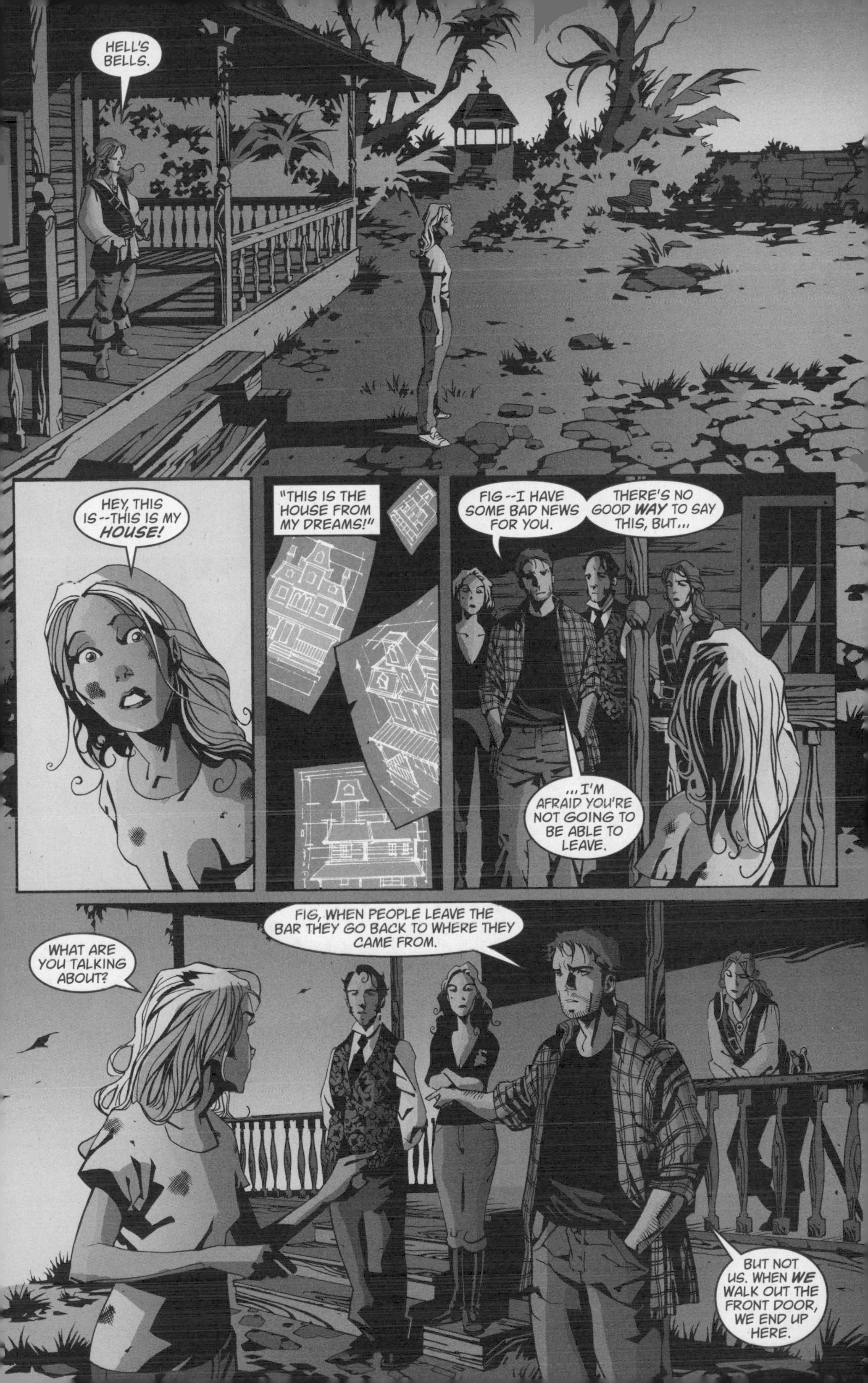
HELL'S BELLS.
HEY, THIS IS--THIS IS MY HOUSE!
"THIS IS THE HOUSE FROM MY DREAMS!"
FIG--I HAVE SOME BAD NEWS FOR YOU.
THERE'S NO GOOD WAY TO SAY THIS, BUT...
...I'M AFRAID YOU'RE NOT GOING TO BE ABLE TO LEAVE.
WHAT ARE YOU TALKING ABOUT?
FIG, WHEN PEOPLE LEAVE THE BAR THEY GO BACK TO WHERE THEY CAME FROM.
BUT NOT US. WHEN WE WALK OUT THE FRONT DOOR, WE END UP HERE.

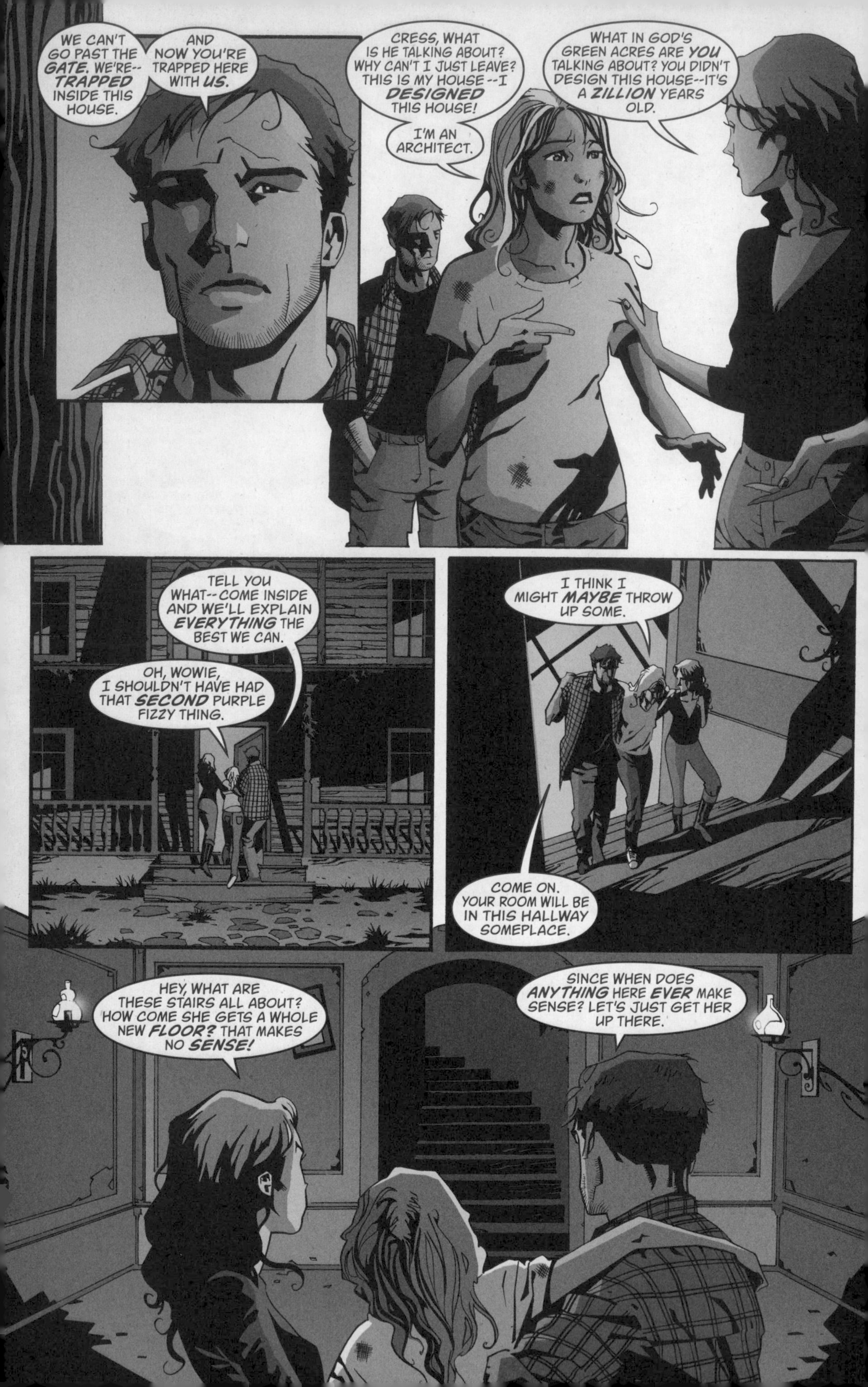
WE CAN'T GO PAST THE GATE. WE'RE-- TRAPPED INSIDE THIS HOUSE.
AND NOW YOU'RE TRAPPED HERE WITH US.
CRESS, WHAT IS HE TALKING ABOUT? WHY CAN'T I JUST LEAVE? THIS IS MY HOUSE --I DESIGNED THIS HOUSE!
I'M AN ARCHITECT.
WHAT IN GOD'S GREEN ACRES ARE YOU TALKING ABOUT? YOU DIDN'T DESIGN THIS HOUSE--IT'S A ZILLION YEARS OLD.
TELL YOU WHAT-- COME INSIDE AND WE'LL EXPLAIN EVERYTHING THE BEST WE CAN.
OH, WOWIE, I SHOULDN'T HAVE HAD THAT SECOND PURPLE FIZZY THING.
I THINK I MIGHT MAYBE THROW UP SOME.
COME ON. YOUR ROOM WILL BE IN THIS HALLWAY SOMEPLACE.
HEY, WHAT ARE THESE STAIRS ALL ABOUT? HOW COME SHE GETS A WHOLE NEW FLOOR? THAT MAKES NO SENSE!
SINCE WHEN DOES ANYTHING HERE EVER MAKE SENSE? LET'S JUST GET HER UP THERE.

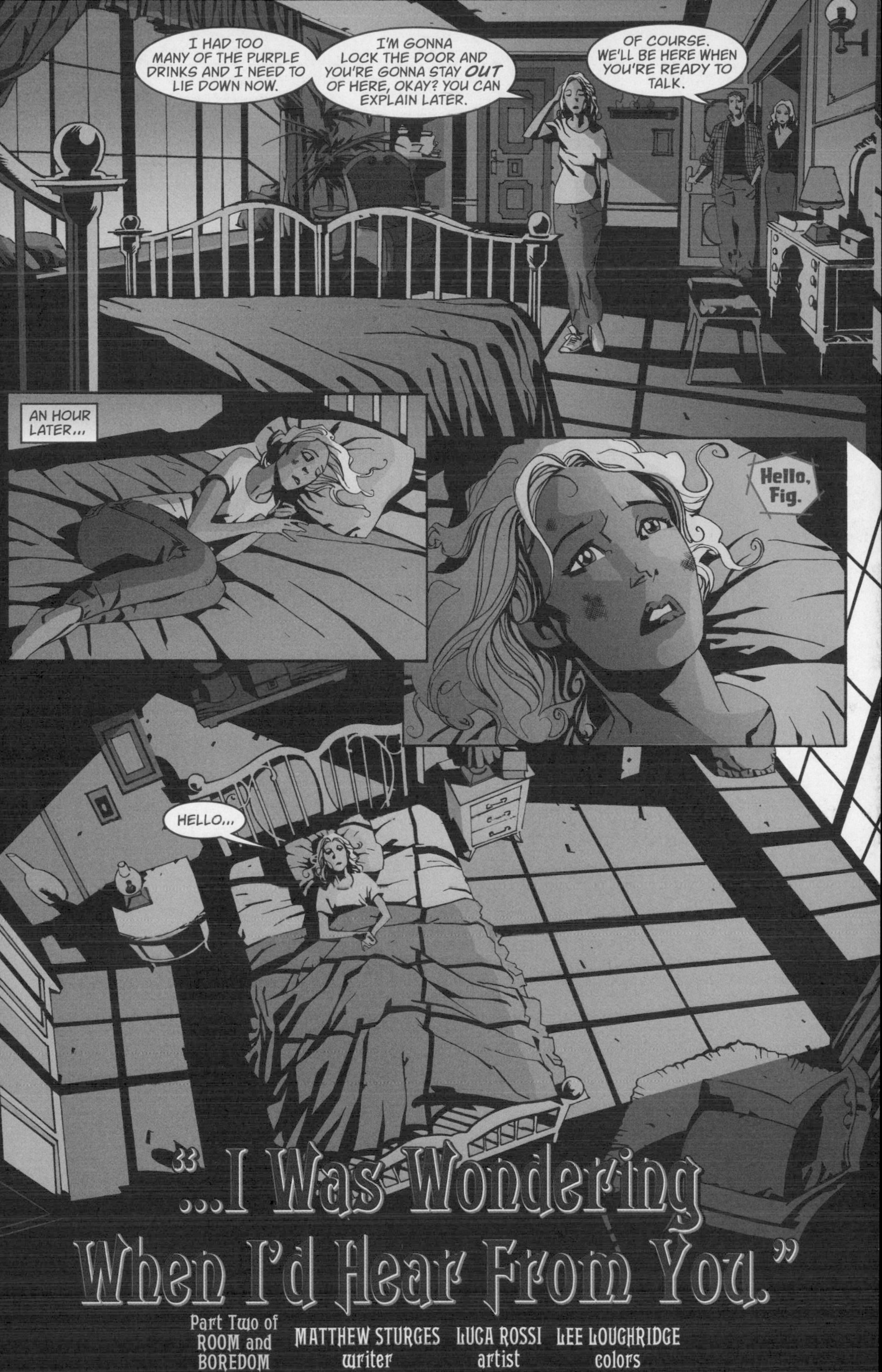

I HAD TOO MANY OF THE PURPLE DRINKS AND I NEED TO LIE DOWN NOW.
I'M GONNA LOCK THE DOOR AND YOU'RE GONNA STAY OUT OF HERE, OKAY? YOU CAN EXPLAIN LATER.
OF COURSE. WE'LL BE HERE WHEN YOU'RE READY TO TALK.
AN HOUR LATER...
Hello, Fig.
HELLO...
"...I Was Wondering When I'd Hear From You."
Part Two of ROOM and BOREDOM
MATTHEW STURGES writer
LUCA ROSSI artist
LEE LOUGHRIDGE colors

Issue #3 cover art by Sam Weber.

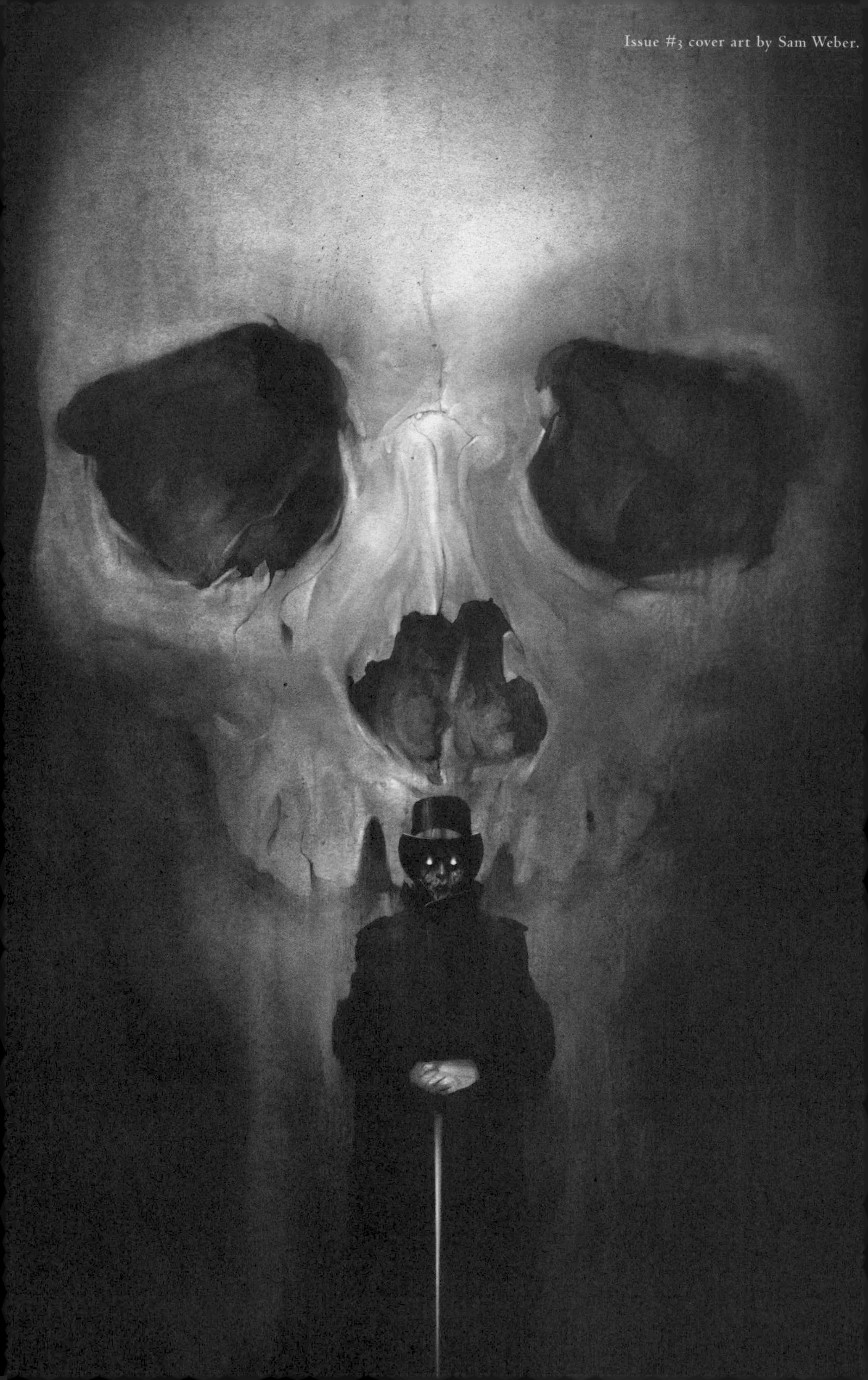

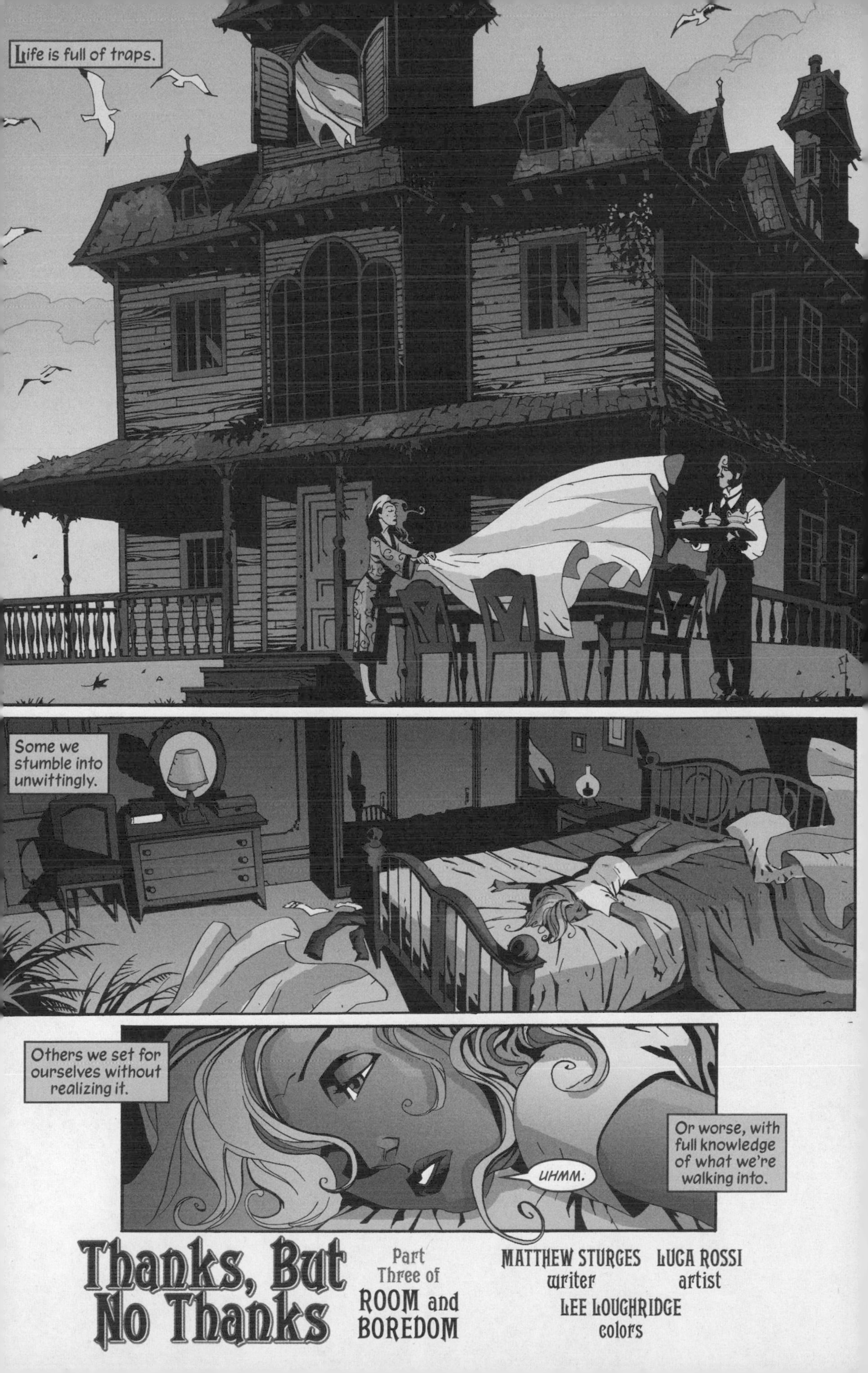

Life is full of traps.
Some we stumble into unwittingly.
Others we set for ourselves without realizing it.
UHMM.
Or worse, with full knowledge of what we're walking into.
Thanks, But No Thanks
Part Three of ROOM and BOREDOM
MATTHEW STURGES writer
LUCA ROSSI artist
LEE LOUGHRIDGE colors

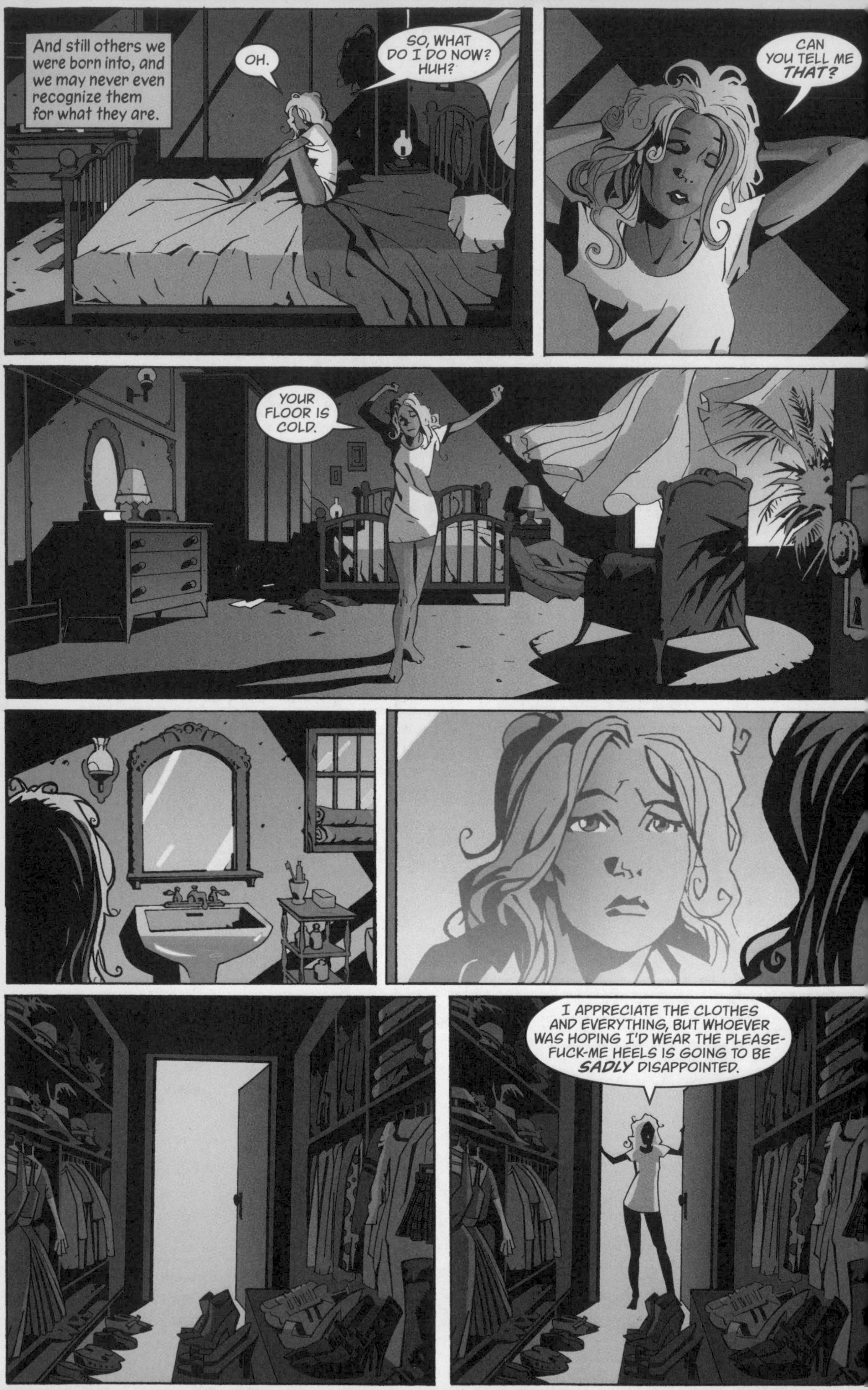
And still others we were born into, and we may never even recognize them for what they are.
OH.
SO, WHAT DO I DO NOW? HUH?
CAN YOU TELL ME *THAT?*
YOUR FLOOR IS COLD.
I APPRECIATE THE CLOTHES AND EVERYTHING, BUT WHOEVER WAS HOPING I'D WEAR THE PLEASE-FUCK-ME HEELS IS GOING TO BE *SADLY* DISAPPOINTED.

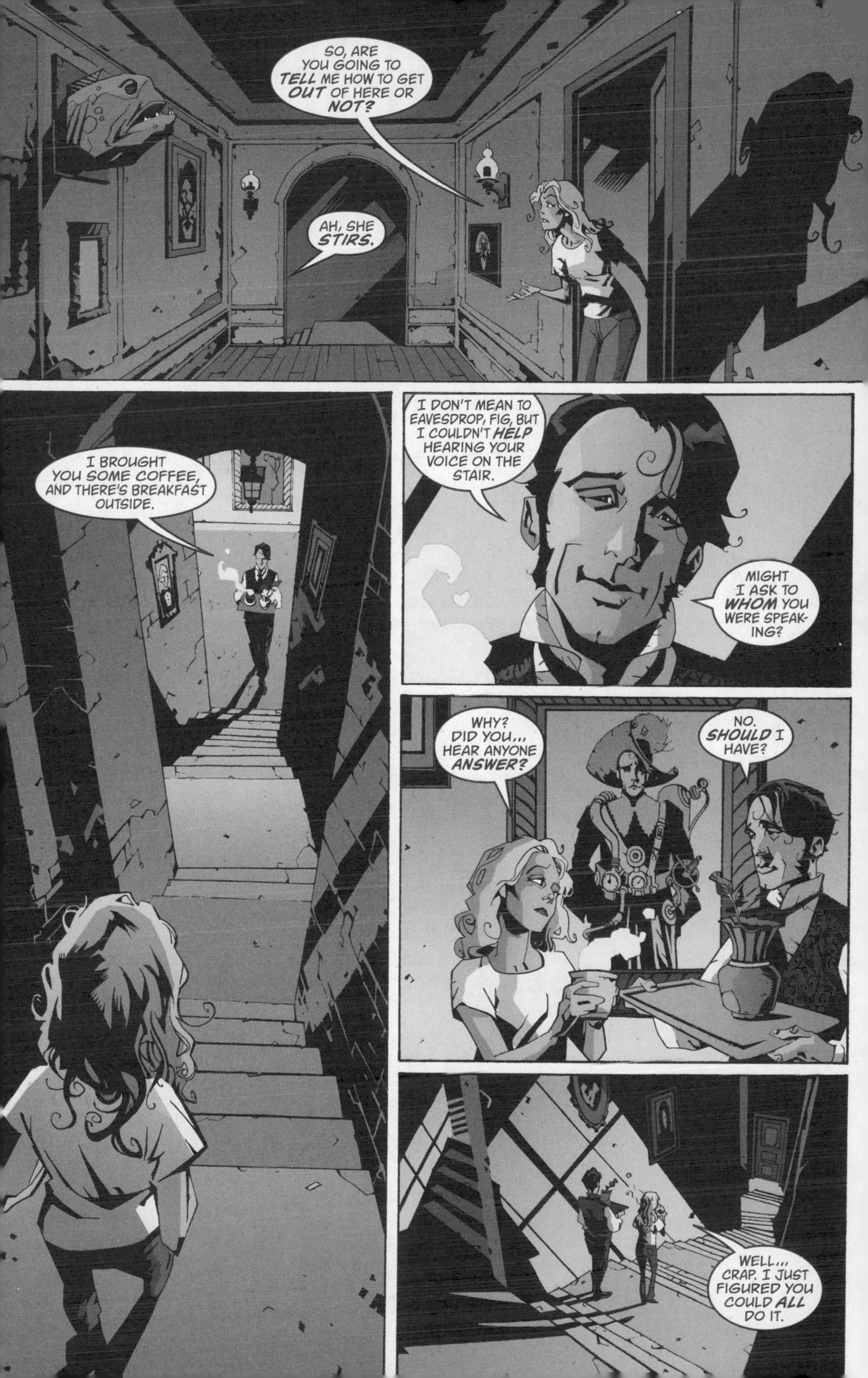

SO, ARE YOU GOING TO TELL ME HOW TO GET OUT OF HERE OR NOT?
AH, SHE STIRS.
I BROUGHT YOU SOME COFFEE, AND THERE'S BREAKFAST OUTSIDE.
I DON'T MEAN TO EAVESDROP, FIG, BUT I COULDN'T HELP HEARING YOUR VOICE ON THE STAIR.
MIGHT I ASK TO WHOM YOU WERE SPEAKING?
WHY? DID YOU... HEAR ANYONE ANSWER?
NO. SHOULD I HAVE?
WELL... CRAP. I JUST FIGURED YOU COULD ALL DO IT.

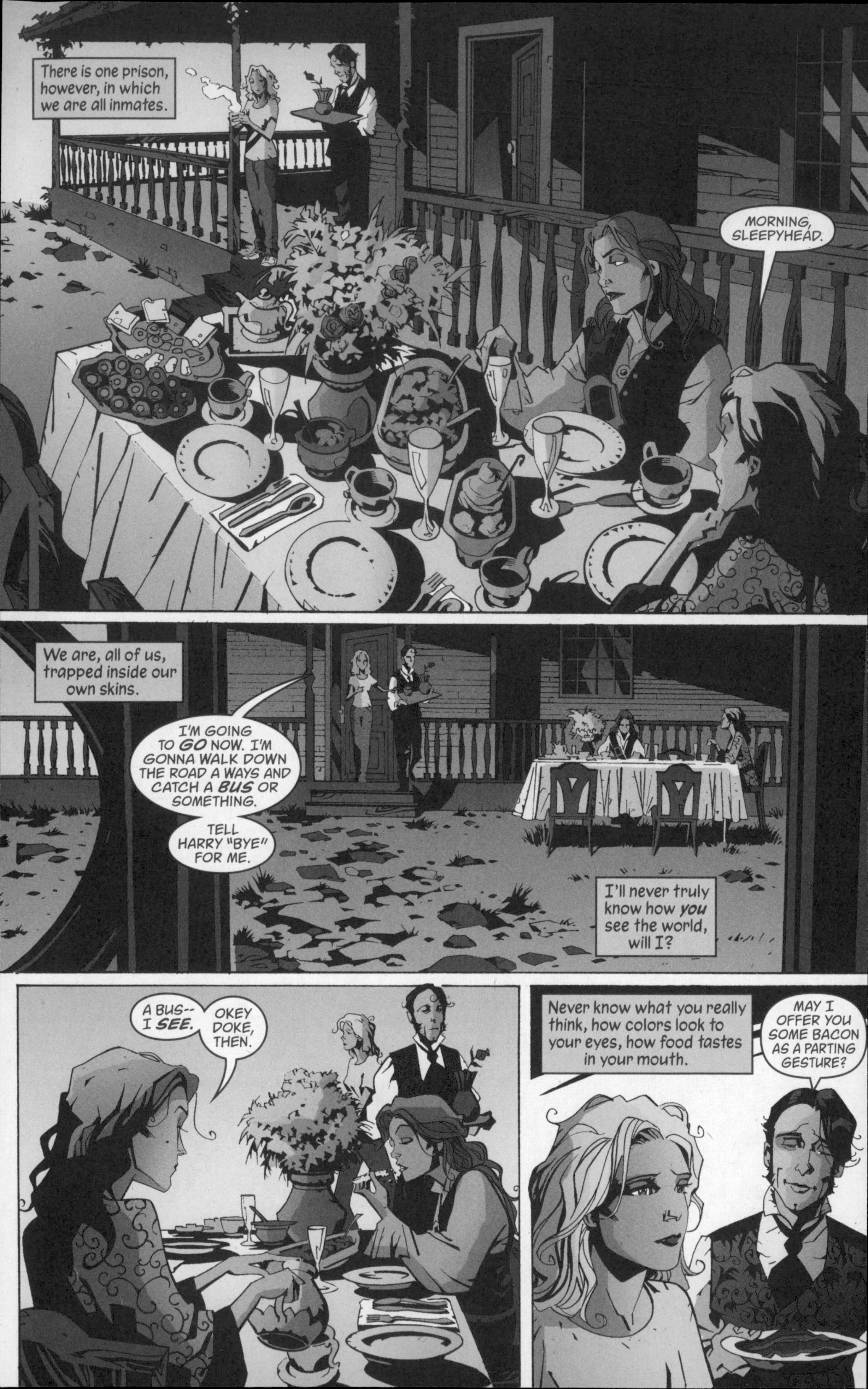
There is one prison, however, in which we are all inmates.
MORNING, SLEEPYHEAD.
We are, all of us, trapped inside our own skins.
I'M GOING TO GO NOW. I'M GONNA WALK DOWN THE ROAD A WAYS AND CATCH A BUS OR SOMETHING.
TELL HARRY "BYE" FOR ME.
I'll never truly know how you see the world, will I?
A BUS-- I SEE.
OKEY DOKE, THEN.
Never know what you really think, how colors look to your eyes, how food tastes in your mouth.
MAY I OFFER YOU SOME BACON AS A PARTING GESTURE?

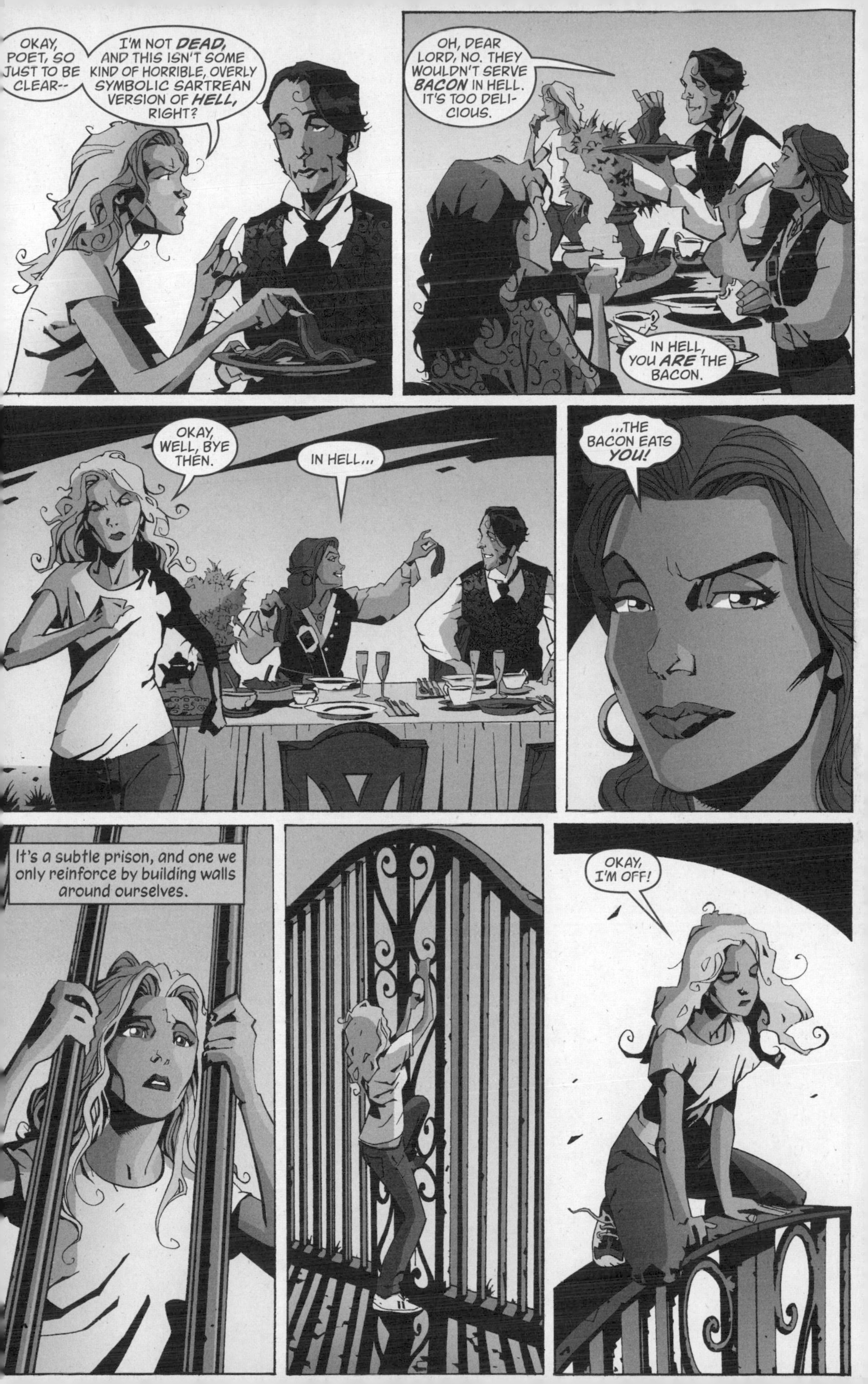
OKAY, POET, SO JUST TO BE CLEAR--
I'M NOT DEAD, AND THIS ISN'T SOME KIND OF HORRIBLE, OVERLY SYMBOLIC SARTREAN VERSION OF HELL, RIGHT?
OH, DEAR LORD, NO. THEY WOULDN'T SERVE BACON IN HELL. IT'S TOO DELICIOUS.
IN HELL, YOU ARE THE BACON.
OKAY, WELL, BYE THEN.
IN HELL...
...THE BACON EATS YOU!
It's a subtle prison, and one we only reinforce by building walls around ourselves.
OKAY, I'M OFF!

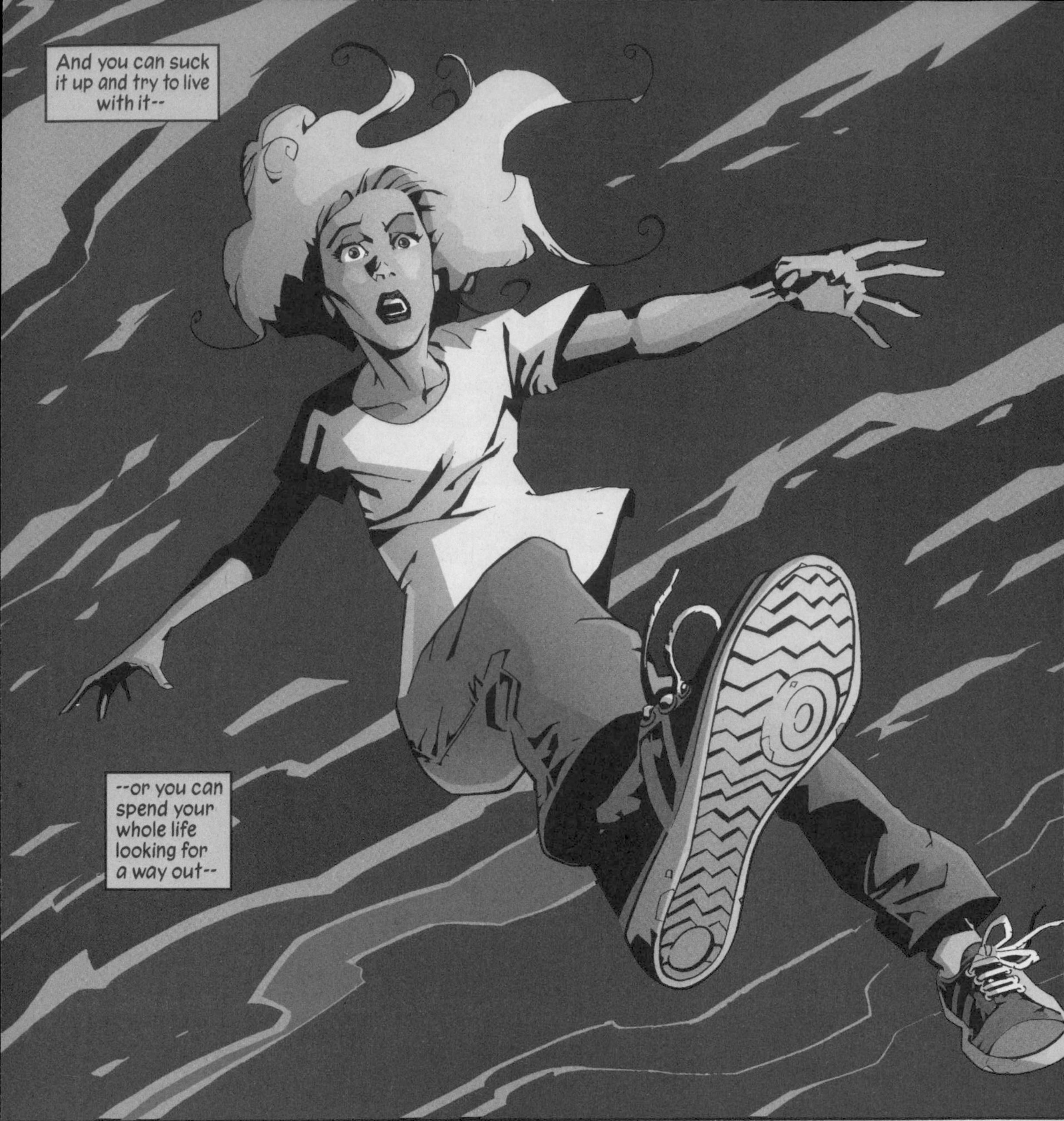
And you can suck it up and try to live with it--
--or you can spend your whole life looking for a way out--

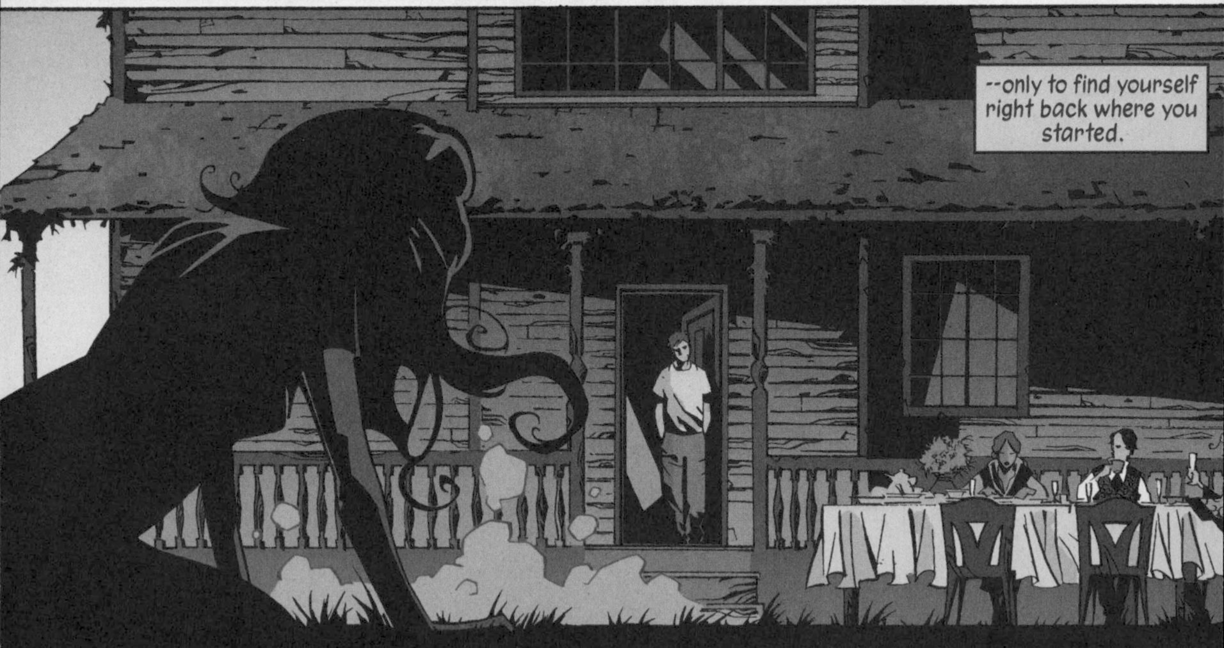
--only to find yourself right back where you started.

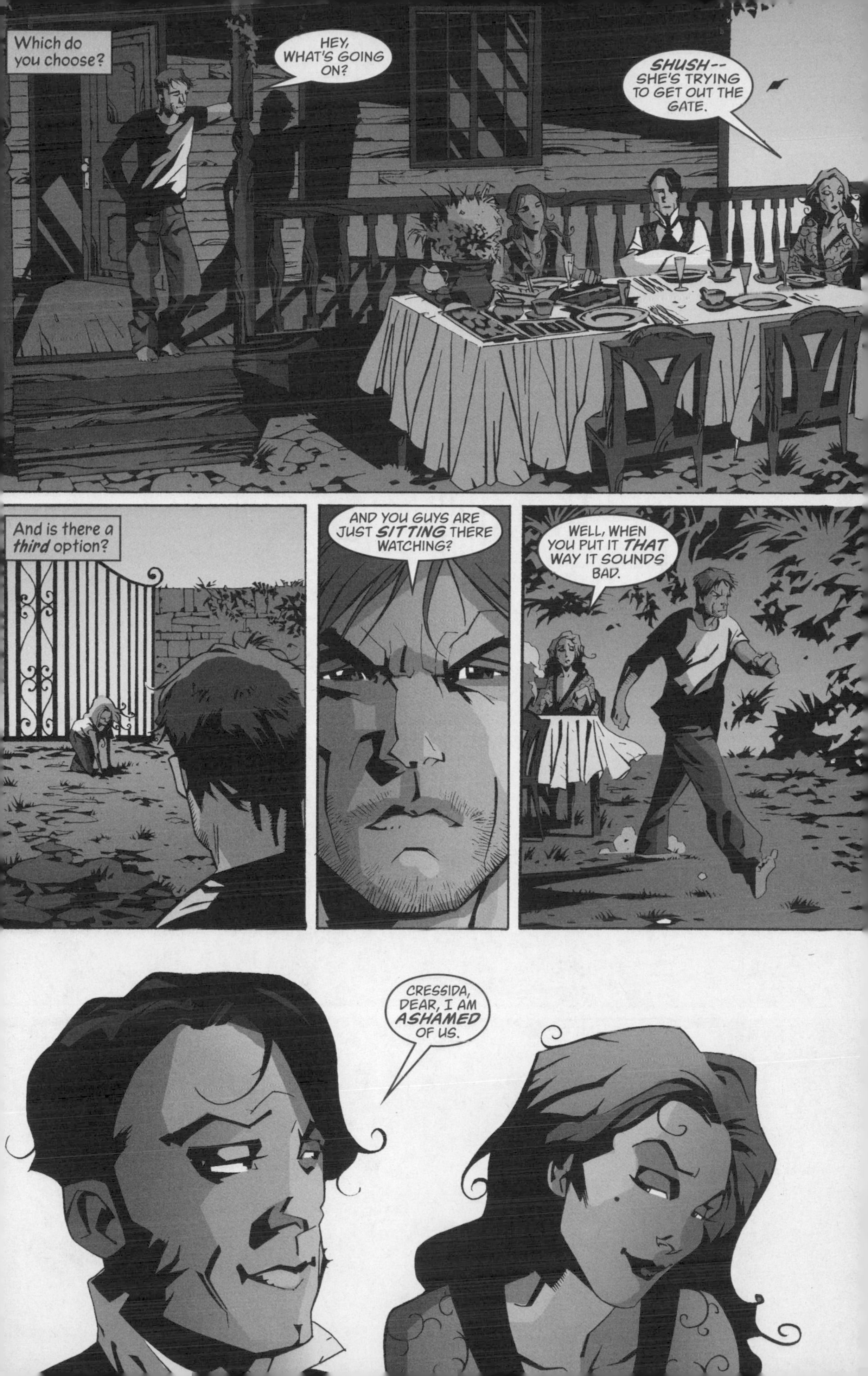

Which do you choose?
HEY, WHAT'S GOING ON?
SHUSH-- SHE'S TRYING TO GET OUT THE GATE.
And is there a *third* option?
AND YOU GUYS ARE JUST *SITTING* THERE WATCHING?
WELL, WHEN YOU PUT IT *THAT* WAY IT SOUNDS BAD.
CRESSIDA, DEAR, I AM *ASHAMED* OF US.

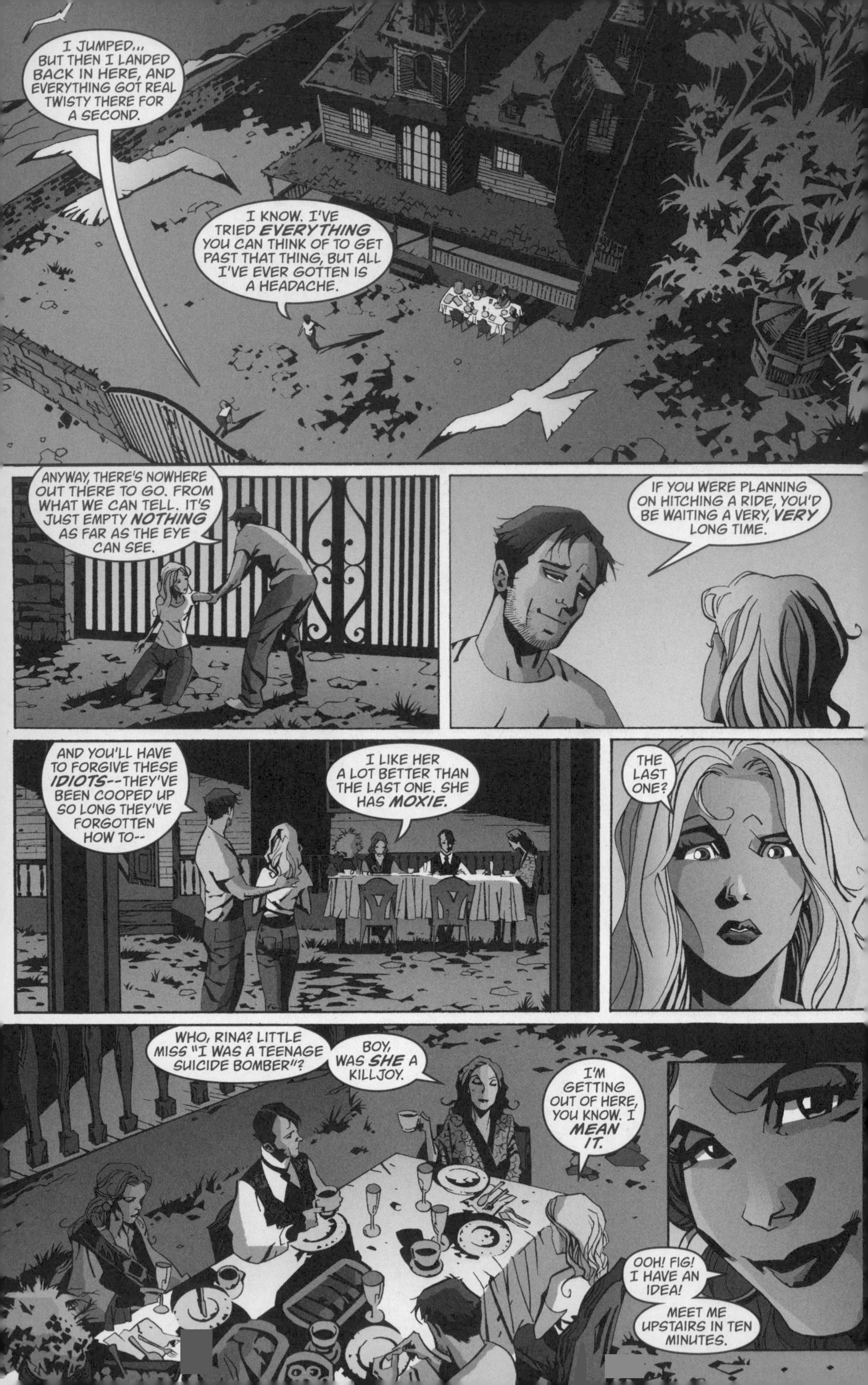

I JUMPED... BUT THEN I LANDED BACK IN HERE, AND EVERYTHING GOT REAL TWISTY THERE FOR A SECOND.
I KNOW. I'VE TRIED EVERYTHING YOU CAN THINK OF TO GET PAST THAT THING, BUT ALL I'VE EVER GOTTEN IS A HEADACHE.
ANYWAY, THERE'S NOWHERE OUT THERE TO GO. FROM WHAT WE CAN TELL, IT'S JUST EMPTY NOTHING AS FAR AS THE EYE CAN SEE.
IF YOU WERE PLANNING ON HITCHING A RIDE, YOU'D BE WAITING A VERY, VERY LONG TIME.
AND YOU'LL HAVE TO FORGIVE THESE IDIOTS--THEY'VE BEEN COOPED UP SO LONG THEY'VE FORGOTTEN HOW TO--
I LIKE HER A LOT BETTER THAN THE LAST ONE. SHE HAS MOXIE.
THE LAST ONE?
WHO, RINA? LITTLE MISS "I WAS A TEENAGE SUICIDE BOMBER"?
BOY, WAS SHE A KILLJOY.
I'M GETTING OUT OF HERE, YOU KNOW. I MEAN IT.
OOH! FIG! I HAVE AN IDEA!
MEET ME UPSTAIRS IN TEN MINUTES.

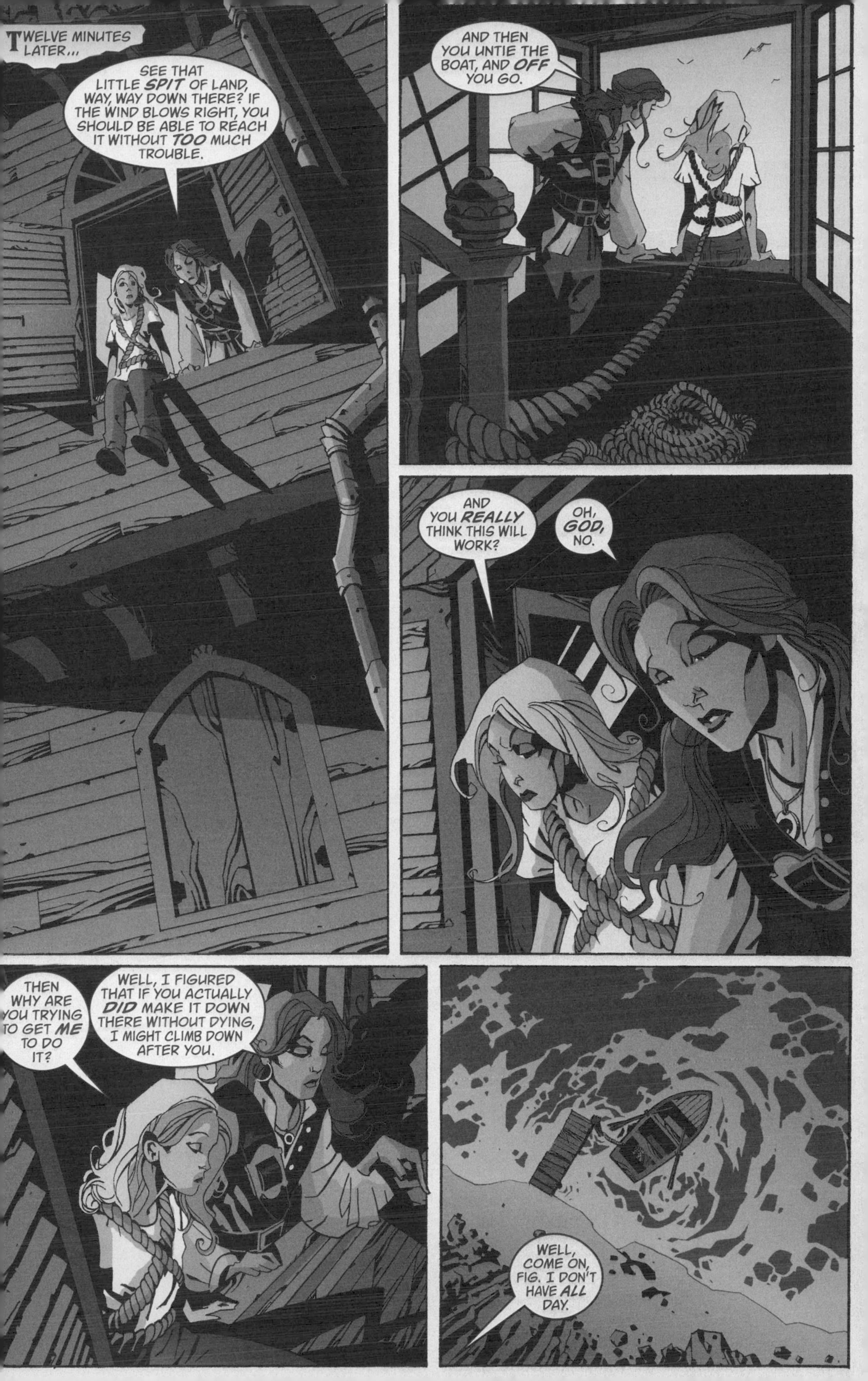
TWELVE MINUTES LATER...
SEE THAT LITTLE SPIT OF LAND, WAY, WAY DOWN THERE? IF THE WIND BLOWS RIGHT, YOU SHOULD BE ABLE TO REACH IT WITHOUT TOO MUCH TROUBLE.
AND THEN YOU UNTIE THE BOAT, AND OFF YOU GO.
AND YOU REALLY THINK THIS WILL WORK?
OH, GOD, NO.
THEN WHY ARE YOU TRYING TO GET ME TO DO IT?
WELL, I FIGURED THAT IF YOU ACTUALLY DID MAKE IT DOWN THERE WITHOUT DYING, I MIGHT CLIMB DOWN AFTER YOU.
WELL, COME ON, FIG. I DON'T HAVE ALL DAY.

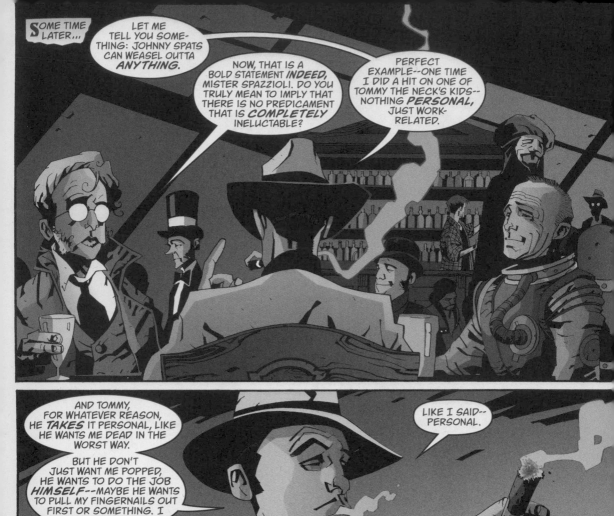

LET ME TELL YOU SOMETHING: JOHNNY SPATS CAN WEASEL OUTTA *ANYTHING.*

NOW, THAT IS A BOLD STATEMENT *INDEED,* MISTER SPAZZIOLI. DO YOU TRULY MEAN TO IMPLY THAT THERE IS NO PREDICAMENT THAT IS *COMPLETELY* INELUCTABLE?

PERFECT EXAMPLE--ONE TIME I DID A HIT ON ONE OF TOMMY THE NECK'S KIDS-- NOTHING *PERSONAL,* JUST WORK- RELATED.

AND TOMMY, FOR WHATEVER REASON, HE *TAKES* IT PERSONAL, LIKE HE WANTS ME DEAD IN THE WORST WAY.

BUT HE DON'T JUST WANT ME POPPED, HE WANTS TO DO THE JOB *HIMSELF*--MAYBE HE WANTS TO PULL MY FINGERNAILS OUT FIRST OR SOMETHING. I DON'T KNOW.

LIKE I SAID-- PERSONAL.

SO HE SENDS HIS BOYS OUT TO COLLECT ME. NOW, *USUALLY* I'M A TOUGH ONE TO NAB, BUT THEY CATCH ME KNEE-DEEP IN THIS WAITRESS WORKS OVER AT CHARLIE'S.

GORGEOUS AS HELL, THIS BROAD WAS. BAZOOMS OUT TO *HERE,* THE WHOLE PACKAGE...

WHAT THE FUCK WAS I TALKING ABOUT?

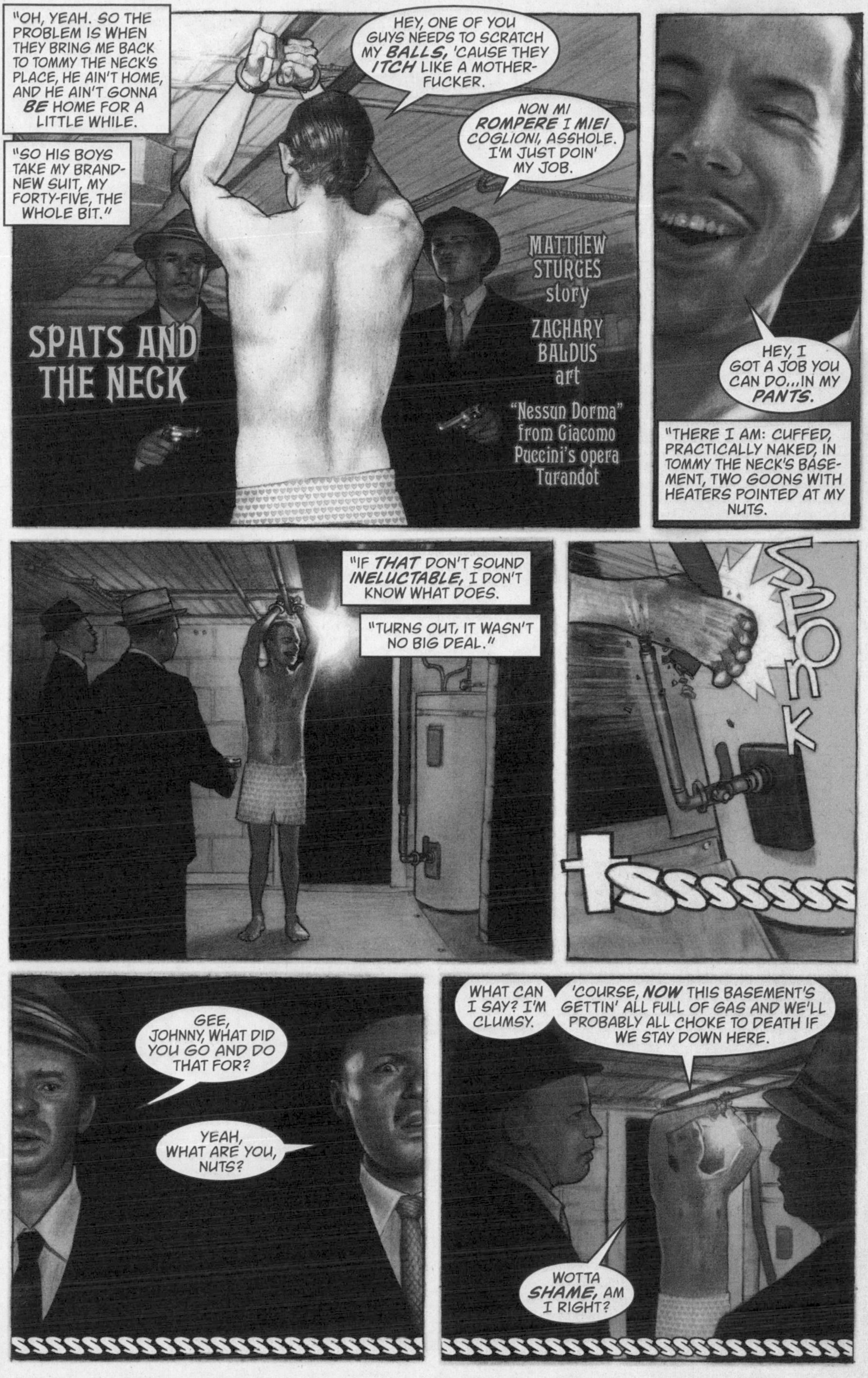
"OH, YEAH. SO THE PROBLEM IS WHEN THEY BRING ME BACK TO TOMMY THE NECK'S PLACE, HE AIN'T HOME, AND HE AIN'T GONNA BE HOME FOR A LITTLE WHILE.
"SO HIS BOYS TAKE MY BRAND-NEW SUIT, MY FORTY-FIVE, THE WHOLE BIT."
HEY, ONE OF YOU GUYS NEEDS TO SCRATCH MY BALLS, 'CAUSE THEY ITCH LIKE A MOTHER-FUCKER.
NON MI ROMPERE I MIEI COGLIONI, ASSHOLE. I'M JUST DOIN' MY JOB.
SPATS AND THE NECK
MATTHEW STURGES story
ZACHARY BALDUS art
"Nessun Dorma" from Giacomo Puccini's opera Turandot
HEY, I GOT A JOB YOU CAN DO...IN MY PANTS.
"THERE I AM: CUFFED, PRACTICALLY NAKED, IN TOMMY THE NECK'S BASE-MENT, TWO GOONS WITH HEATERS POINTED AT MY NUTS.
"IF THAT DON'T SOUND INELUCTABLE, I DON'T KNOW WHAT DOES.
"TURNS OUT, IT WASN'T NO BIG DEAL."
SPONK
tSSSSSSS
GEE, JOHNNY, WHAT DID YOU GO AND DO THAT FOR?
YEAH, WHAT ARE YOU, NUTS?
SSSSSSSSSSSSSSSSSSSSSSSSSSSS
WHAT CAN I SAY? I'M CLUMSY.
'COURSE, NOW THIS BASEMENT'S GETTIN' ALL FULL OF GAS AND WE'LL PROBABLY ALL CHOKE TO DEATH IF WE STAY DOWN HERE.
WOTTA SHAME, AM I RIGHT?
SSSSSSSSSSSSSSSSSSSSSSSSSSSSS

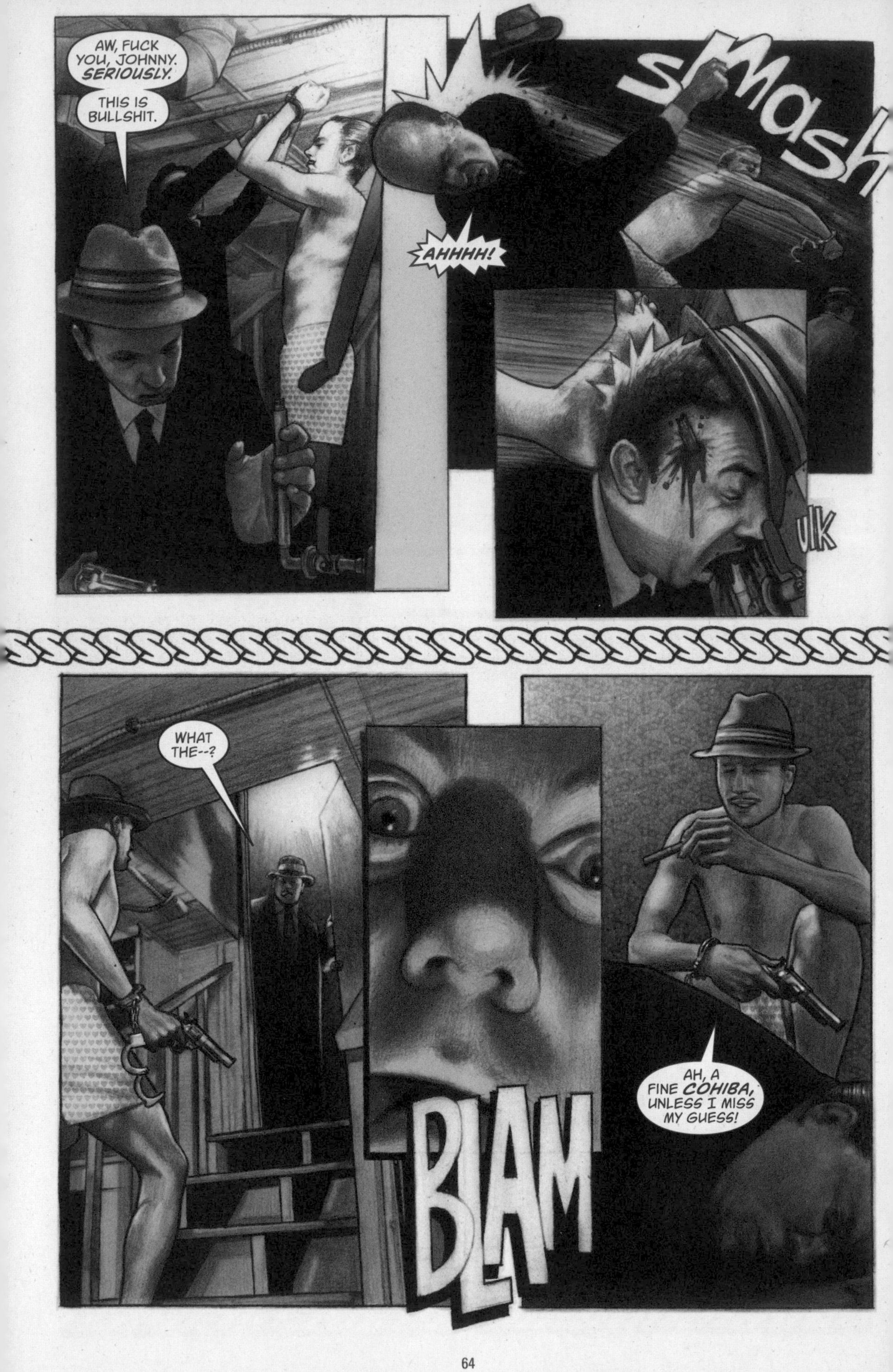
AW, FUCK YOU, JOHNNY. SERIOUSLY.
THIS IS BULLSHIT.
sMash
AHHHH!
UIK
SSSSSSSSSSSSSSSSSSSSSSSSSSSSSS
WHAT THE--?
BLAM
AH, A FINE COHIBA, UNLESS I MISS MY GUESS!

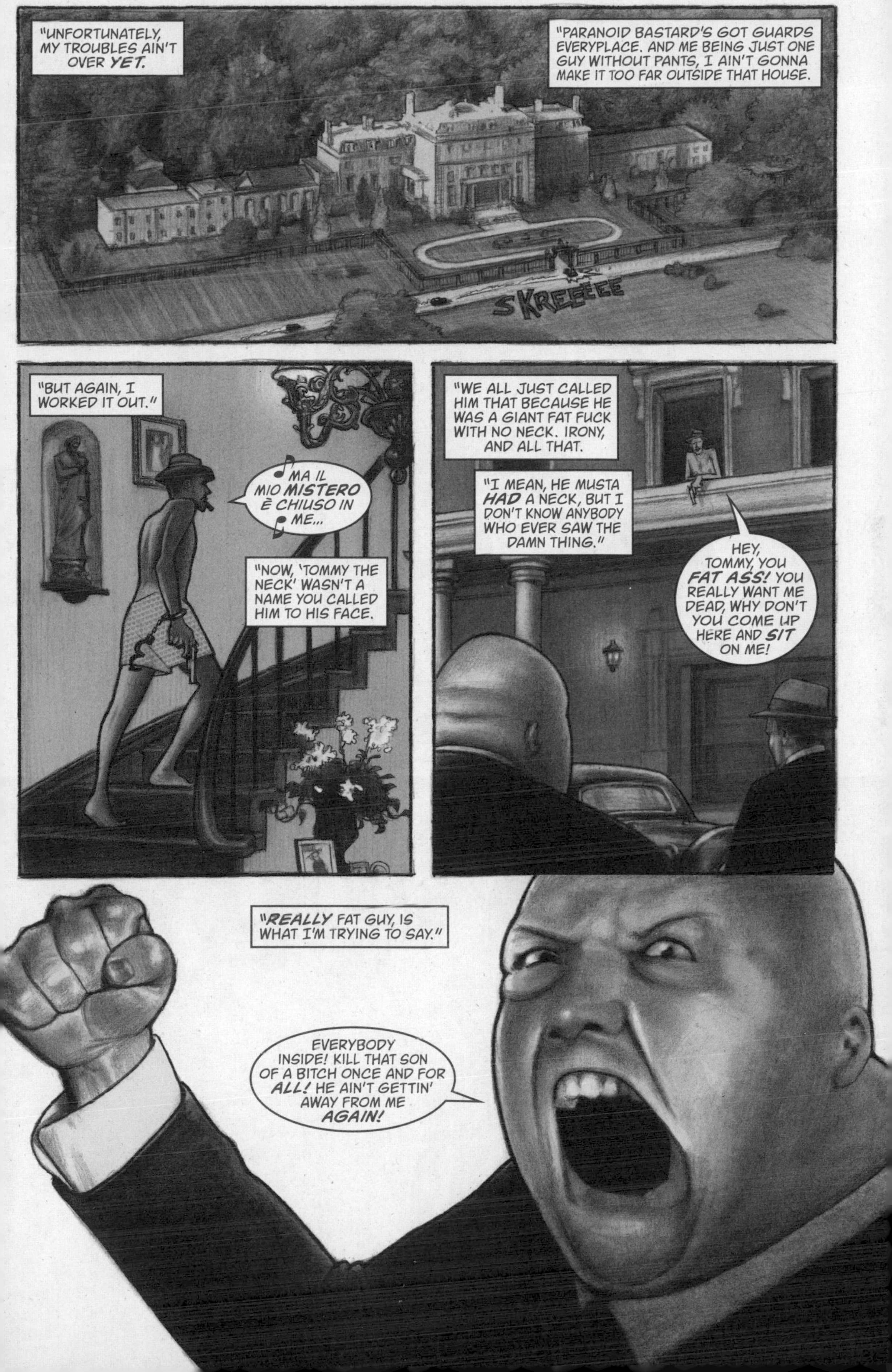
"UNFORTUNATELY, MY TROUBLES AIN'T OVER YET.
"PARANOID BASTARD'S GOT GUARDS EVERYPLACE. AND ME BEING JUST ONE GUY WITHOUT PANTS, I AIN'T GONNA MAKE IT TOO FAR OUTSIDE THAT HOUSE.
SKREEEEE
"BUT AGAIN, I WORKED IT OUT."
MA IL MIO MISTERO È CHIUSO IN ME...
"NOW, 'TOMMY THE NECK' WASN'T A NAME YOU CALLED HIM TO HIS FACE.
"WE ALL JUST CALLED HIM THAT BECAUSE HE WAS A GIANT FAT FUCK WITH NO NECK. IRONY, AND ALL THAT.
"I MEAN, HE MUSTA HAD A NECK, BUT I DON'T KNOW ANYBODY WHO EVER SAW THE DAMN THING."
HEY, TOMMY, YOU FAT ASS! YOU REALLY WANT ME DEAD, WHY DON'T YOU COME UP HERE AND SIT ON ME!
"REALLY FAT GUY, IS WHAT I'M TRYING TO SAY."
EVERYBODY INSIDE! KILL THAT SON OF A BITCH ONCE AND FOR ALL! HE AIN'T GETTIN' AWAY FROM ME AGAIN!

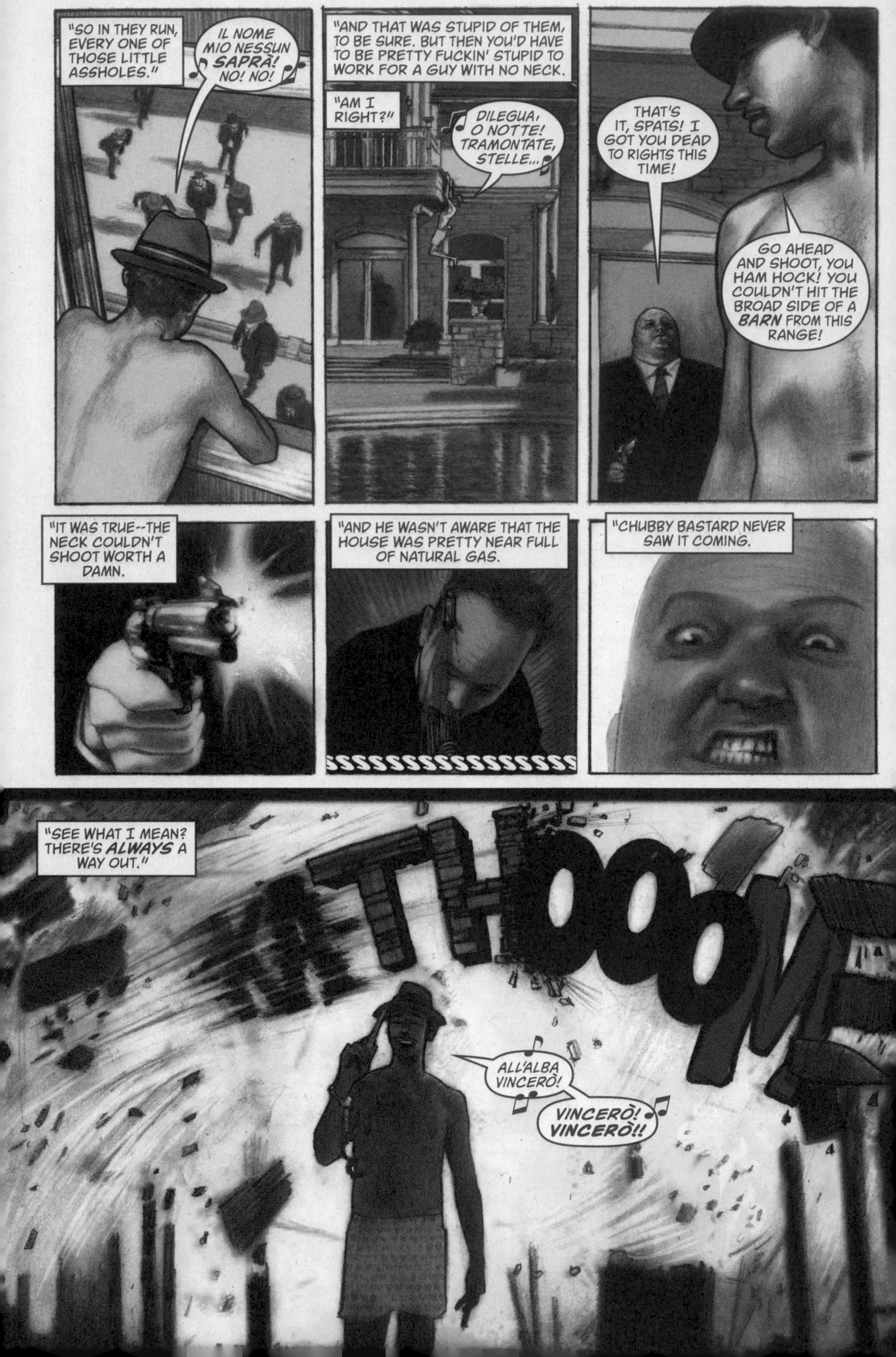
"SO IN THEY RUN, EVERY ONE OF THOSE LITTLE ASSHOLES."
IL NOME MIO NESSUN SAPRÀ! NO! NO!
"AND THAT WAS STUPID OF THEM, TO BE SURE. BUT THEN YOU'D HAVE TO BE PRETTY FUCKIN' STUPID TO WORK FOR A GUY WITH NO NECK.
"AM I RIGHT?"
DILEGUA, O NOTTE! TRAMONTATE, STELLE...
THAT'S IT, SPATS! I GOT YOU DEAD TO RIGHTS THIS TIME!
GO AHEAD AND SHOOT, YOU HAM HOCK! YOU COULDN'T HIT THE BROAD SIDE OF A BARN FROM THIS RANGE!
"IT WAS TRUE--THE NECK COULDN'T SHOOT WORTH A DAMN.
"AND HE WASN'T AWARE THAT THE HOUSE WAS PRETTY NEAR FULL OF NATURAL GAS.
SSSSSSSSSSSSSSSSSSSS
"CHUBBY BASTARD NEVER SAW IT COMING.
"SEE WHAT I MEAN? THERE'S ALWAYS A WAY OUT."
THOOM
ALL'ALBA VINCERÒ!
VINCERÒ! VINCERÒ!!

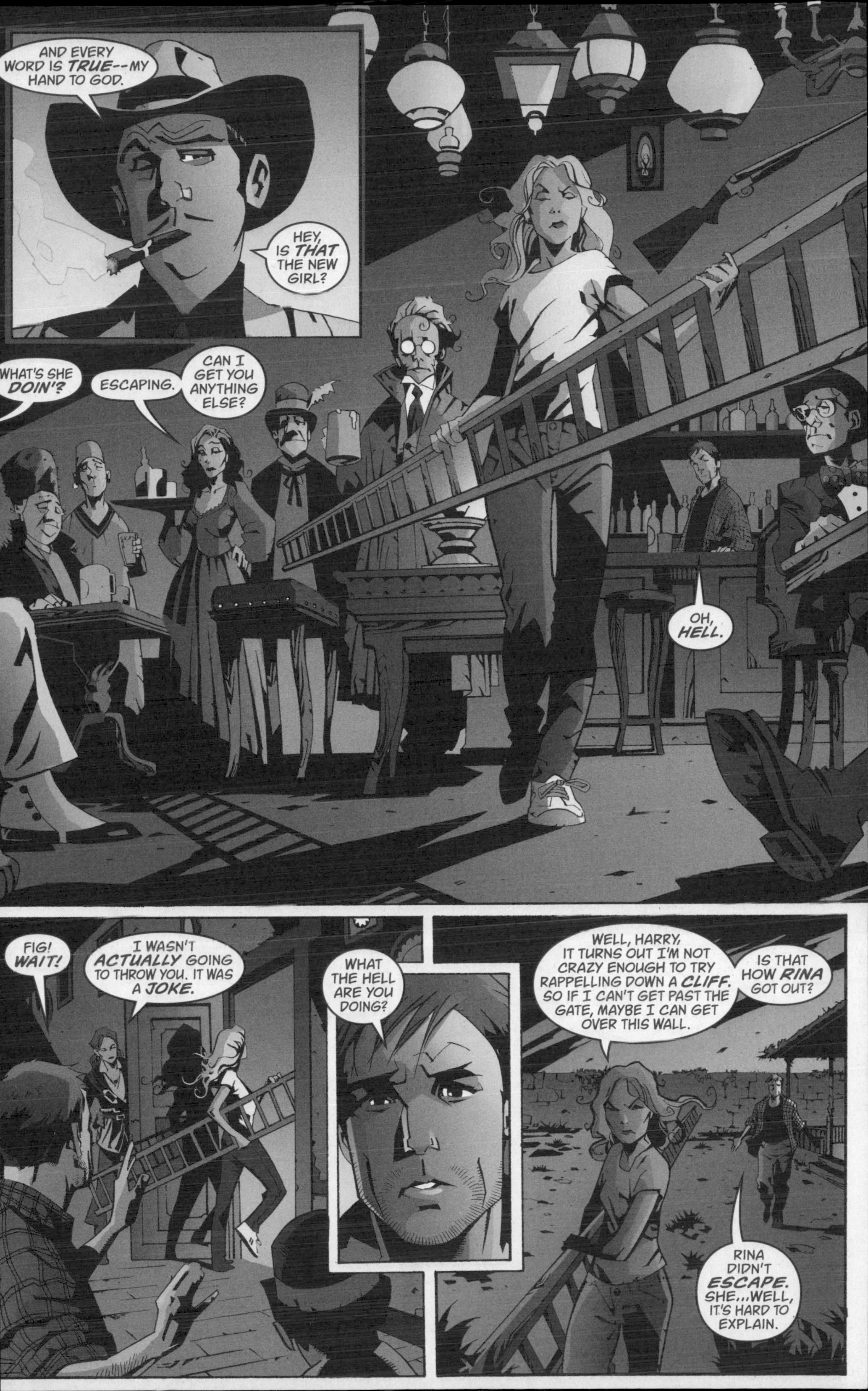

AND EVERY WORD IS TRUE--MY HAND TO GOD.
HEY, IS THAT THE NEW GIRL?
WHAT'S SHE DOIN'?
ESCAPING.
CAN I GET YOU ANYTHING ELSE?
OH, HELL.
FIG! WAIT!
I WASN'T ACTUALLY GOING TO THROW YOU. IT WAS A JOKE.
WHAT THE HELL ARE YOU DOING?
WELL, HARRY, IT TURNS OUT I'M NOT CRAZY ENOUGH TO TRY RAPPELLING DOWN A CLIFF. SO IF I CAN'T GET PAST THE GATE, MAYBE I CAN GET OVER THIS WALL.
IS THAT HOW RINA GOT OUT?
RINA DIDN'T ESCAPE. SHE...WELL, IT'S HARD TO EXPLAIN.

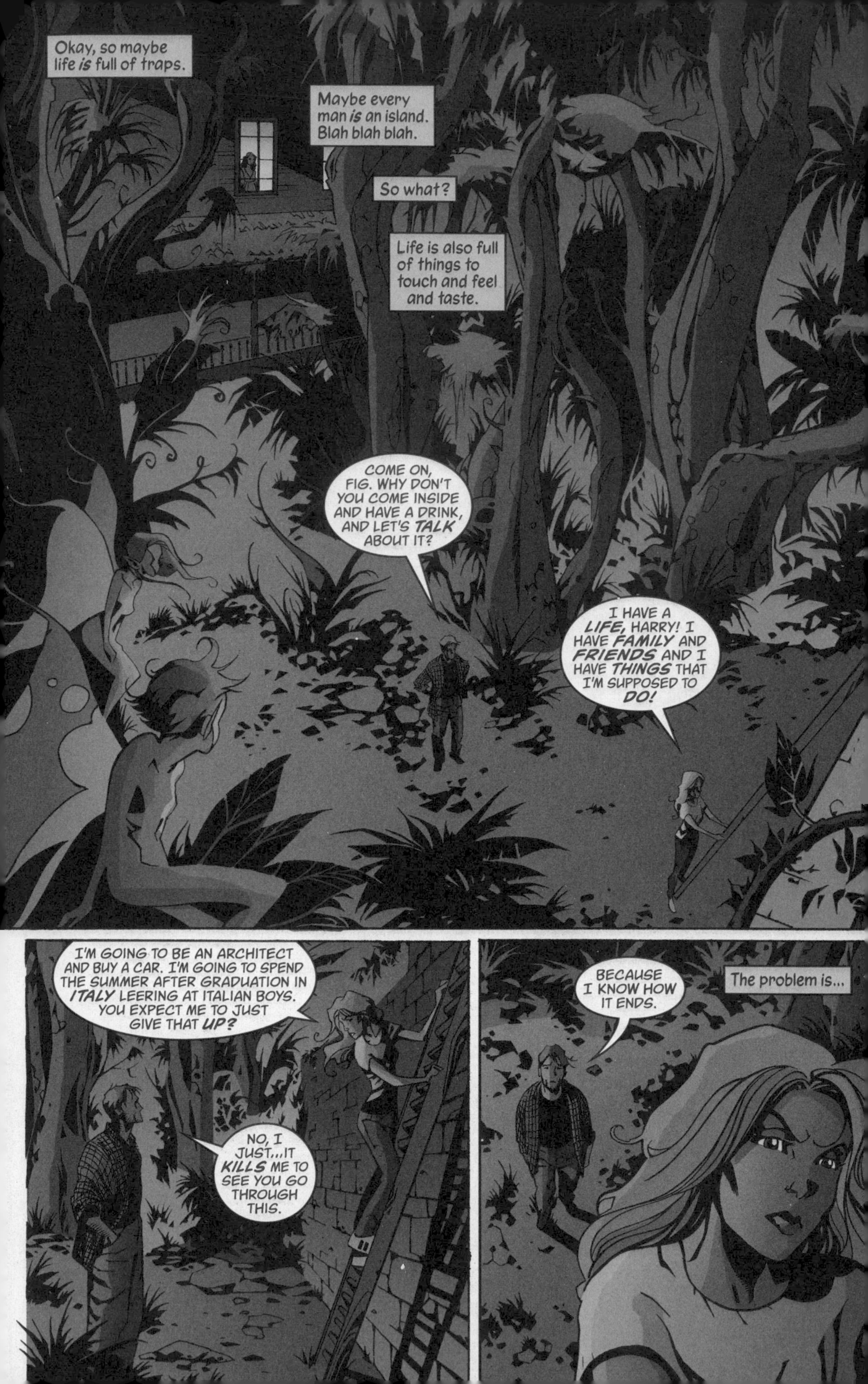
Okay, so maybe life *is* full of traps.
Maybe every man *is* an island. Blah blah blah.
So what?
Life is also full of things to touch and feel and taste.
COME ON, FIG. WHY DON'T YOU COME INSIDE AND HAVE A DRINK, AND LET'S *TALK* ABOUT IT?
I HAVE A *LIFE,* HARRY! I HAVE *FAMILY* AND *FRIENDS* AND I HAVE *THINGS* THAT I'M SUPPOSED TO *DO!*
I'M GOING TO BE AN ARCHITECT AND BUY A CAR. I'M GOING TO SPEND THE SUMMER AFTER GRADUATION IN *ITALY* LEERING AT ITALIAN BOYS. YOU EXPECT ME TO JUST GIVE THAT *UP?*
NO, I JUST...IT *KILLS* ME TO SEE YOU GO THROUGH THIS.
BECAUSE I KNOW HOW IT ENDS.
The problem is...

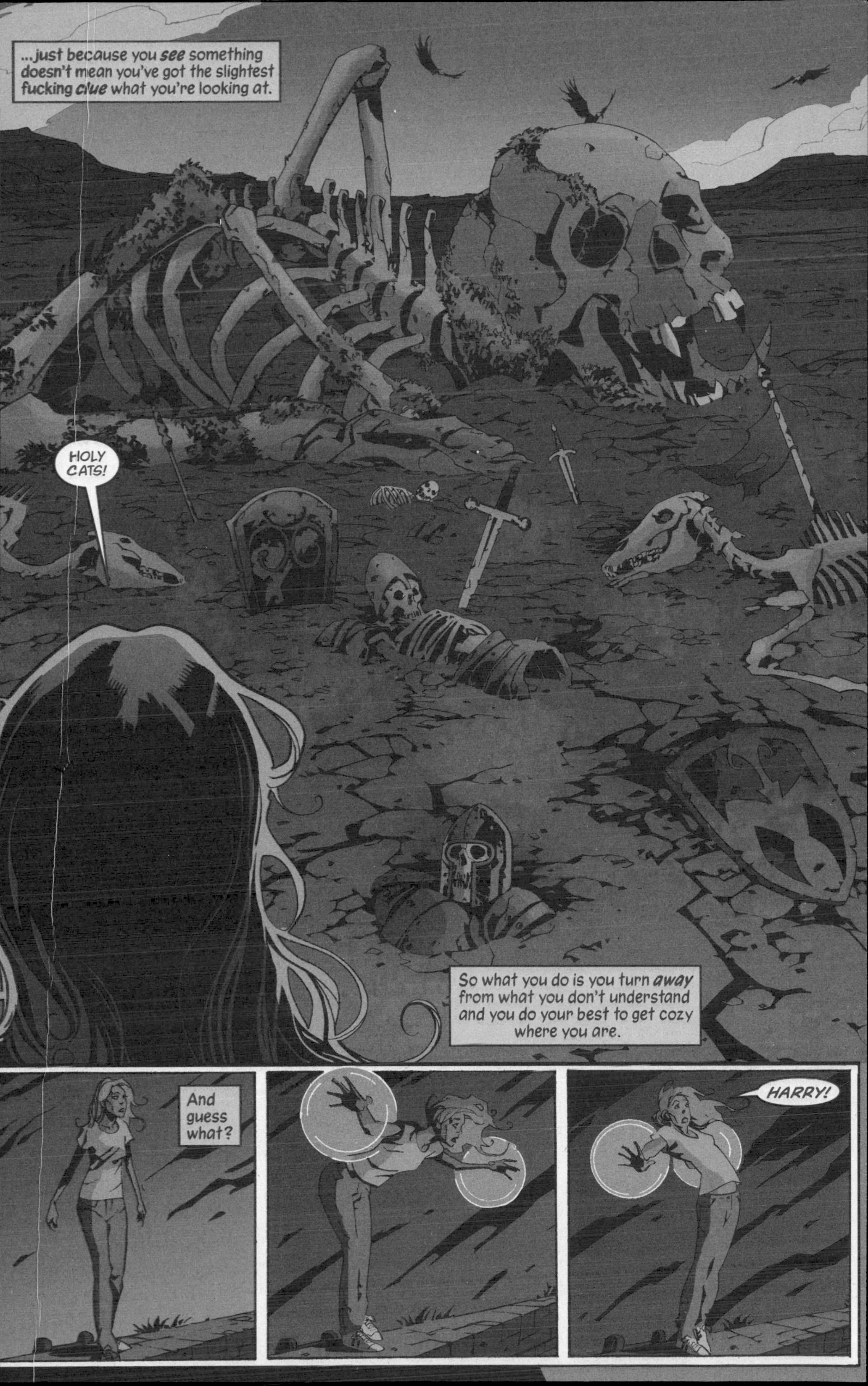
...just because you see something doesn't mean you've got the slightest fucking clue what you're looking at.
HOLY CATS!
So what you do is you turn away from what you don't understand and you do your best to get cozy where you are.
And guess what?
HARRY!

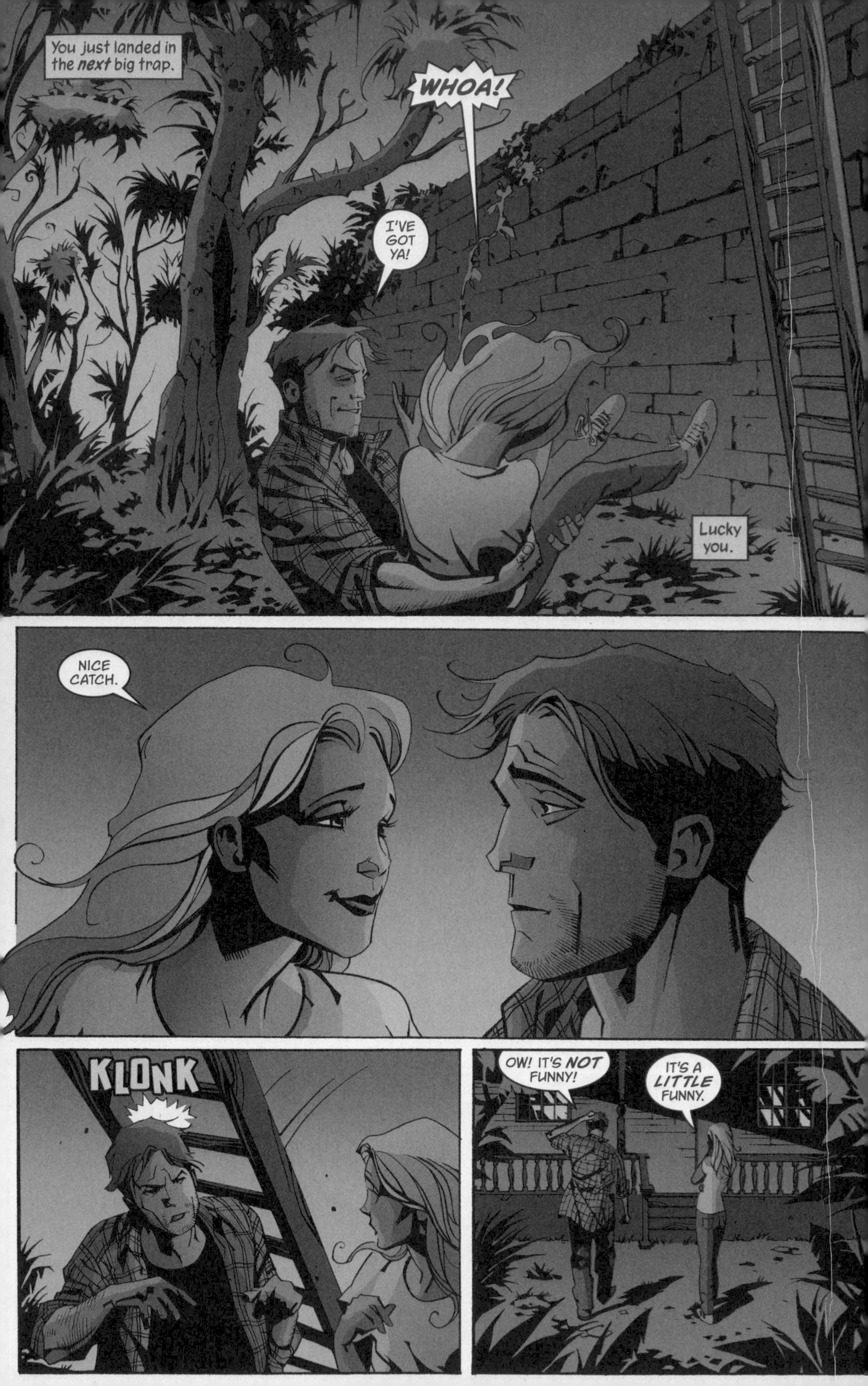
You just landed in the *next* big trap.
WHOA!
I'VE GOT YA!
Lucky you.
NICE CATCH.
KLONK
OW! IT'S *NOT* FUNNY!
IT'S A *LITTLE* FUNNY.

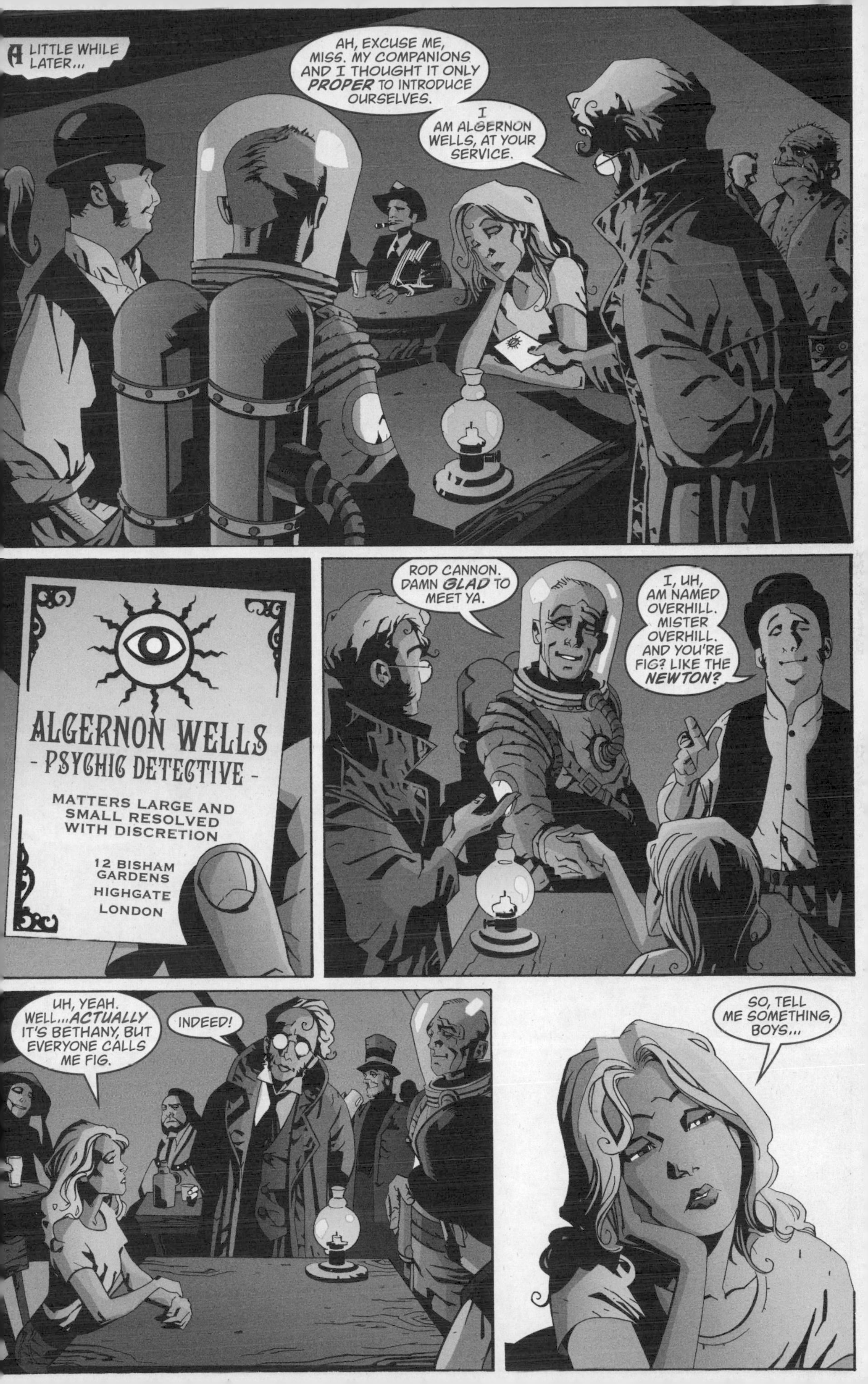
A LITTLE WHILE LATER...
AH, EXCUSE ME, MISS. MY COMPANIONS AND I THOUGHT IT ONLY PROPER TO INTRODUCE OURSELVES.
I AM ALGERNON WELLS, AT YOUR SERVICE.
ALGERNON WELLS
- PSYCHIC DETECTIVE -
MATTERS LARGE AND SMALL RESOLVED WITH DISCRETION
12 BISHAM GARDENS
HIGHGATE
LONDON
ROD CANNON. DAMN GLAD TO MEET YA.
I, UH, AM NAMED OVERHILL. MISTER OVERHILL. AND YOU'RE FIG? LIKE THE NEWTON?
UH, YEAH. WELL...ACTUALLY IT'S BETHANY, BUT EVERYONE CALLS ME FIG.
INDEED!
SO, TELL ME SOMETHING, BOYS...

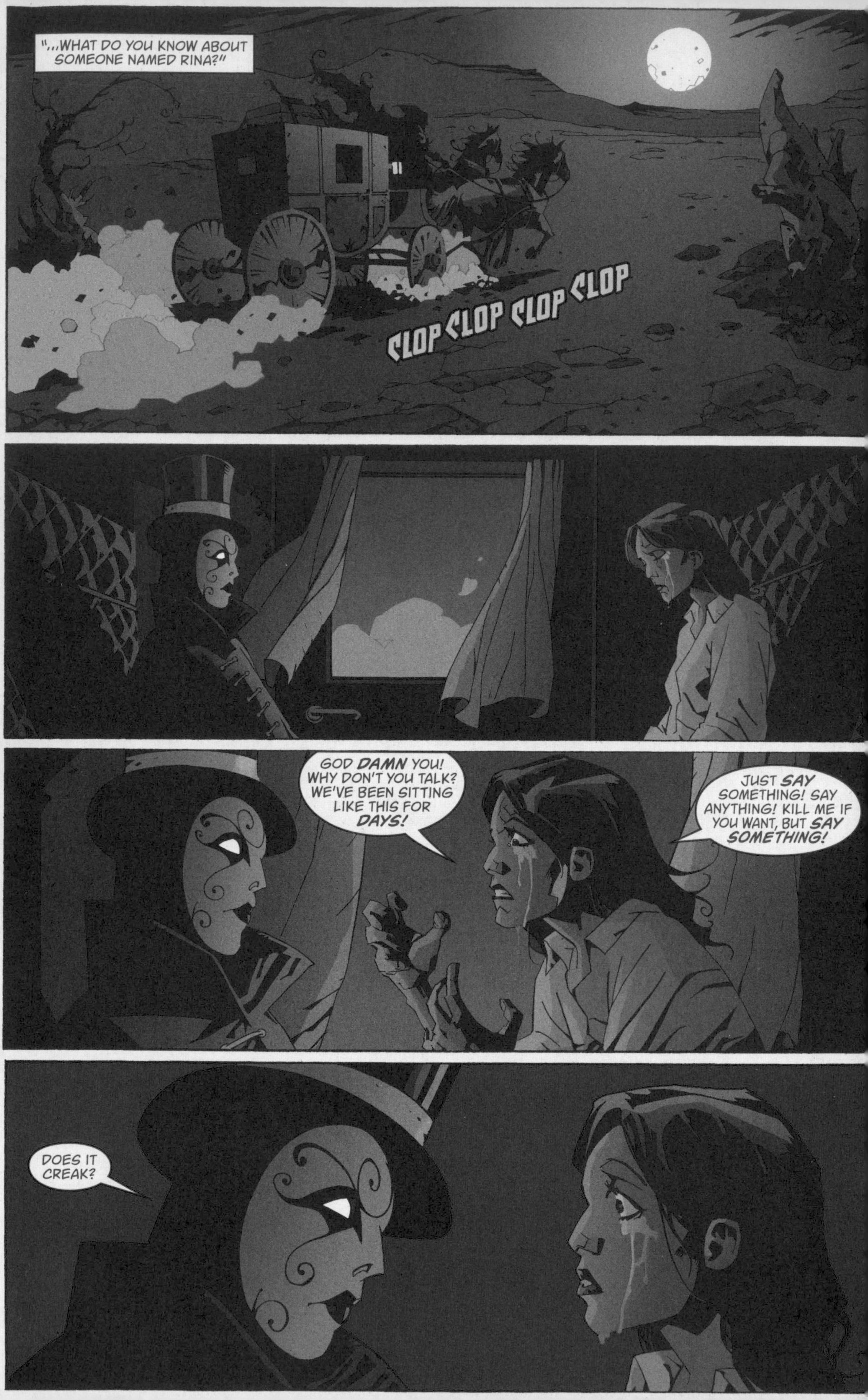
"...WHAT DO YOU KNOW ABOUT SOMEONE NAMED RINA?"
CLOP CLOP CLOP CLOP
GOD DAMN YOU! WHY DON'T YOU TALK? WE'VE BEEN SITTING LIKE THIS FOR DAYS!
JUST SAY SOMETHING! SAY ANYTHING! KILL ME IF YOU WANT, BUT SAY SOMETHING!
DOES IT CREAK?

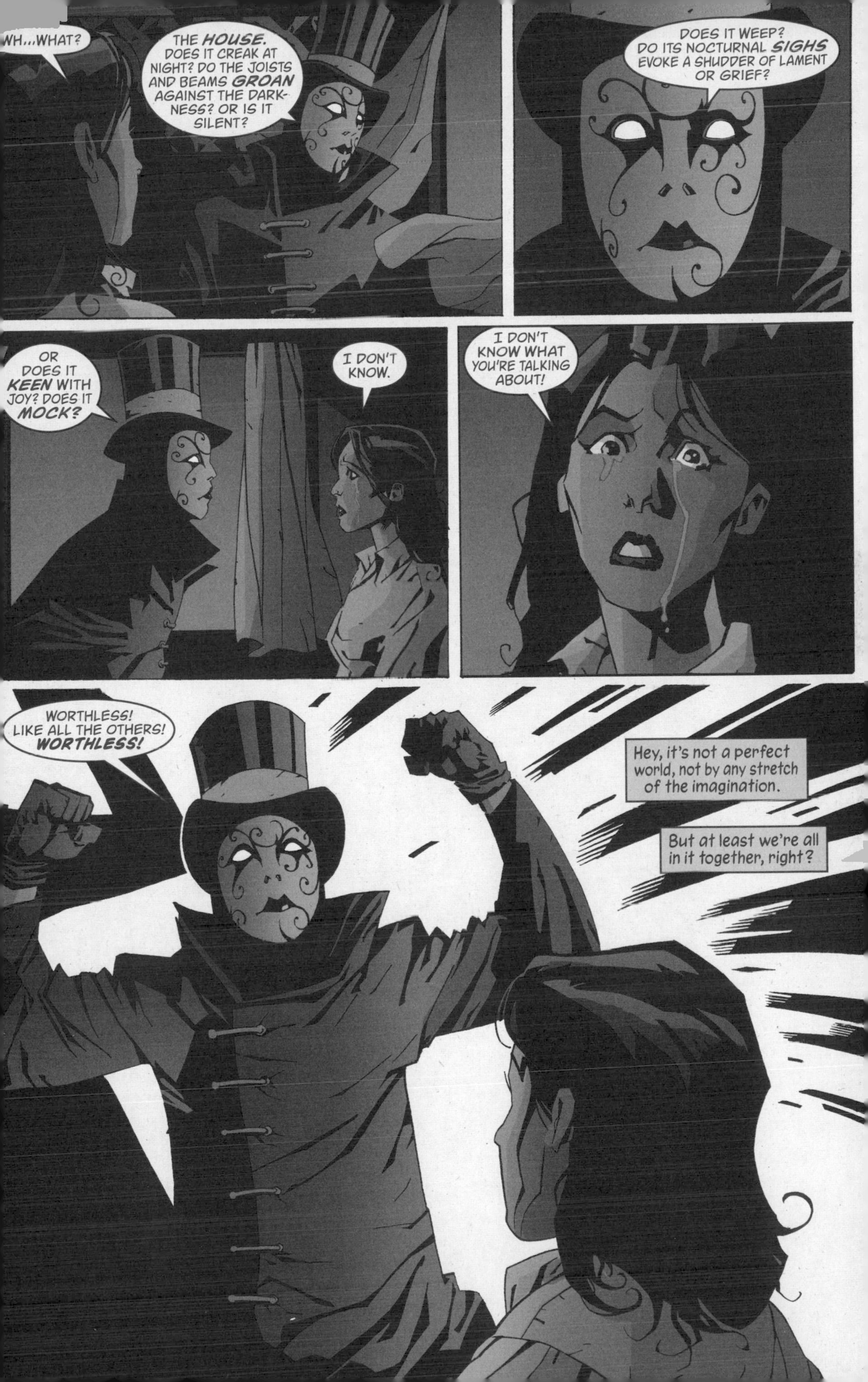
WH...WHAT?
THE HOUSE. DOES IT CREAK AT NIGHT? DO THE JOISTS AND BEAMS GROAN AGAINST THE DARKNESS? OR IS IT SILENT?
DOES IT WEEP? DO ITS NOCTURNAL SIGHS EVOKE A SHUDDER OF LAMENT OR GRIEF?
OR DOES IT KEEN WITH JOY? DOES IT MOCK?
I DON'T KNOW.
I DON'T KNOW WHAT YOU'RE TALKING ABOUT!
WORTHLESS! LIKE ALL THE OTHERS! WORTHLESS!
Hey, it's not a perfect world, not by any stretch of the imagination.
But at least we're all in it together, right?

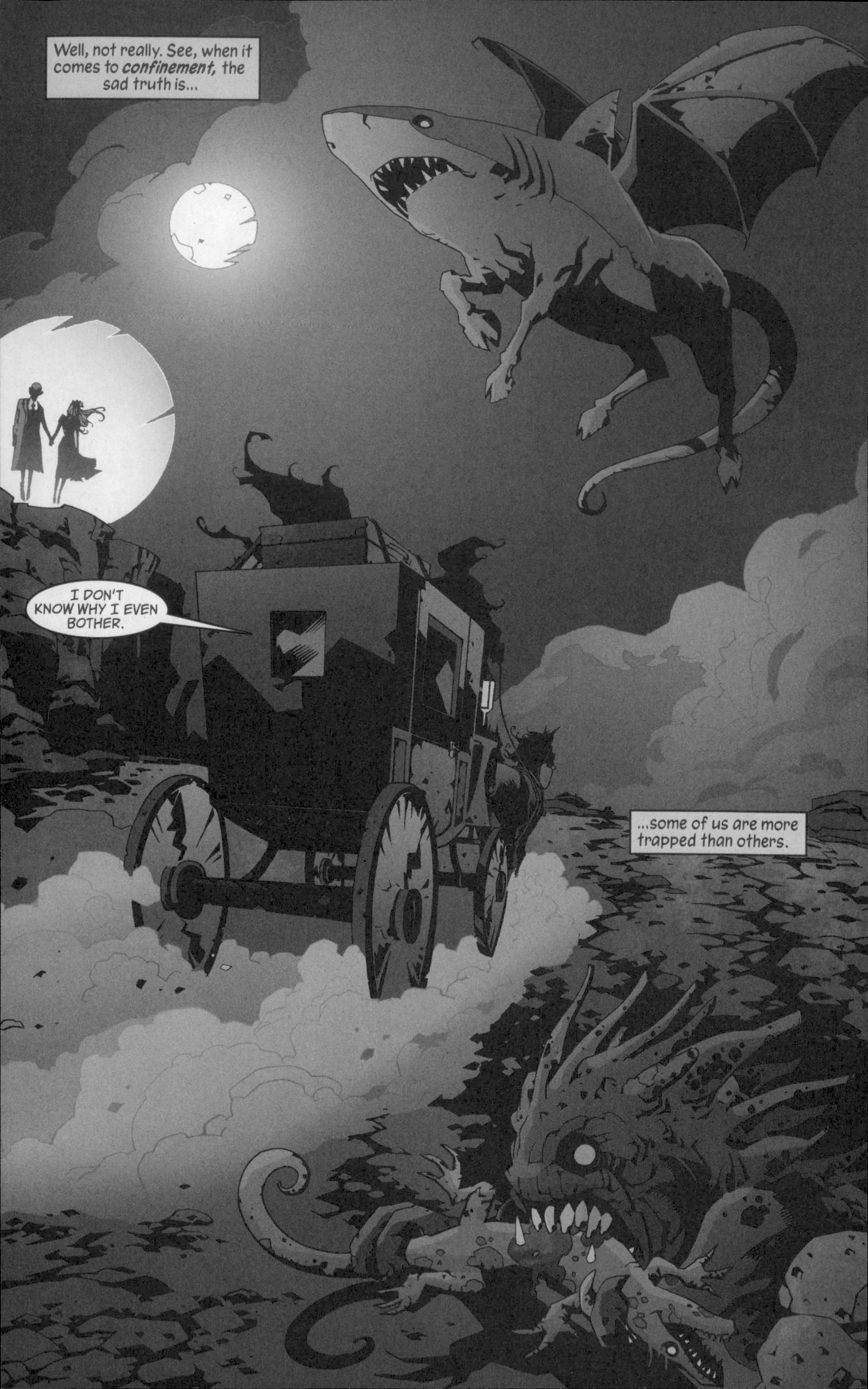
Well, not really. See, when it comes to *confinement,* the sad truth is...
I DON'T KNOW WHY I EVEN BOTHER.
...some of us are more trapped than others.

Issue #4 cover art by Sam Weber.

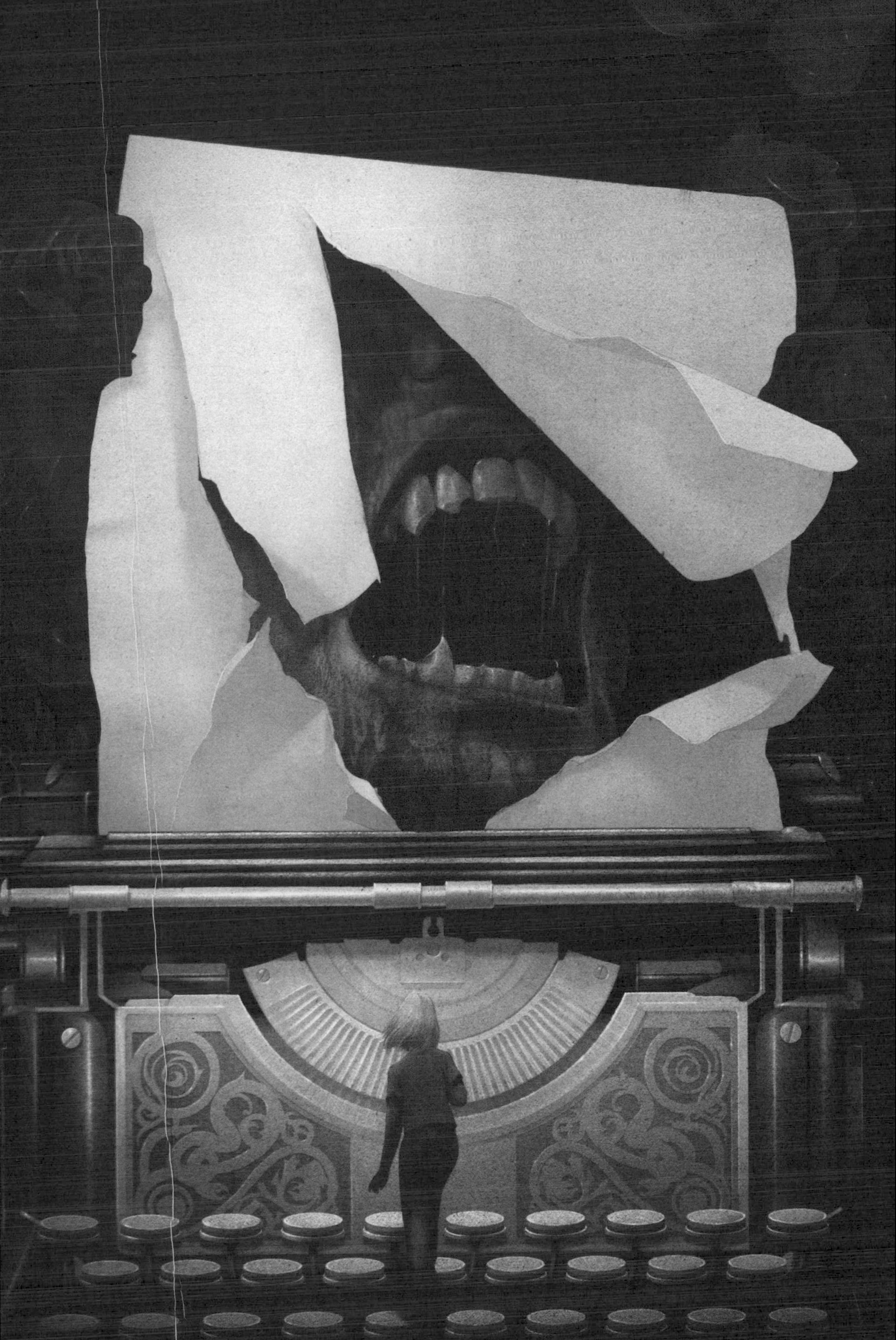

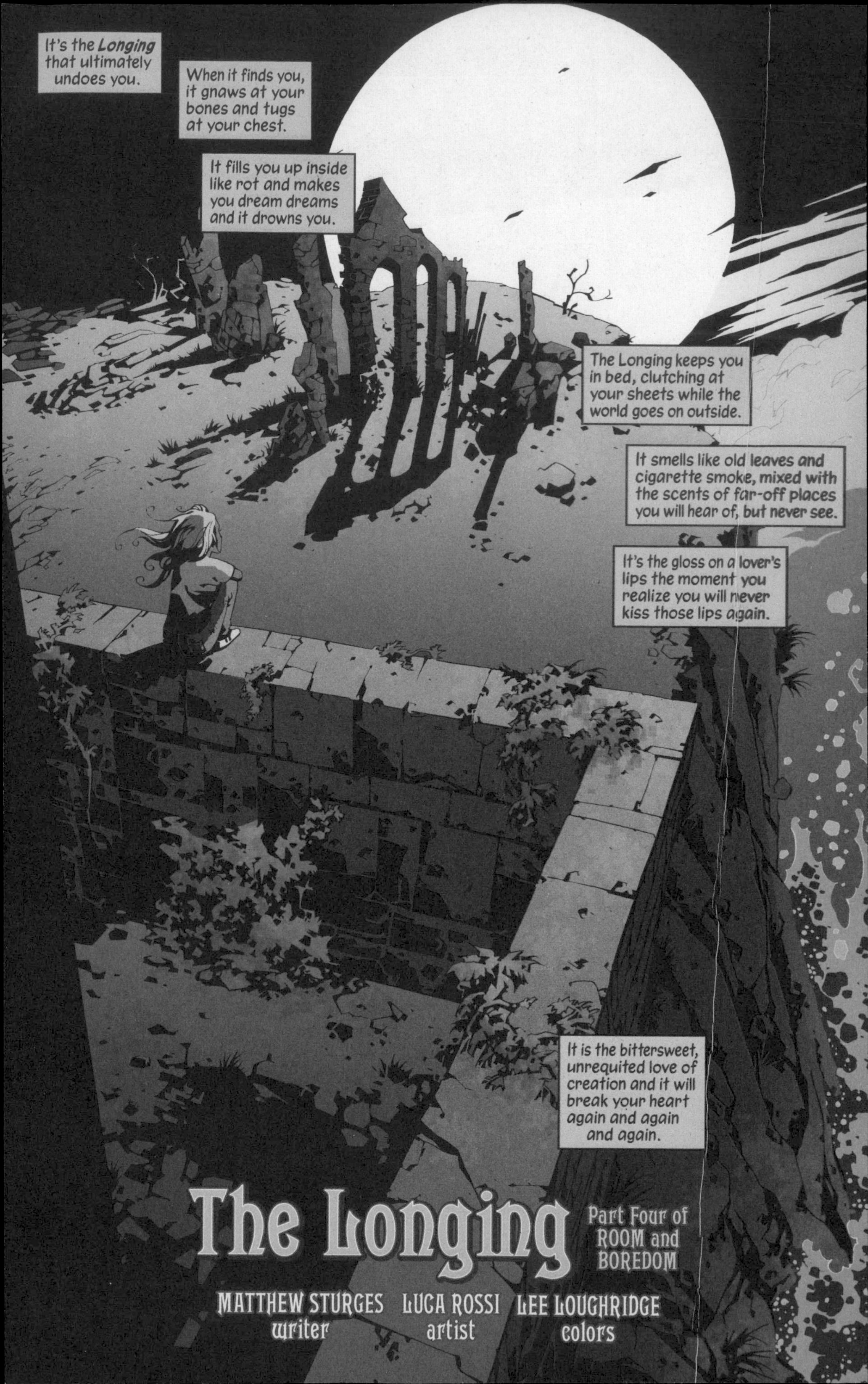
It's the *Longing* that ultimately undoes you.
When it finds you, it gnaws at your bones and tugs at your chest.
It fills you up inside like rot and makes you dream dreams and it drowns you.
The Longing keeps you in bed, clutching at your sheets while the world goes on outside.
It smells like old leaves and cigarette smoke, mixed with the scents of far-off places you will hear of, but never see.
It's the gloss on a lover's lips the moment you realize you will never kiss those lips again.
It is the bittersweet, unrequited love of creation and it will break your heart again and again and again.
The Longing
Part Four of ROOM and BOREDOM
MATTHEW STURGES writer
LUCA ROSSI artist
LEE LOUGHRIDGE colors

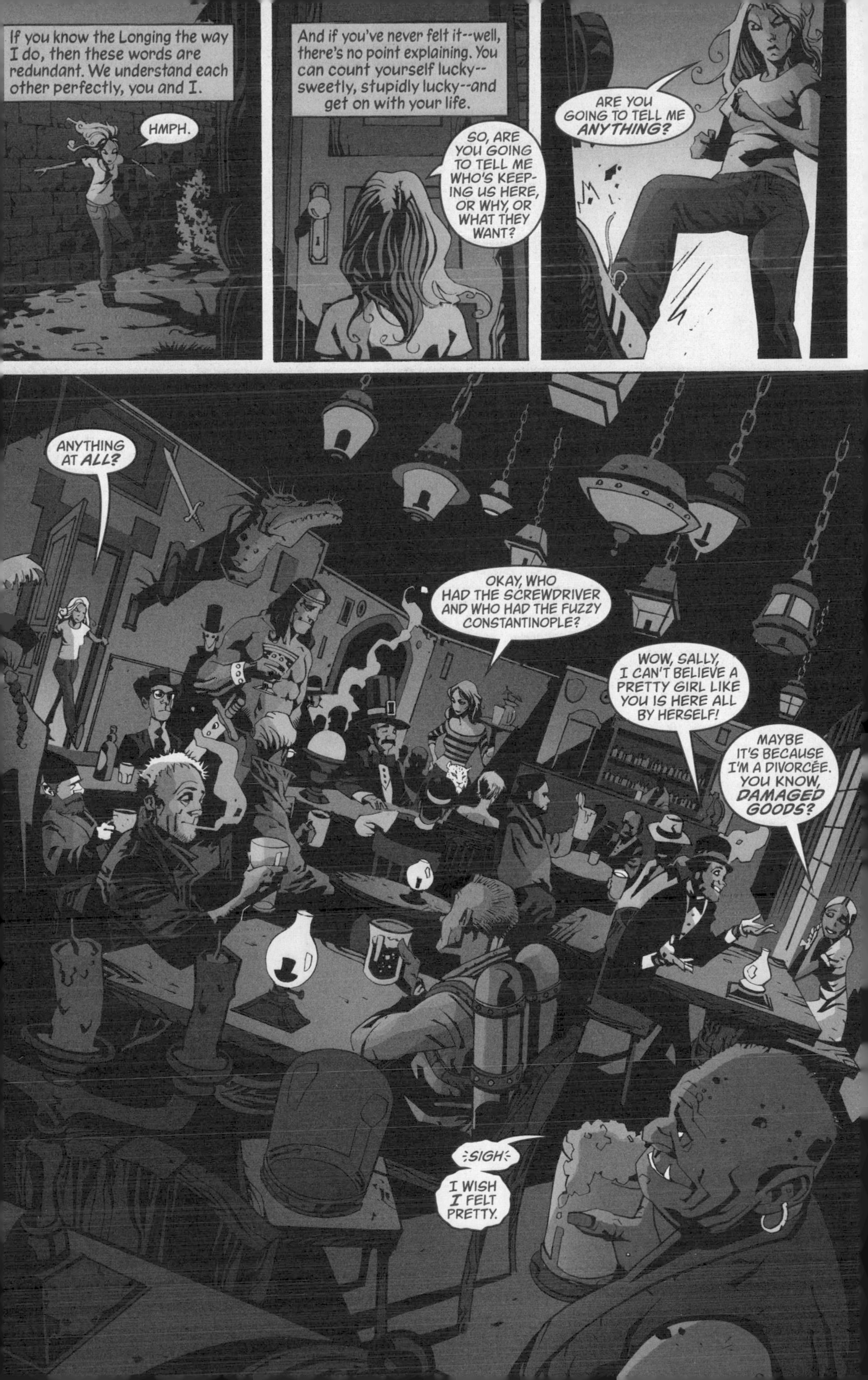
If you know the Longing the way I do, then these words are redundant. We understand each other perfectly, you and I.
HMPH.
And if you've never felt it--well, there's no point explaining. You can count yourself lucky--sweetly, stupidly lucky--and get on with your life.
SO, ARE YOU GOING TO TELL ME WHO'S KEEPING US HERE, OR WHY, OR WHAT THEY WANT?
ARE YOU GOING TO TELL ME ANYTHING?
ANYTHING AT ALL?
OKAY, WHO HAD THE SCREWDRIVER AND WHO HAD THE FUZZY CONSTANTINOPLE?
WOW, SALLY, I CAN'T BELIEVE A PRETTY GIRL LIKE YOU IS HERE ALL BY HERSELF!
MAYBE IT'S BECAUSE I'M A DIVORCÉE. YOU KNOW, DAMAGED GOODS?
SIGH
I WISH I FELT PRETTY.

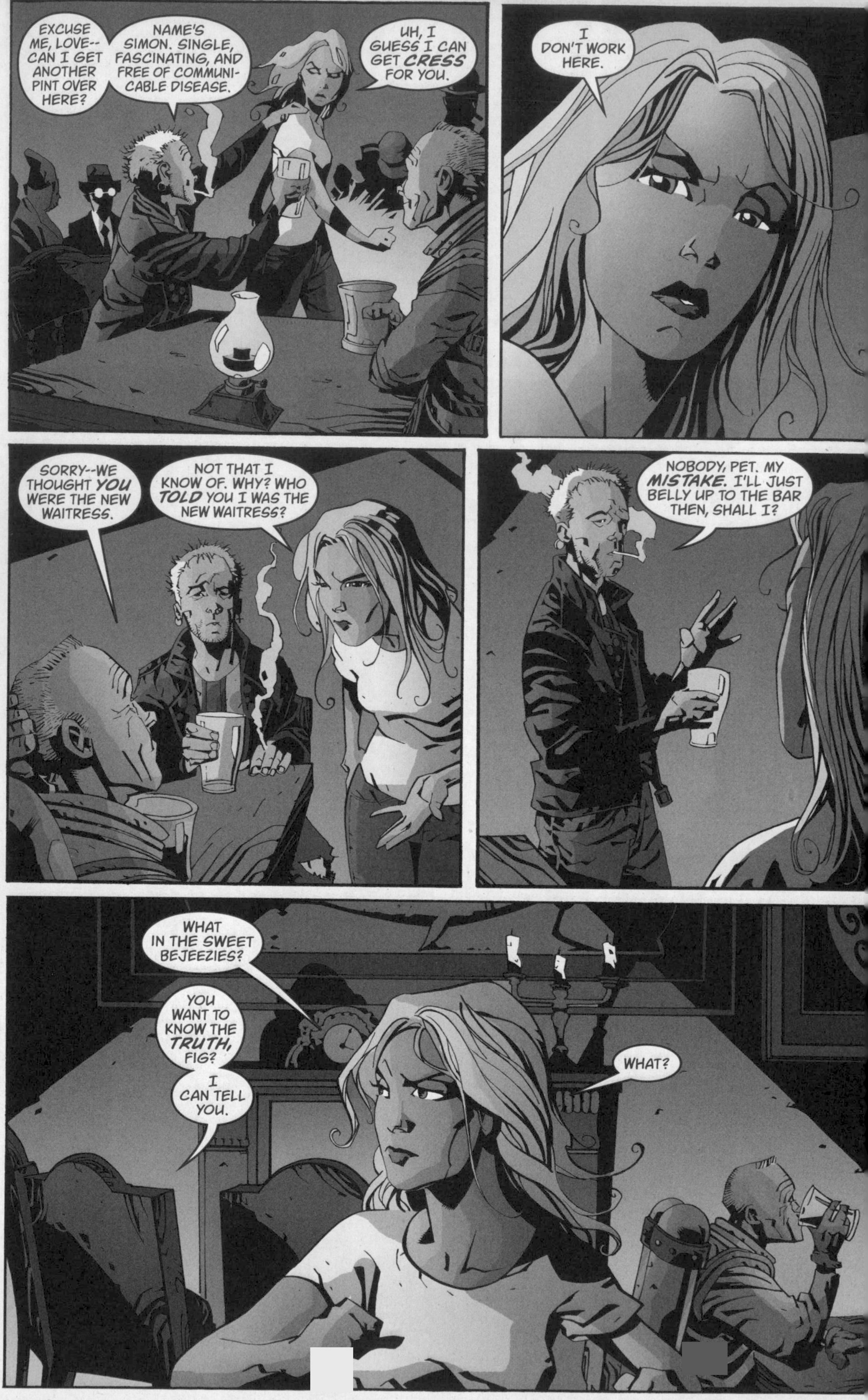
EXCUSE ME, LOVE-- CAN I GET ANOTHER PINT OVER HERE?
NAME'S SIMON. SINGLE, FASCINATING, AND FREE OF COMMUNI-CABLE DISEASE.
UH, I GUESS I CAN GET CRESS FOR YOU.
I DON'T WORK HERE.
SORRY--WE THOUGHT YOU WERE THE NEW WAITRESS.
NOT THAT I KNOW OF. WHY? WHO TOLD YOU I WAS THE NEW WAITRESS?
NOBODY, PET. MY MISTAKE. I'LL JUST BELLY UP TO THE BAR THEN, SHALL I?
WHAT IN THE SWEET BEJEEZIES?
YOU WANT TO KNOW THE TRUTH, FIG?
I CAN TELL YOU.
WHAT?

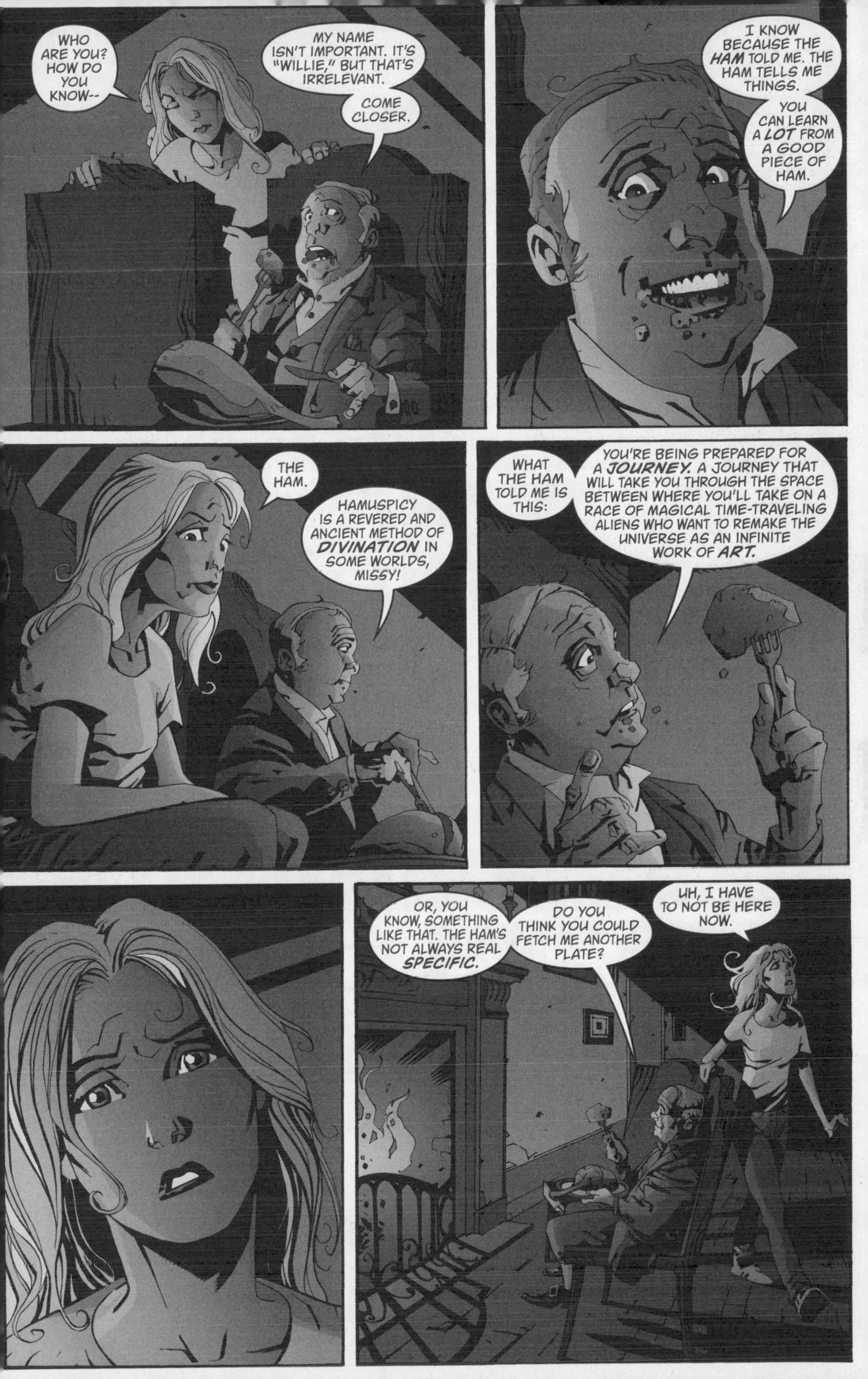
WHO ARE YOU? HOW DO YOU KNOW--
MY NAME ISN'T IMPORTANT. IT'S "WILLIE," BUT THAT'S IRRELEVANT.
COME CLOSER.
I KNOW BECAUSE THE HAM TOLD ME. THE HAM TELLS ME THINGS.
YOU CAN LEARN A LOT FROM A GOOD PIECE OF HAM.
THE HAM.
HAMUSPICY IS A REVERED AND ANCIENT METHOD OF DIVINATION IN SOME WORLDS, MISSY!
WHAT THE HAM TOLD ME IS THIS:
YOU'RE BEING PREPARED FOR A JOURNEY. A JOURNEY THAT WILL TAKE YOU THROUGH THE SPACE BETWEEN WHERE YOU'LL TAKE ON A RACE OF MAGICAL TIME-TRAVELING ALIENS WHO WANT TO REMAKE THE UNIVERSE AS AN INFINITE WORK OF ART.
OR, YOU KNOW, SOMETHING LIKE THAT. THE HAM'S NOT ALWAYS REAL SPECIFIC.
DO YOU THINK YOU COULD FETCH ME ANOTHER PLATE?
UH, I HAVE TO NOT BE HERE NOW.

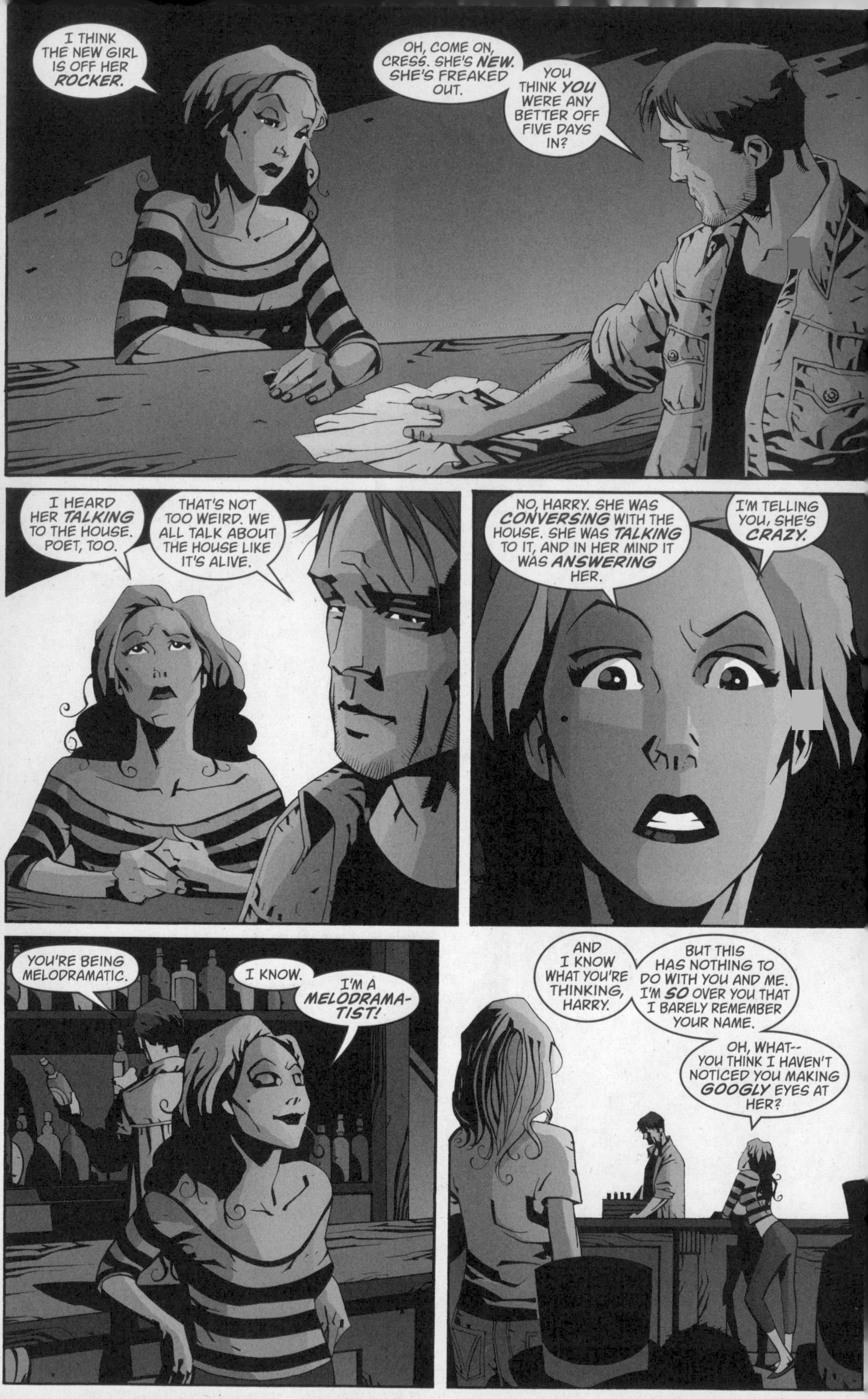
I THINK THE NEW GIRL IS OFF HER ROCKER.
OH, COME ON, CRESS. SHE'S NEW. SHE'S FREAKED OUT.
YOU THINK YOU WERE ANY BETTER OFF FIVE DAYS IN?
I HEARD HER TALKING TO THE HOUSE. POET, TOO.
THAT'S NOT TOO WEIRD. WE ALL TALK ABOUT THE HOUSE LIKE IT'S ALIVE.
NO, HARRY. SHE WAS CONVERSING WITH THE HOUSE. SHE WAS TALKING TO IT, AND IN HER MIND IT WAS ANSWERING HER.
I'M TELLING YOU, SHE'S CRAZY.
YOU'RE BEING MELODRAMATIC.
I KNOW.
I'M A MELODRAMA-TIST!
AND I KNOW WHAT YOU'RE THINKING, HARRY.
BUT THIS HAS NOTHING TO DO WITH YOU AND ME. I'M SO OVER YOU THAT I BARELY REMEMBER YOUR NAME.
OH, WHAT-- YOU THINK I HAVEN'T NOTICED YOU MAKING GOOGLY EYES AT HER?

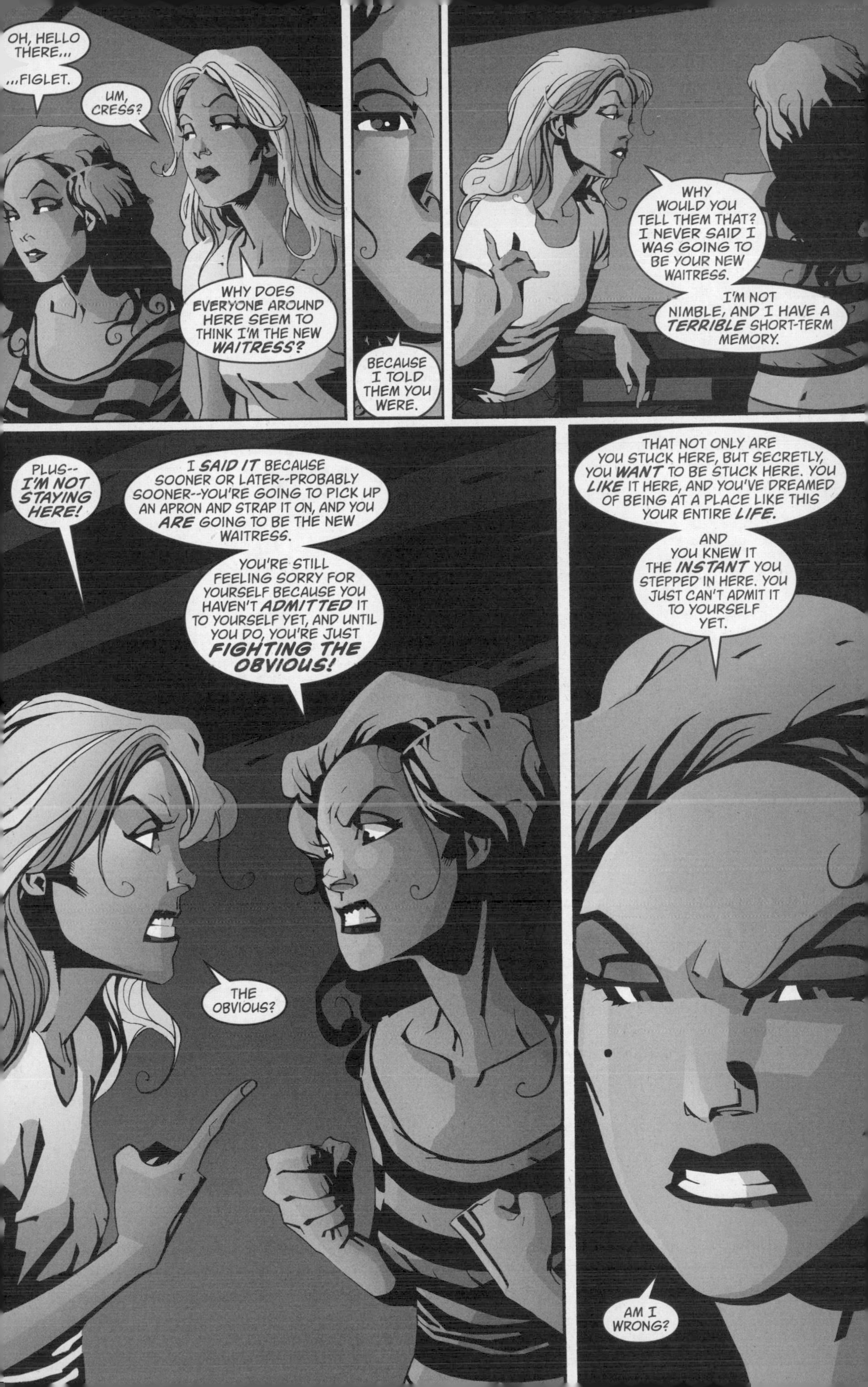
OH, HELLO THERE...
...FIGLET.
UM, CRESS?
WHY DOES EVERYONE AROUND HERE SEEM TO THINK I'M THE NEW WAITRESS?
BECAUSE I TOLD THEM YOU WERE.
WHY WOULD YOU TELL THEM THAT? I NEVER SAID I WAS GOING TO BE YOUR NEW WAITRESS.
I'M NOT NIMBLE, AND I HAVE A TERRIBLE SHORT-TERM MEMORY.
PLUS-- I'M NOT STAYING HERE!
I SAID IT BECAUSE SOONER OR LATER--PROBABLY SOONER--YOU'RE GOING TO PICK UP AN APRON AND STRAP IT ON, AND YOU ARE GOING TO BE THE NEW WAITRESS.
YOU'RE STILL FEELING SORRY FOR YOURSELF BECAUSE YOU HAVEN'T ADMITTED IT TO YOURSELF YET, AND UNTIL YOU DO, YOU'RE JUST FIGHTING THE OBVIOUS!
THE OBVIOUS?
THAT NOT ONLY ARE YOU STUCK HERE, BUT SECRETLY, YOU WANT TO BE STUCK HERE. YOU LIKE IT HERE, AND YOU'VE DREAMED OF BEING AT A PLACE LIKE THIS YOUR ENTIRE LIFE.
AND YOU KNEW IT THE INSTANT YOU STEPPED IN HERE. YOU JUST CAN'T ADMIT IT TO YOURSELF YET.
AM I WRONG?

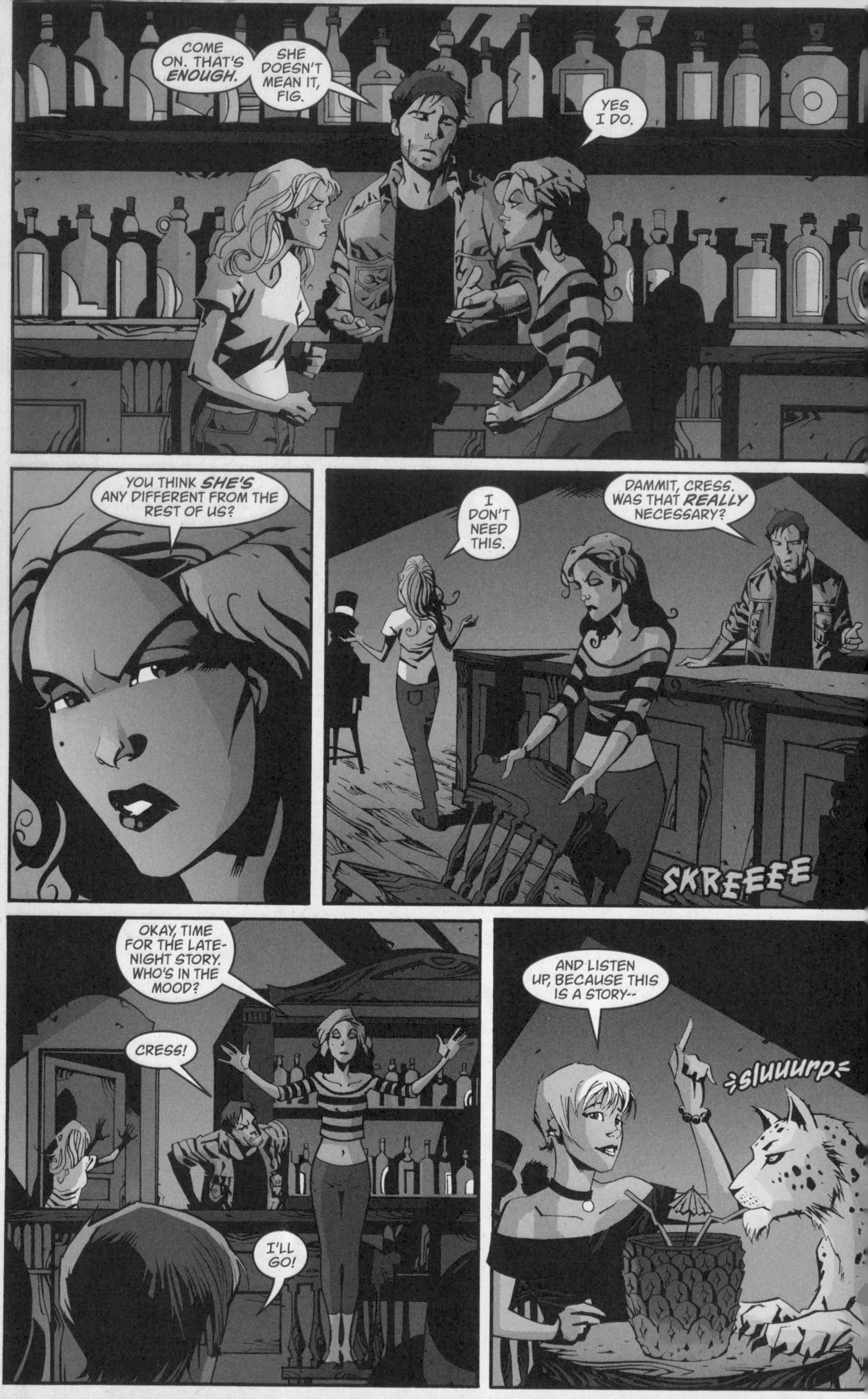
COME ON. THAT'S ENOUGH.
SHE DOESN'T MEAN IT, FIG.
YES I DO.
YOU THINK SHE'S ANY DIFFERENT FROM THE REST OF US?
I DON'T NEED THIS.
DAMMIT, CRESS. WAS THAT REALLY NECESSARY?
SKREEEEE
OKAY, TIME FOR THE LATE-NIGHT STORY. WHO'S IN THE MOOD?
CRESS!
I'LL GO!
AND LISTEN UP, BECAUSE THIS IS A STORY--
sluuurp

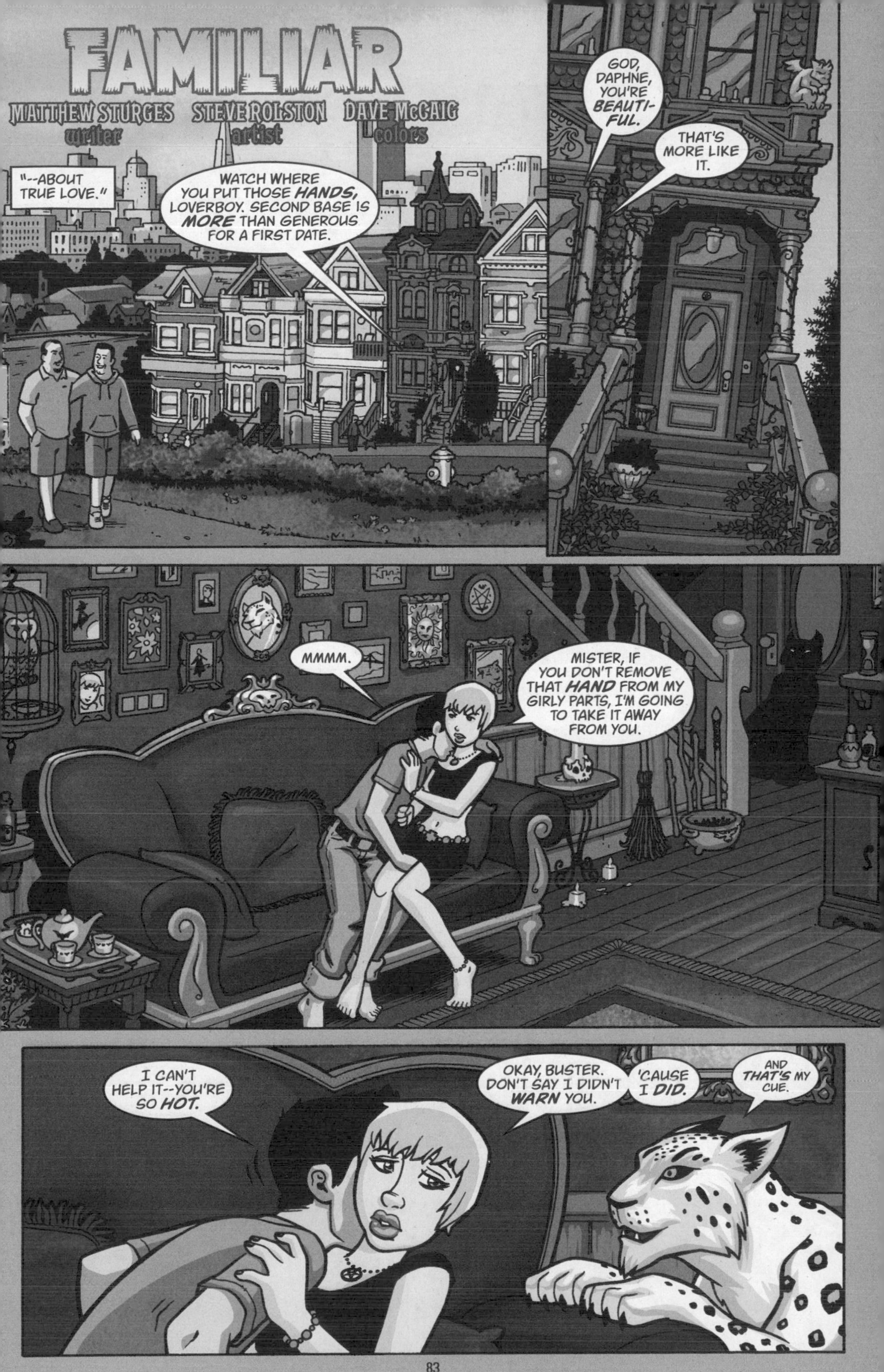
FAMILIAR
MATTHEW STURGES writer
STEVE ROLSTON artist
DAVE McCAIG colors
"--ABOUT TRUE LOVE."
WATCH WHERE YOU PUT THOSE HANDS, LOVERBOY. SECOND BASE IS MORE THAN GENEROUS FOR A FIRST DATE.
GOD, DAPHNE, YOU'RE BEAUTIFUL.
THAT'S MORE LIKE IT.
MMMM.
MISTER, IF YOU DON'T REMOVE THAT HAND FROM MY GIRLY PARTS, I'M GOING TO TAKE IT AWAY FROM YOU.
I CAN'T HELP IT--YOU'RE SO HOT.
OKAY, BUSTER. DON'T SAY I DIDN'T WARN YOU.
'CAUSE I DID.
AND THAT'S MY CUE.

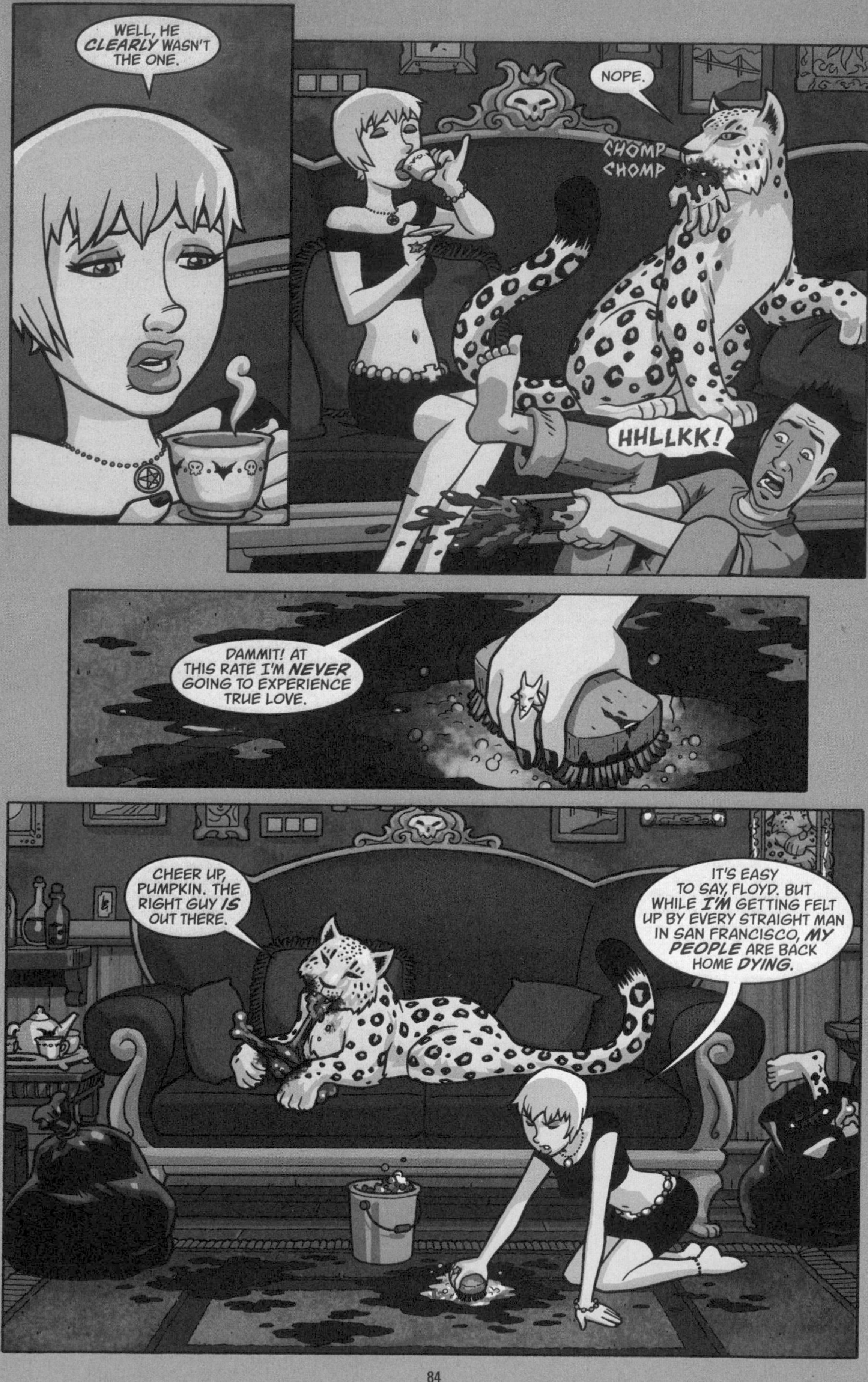
WELL, HE CLEARLY WASN'T THE ONE.
NOPE.
CHOMP CHOMP
HHLLKK!
DAMMIT! AT THIS RATE I'M NEVER GOING TO EXPERIENCE TRUE LOVE.
CHEER UP, PUMPKIN. THE RIGHT GUY IS OUT THERE.
IT'S EASY TO SAY, FLOYD. BUT WHILE I'M GETTING FELT UP BY EVERY STRAIGHT MAN IN SAN FRANCISCO, MY PEOPLE ARE BACK HOME DYING.

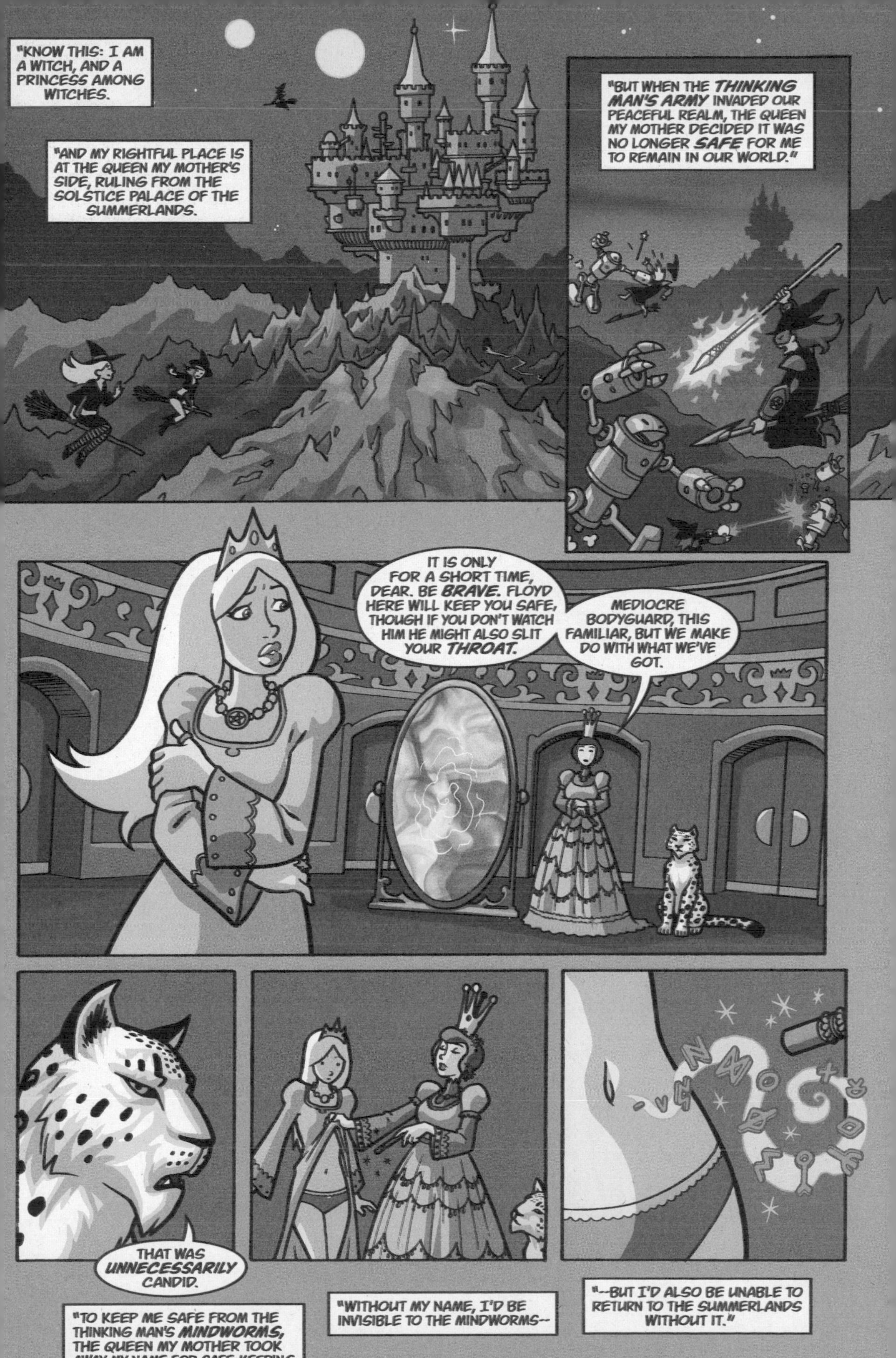
"KNOW THIS: I AM A WITCH, AND A PRINCESS AMONG WITCHES.
"AND MY RIGHTFUL PLACE IS AT THE QUEEN MY MOTHER'S SIDE, RULING FROM THE SOLSTICE PALACE OF THE SUMMERLANDS.
"BUT WHEN THE THINKING MAN'S ARMY INVADED OUR PEACEFUL REALM, THE QUEEN MY MOTHER DECIDED IT WAS NO LONGER SAFE FOR ME TO REMAIN IN OUR WORLD."
IT IS ONLY FOR A SHORT TIME, DEAR. BE BRAVE. FLOYD HERE WILL KEEP YOU SAFE, THOUGH IF YOU DON'T WATCH HIM HE MIGHT ALSO SLIT YOUR THROAT.
MEDIOCRE BODYGUARD, THIS FAMILIAR, BUT WE MAKE DO WITH WHAT WE'VE GOT.
THAT WAS UNNECESSARILY CANDID.
"TO KEEP ME SAFE FROM THE THINKING MAN'S MINDWORMS, THE QUEEN MY MOTHER TOOK AWAY MY NAME FOR SAFE-KEEPING.
"WITHOUT MY NAME, I'D BE INVISIBLE TO THE MINDWORMS--
"--BUT I'D ALSO BE UNABLE TO RETURN TO THE SUMMERLANDS WITHOUT IT."

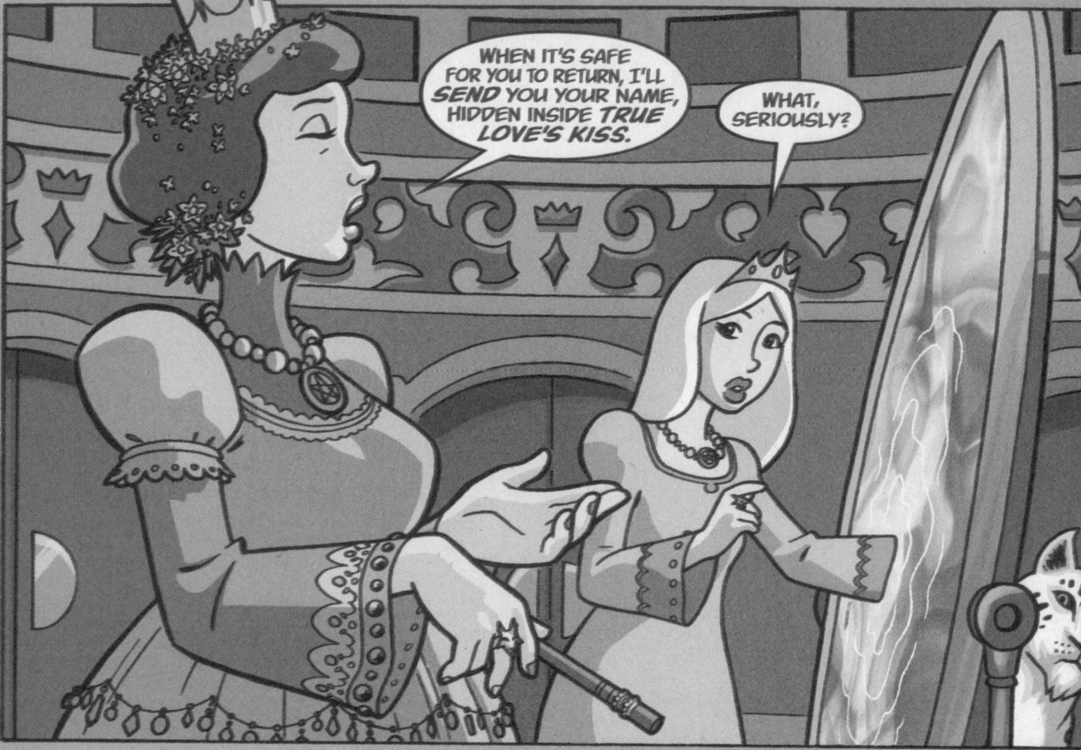
WHEN IT'S SAFE FOR YOU TO RETURN, I'LL SEND YOU YOUR NAME, HIDDEN INSIDE TRUE LOVE'S KISS.
WHAT, SERIOUSLY?

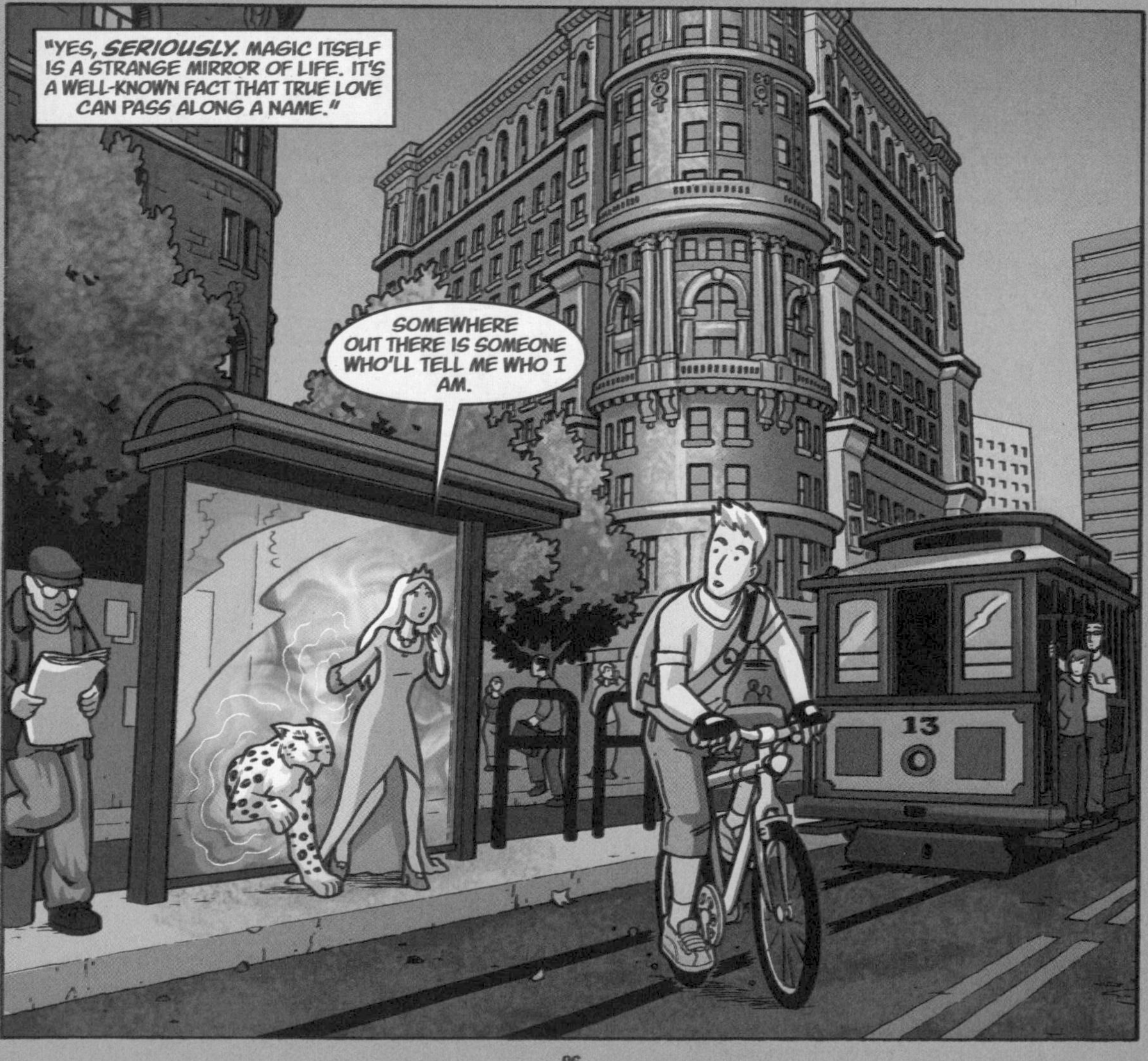
"YES, SERIOUSLY. MAGIC ITSELF IS A STRANGE MIRROR OF LIFE. IT'S A WELL-KNOWN FACT THAT TRUE LOVE CAN PASS ALONG A NAME."
SOMEWHERE OUT THERE IS SOMEONE WHO'LL TELL ME WHO I AM.
13

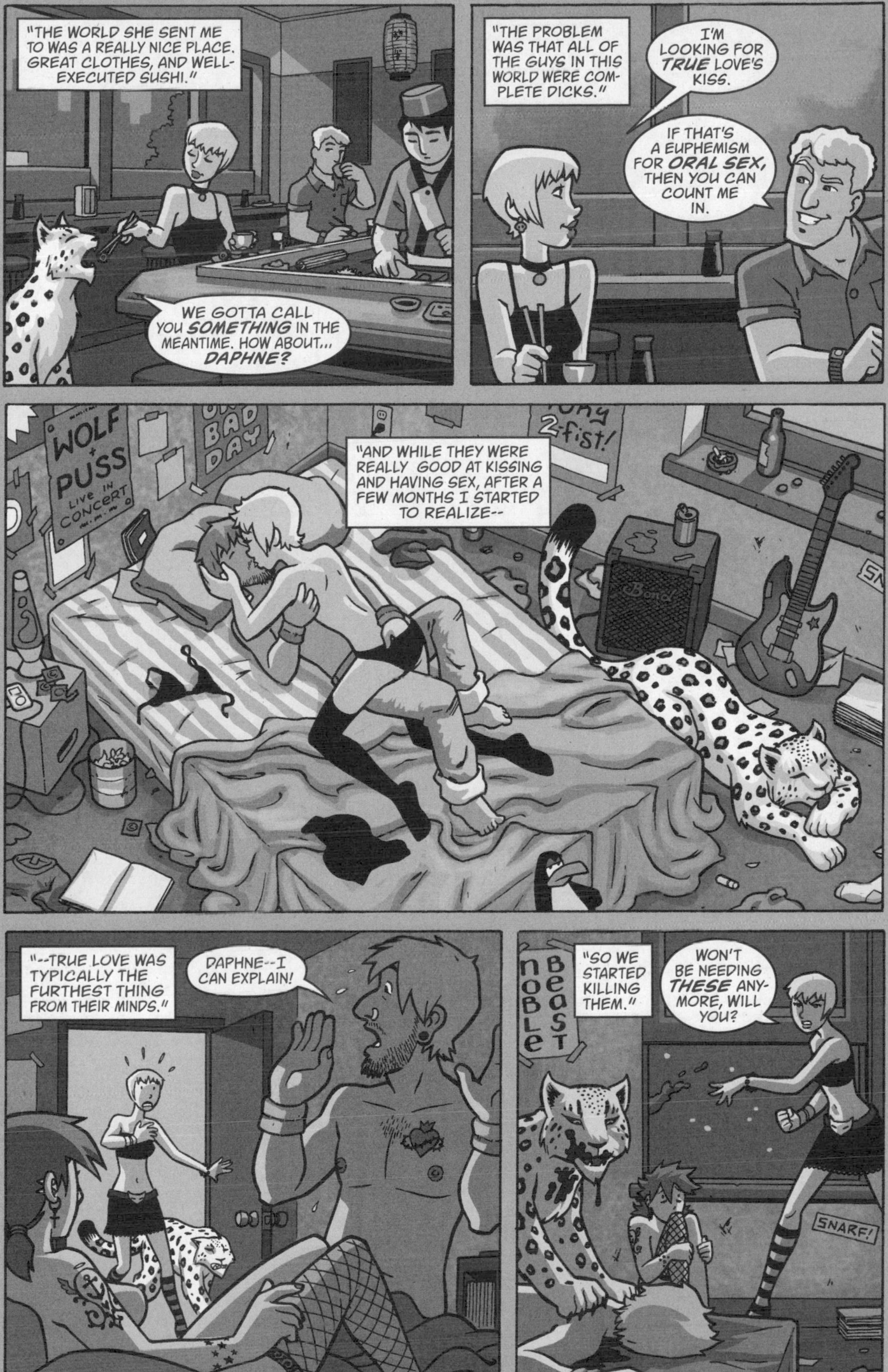
"THE WORLD SHE SENT ME TO WAS A REALLY NICE PLACE. GREAT CLOTHES, AND WELL-EXECUTED SUSHI."
WE GOTTA CALL YOU SOMETHING IN THE MEANTIME. HOW ABOUT... DAPHNE?
"THE PROBLEM WAS THAT ALL OF THE GUYS IN THIS WORLD WERE COMPLETE DICKS."
I'M LOOKING FOR TRUE LOVE'S KISS.
IF THAT'S A EUPHEMISM FOR ORAL SEX, THEN YOU CAN COUNT ME IN.
WOLF + PUSS Live in Concert
BAD DAY
2-fist!
"AND WHILE THEY WERE REALLY GOOD AT KISSING AND HAVING SEX, AFTER A FEW MONTHS I STARTED TO REALIZE--
Bond
"--TRUE LOVE WAS TYPICALLY THE FURTHEST THING FROM THEIR MINDS."
DAPHNE--I CAN EXPLAIN!
noBLe BeaST
"SO WE STARTED KILLING THEM."
WON'T BE NEEDING THESE ANYMORE, WILL YOU?
SNARF!

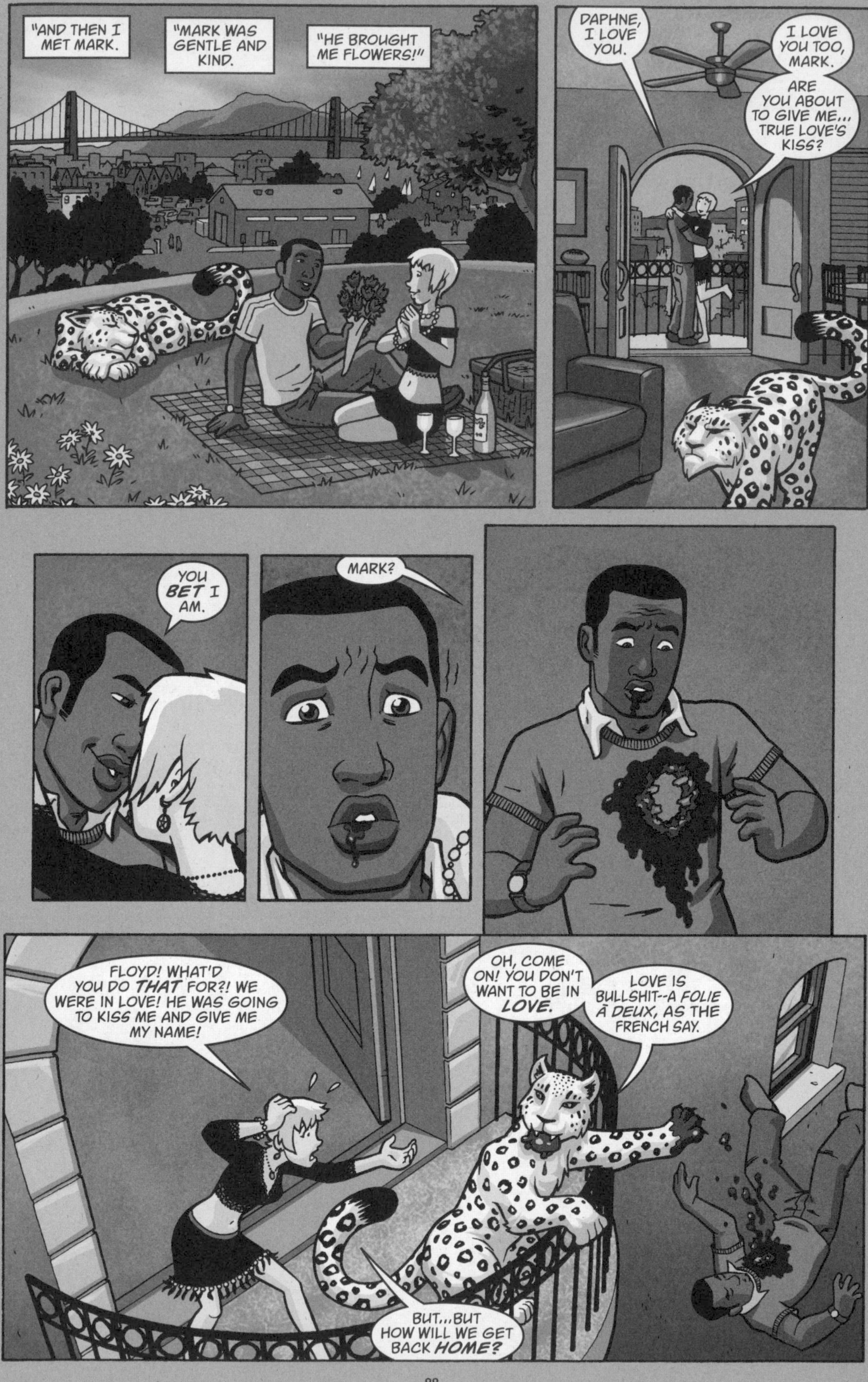
"AND THEN I MET MARK.
"MARK WAS GENTLE AND KIND.
"HE BROUGHT ME FLOWERS!"
DAPHNE, I LOVE YOU.
I LOVE YOU TOO, MARK.
ARE YOU ABOUT TO GIVE ME... TRUE LOVE'S KISS?
YOU *BET* I AM.
MARK?
FLOYD! WHAT'D YOU DO *THAT* FOR?! WE WERE IN LOVE! HE WAS GOING TO KISS ME AND GIVE ME MY NAME!
OH, COME ON! YOU DON'T WANT TO BE IN *LOVE*.
LOVE IS BULLSHIT--A *FOLIE Ã DEUX*, AS THE FRENCH SAY.
BUT...BUT HOW WILL WE GET BACK *HOME*?

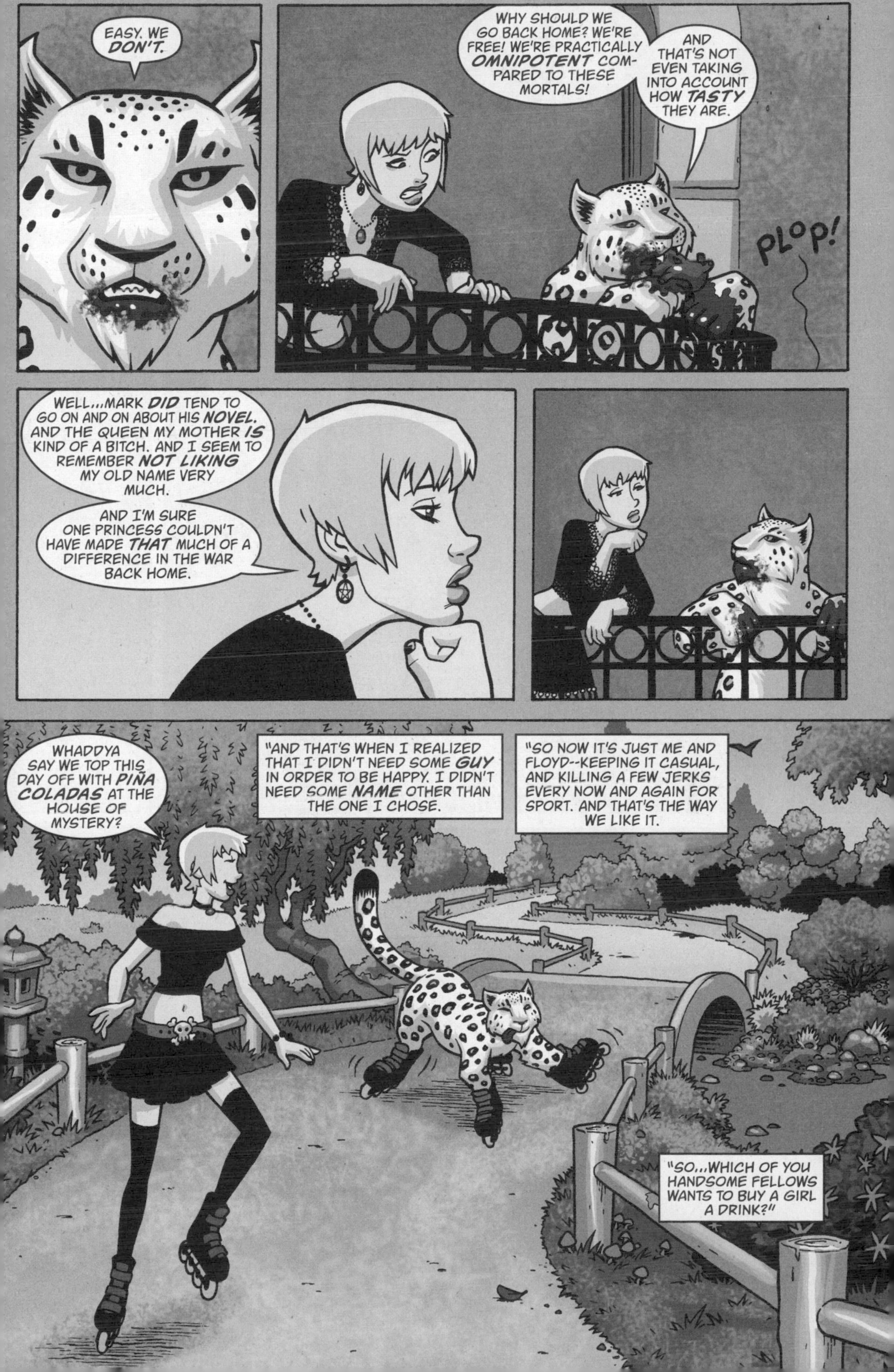
EASY. WE DON'T.
WHY SHOULD WE GO BACK HOME? WE'RE FREE! WE'RE PRACTICALLY OMNIPOTENT COMPARED TO THESE MORTALS!
AND THAT'S NOT EVEN TAKING INTO ACCOUNT HOW TASTY THEY ARE.
PLOP!
WELL...MARK DID TEND TO GO ON AND ON ABOUT HIS NOVEL. AND THE QUEEN MY MOTHER IS KIND OF A BITCH. AND I SEEM TO REMEMBER NOT LIKING MY OLD NAME VERY MUCH.
AND I'M SURE ONE PRINCESS COULDN'T HAVE MADE THAT MUCH OF A DIFFERENCE IN THE WAR BACK HOME.
WHADDYA SAY WE TOP THIS DAY OFF WITH PIÑA COLADAS AT THE HOUSE OF MYSTERY?
"AND THAT'S WHEN I REALIZED THAT I DIDN'T NEED SOME GUY IN ORDER TO BE HAPPY. I DIDN'T NEED SOME NAME OTHER THAN THE ONE I CHOSE.
"SO NOW IT'S JUST ME AND FLOYD--KEEPING IT CASUAL, AND KILLING A FEW JERKS EVERY NOW AND AGAIN FOR SPORT. AND THAT'S THE WAY WE LIKE IT.
"SO...WHICH OF YOU HANDSOME FELLOWS WANTS TO BUY A GIRL A DRINK?"

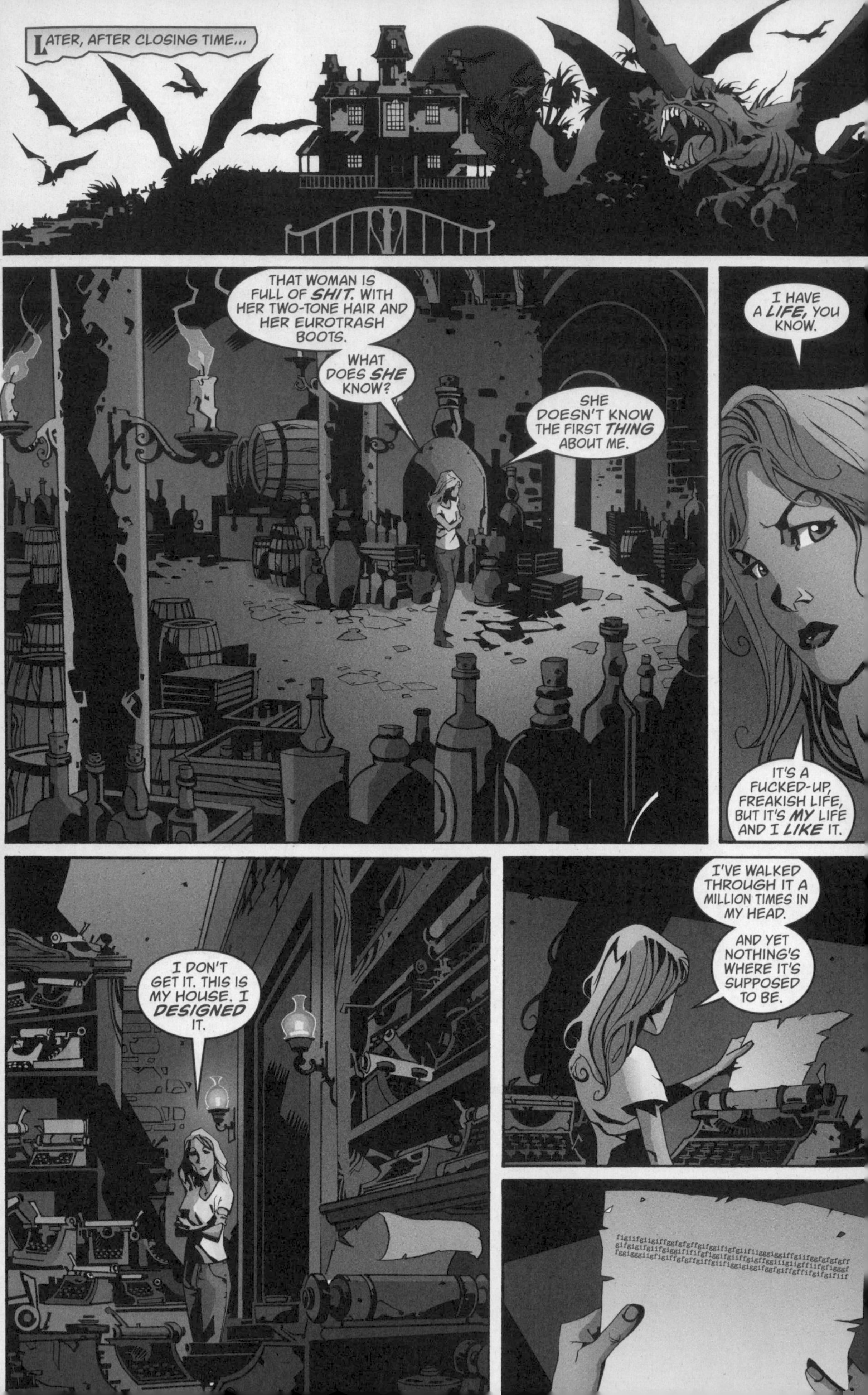
LATER, AFTER CLOSING TIME...
THAT WOMAN IS FULL OF SHIT. WITH HER TWO-TONE HAIR AND HER EUROTRASH BOOTS.
WHAT DOES SHE KNOW?
SHE DOESN'T KNOW THE FIRST THING ABOUT ME.
I HAVE A LIFE, YOU KNOW.
IT'S A FUCKED-UP, FREAKISH LIFE, BUT IT'S MY LIFE AND I LIKE IT.
I DON'T GET IT. THIS IS MY HOUSE. I DESIGNED IT.
I'VE WALKED THROUGH IT A MILLION TIMES IN MY HEAD.
AND YET NOTHING'S WHERE IT'S SUPPOSED TO BE.

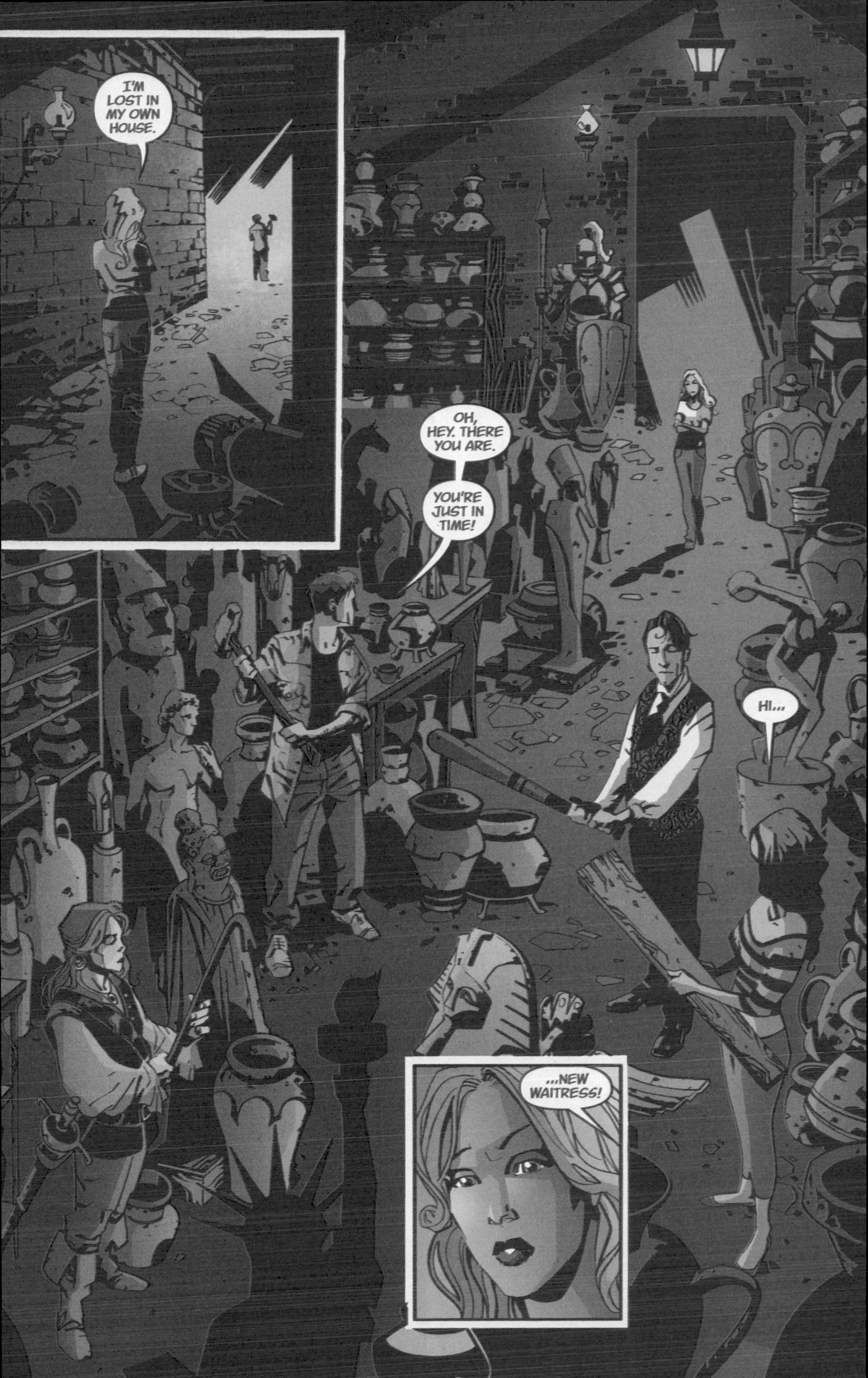
I'M LOST IN MY OWN HOUSE.
OH, HEY. THERE YOU ARE.
YOU'RE JUST IN TIME!
HI...
...NEW WAITRESS!

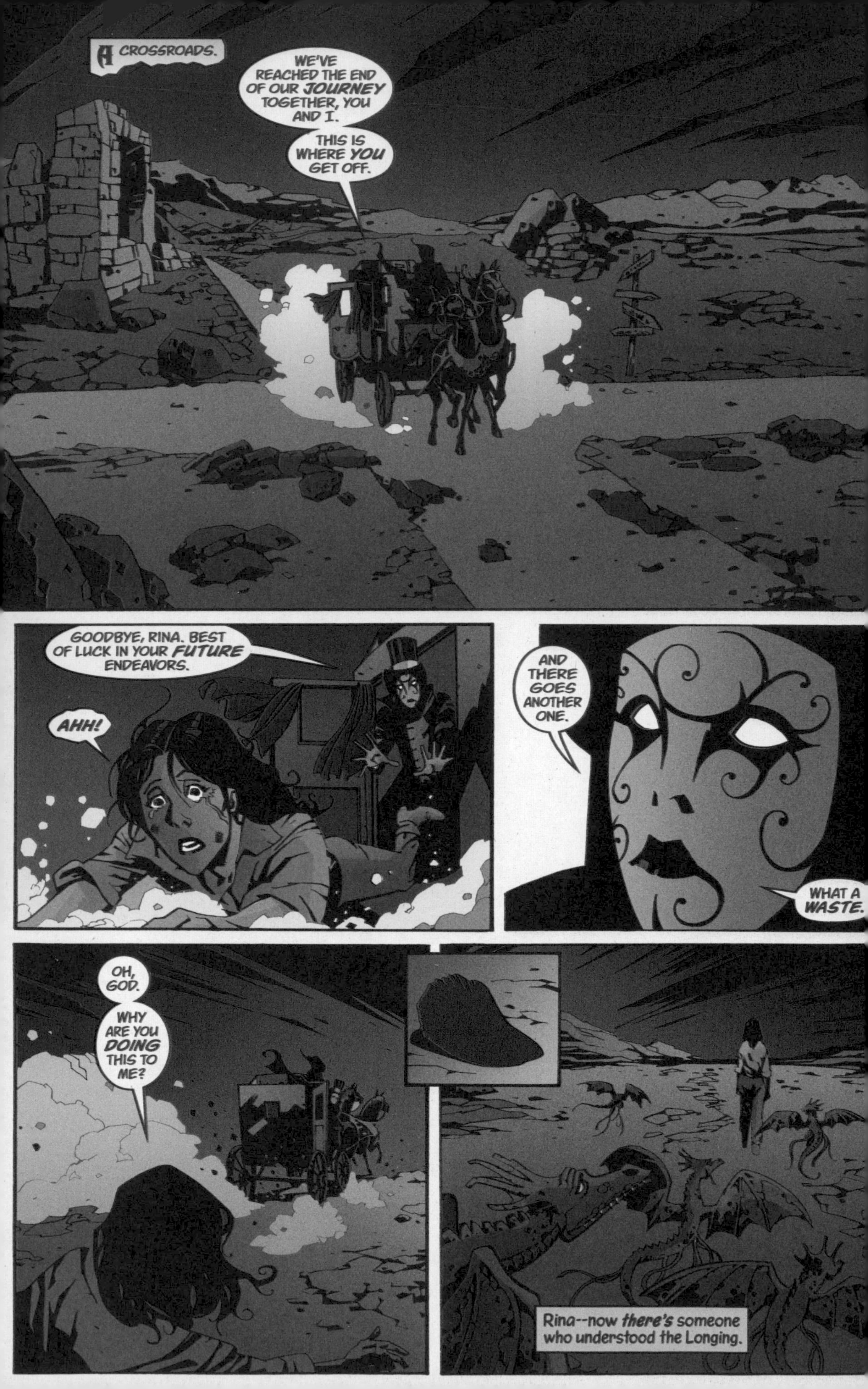
A CROSSROADS.
WE'VE REACHED THE END OF OUR JOURNEY TOGETHER, YOU AND I.
THIS IS WHERE YOU GET OFF.
GOODBYE, RINA. BEST OF LUCK IN YOUR FUTURE ENDEAVORS.
AHH!
AND THERE GOES ANOTHER ONE.
WHAT A WASTE.
OH, GOD.
WHY ARE YOU DOING THIS TO ME?
Rina--now there's someone who understood the Longing.

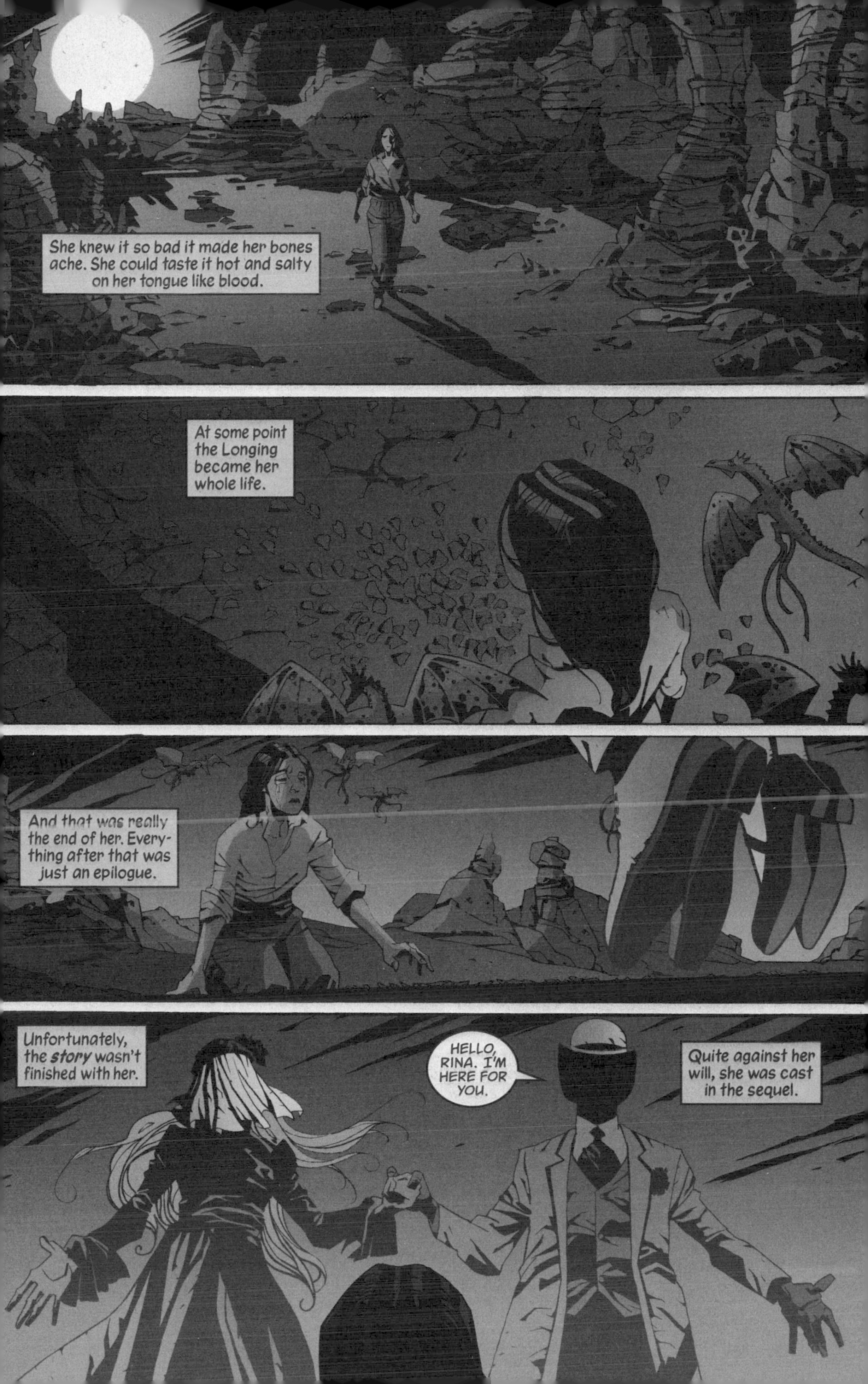
She knew it so bad it made her bones ache. She could taste it hot and salty on her tongue like blood.
At some point the Longing became her whole life.
And that was really the end of her. Everything after that was just an epilogue.
Unfortunately, the *story* wasn't finished with her.
HELLO, RINA. I'M HERE FOR YOU.
Quite against her will, she was cast in the sequel.

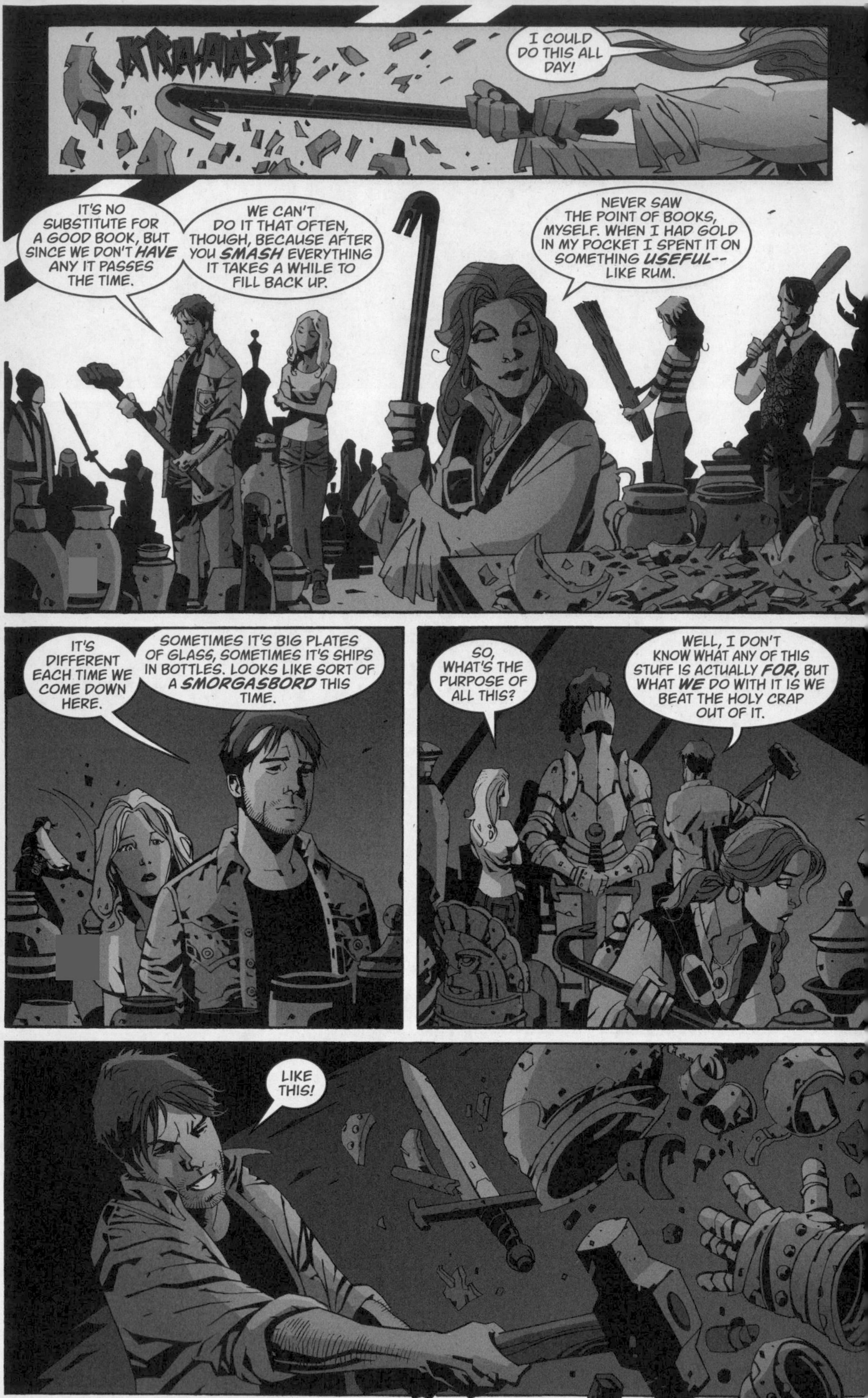
KRAAASH
I COULD DO THIS ALL DAY!
IT'S NO SUBSTITUTE FOR A GOOD BOOK, BUT SINCE WE DON'T HAVE ANY IT PASSES THE TIME.
WE CAN'T DO IT THAT OFTEN, THOUGH, BECAUSE AFTER YOU SMASH EVERYTHING IT TAKES A WHILE TO FILL BACK UP.
NEVER SAW THE POINT OF BOOKS, MYSELF. WHEN I HAD GOLD IN MY POCKET I SPENT IT ON SOMETHING USEFUL-- LIKE RUM.
IT'S DIFFERENT EACH TIME WE COME DOWN HERE.
SOMETIMES IT'S BIG PLATES OF GLASS, SOMETIMES IT'S SHIPS IN BOTTLES. LOOKS LIKE SORT OF A SMORGASBORD THIS TIME.
SO, WHAT'S THE PURPOSE OF ALL THIS?
WELL, I DON'T KNOW WHAT ANY OF THIS STUFF IS ACTUALLY FOR, BUT WHAT WE DO WITH IT IS WE BEAT THE HOLY CRAP OUT OF IT.
LIKE THIS!

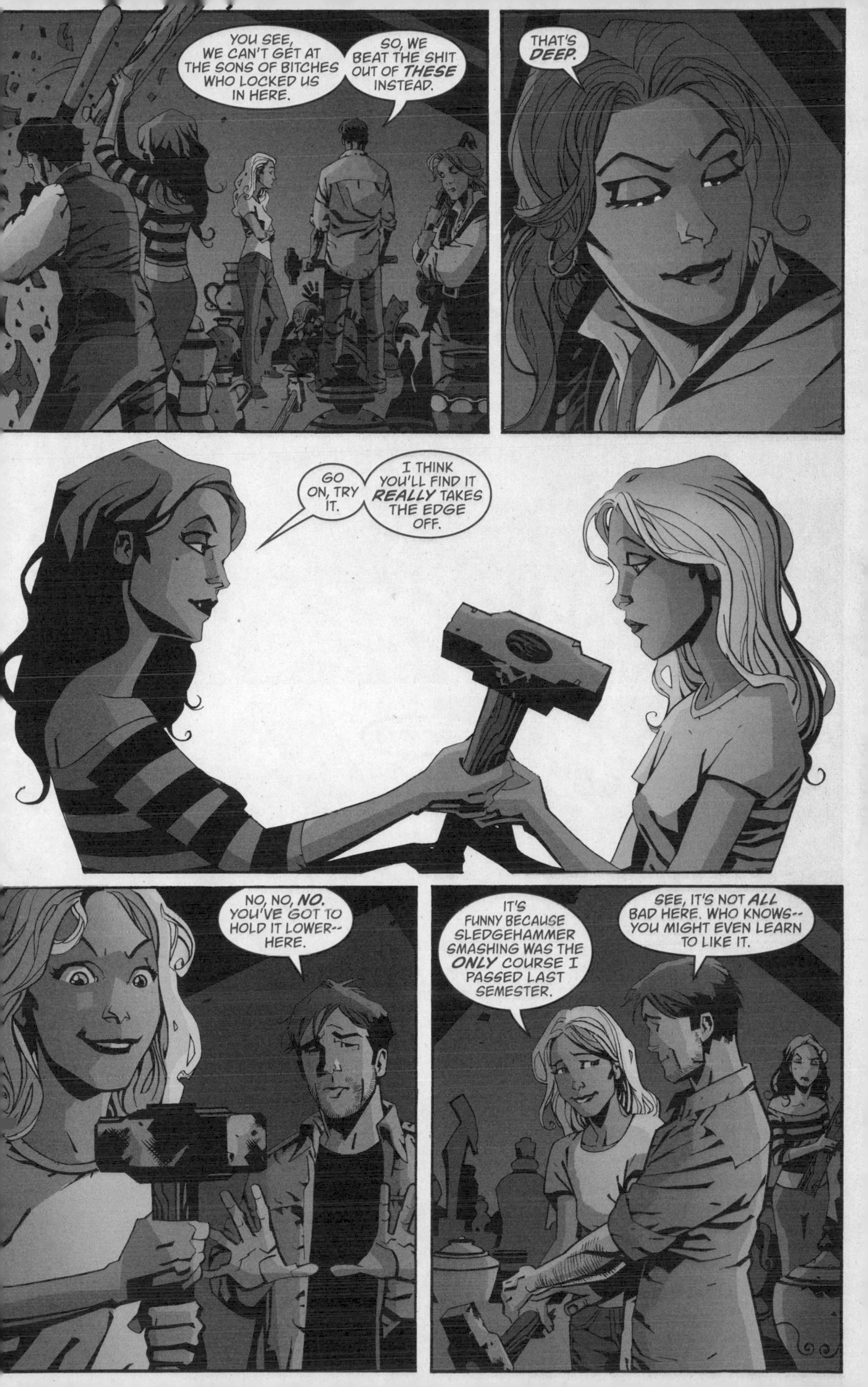
YOU SEE, WE CAN'T GET AT THE SONS OF BITCHES WHO LOCKED US IN HERE.
SO, WE BEAT THE SHIT OUT OF THESE INSTEAD.
THAT'S DEEP.
GO ON, TRY IT.
I THINK YOU'LL FIND IT REALLY TAKES THE EDGE OFF.
NO, NO, NO. YOU'VE GOT TO HOLD IT LOWER-- HERE.
IT'S FUNNY BECAUSE SLEDGEHAMMER SMASHING WAS THE ONLY COURSE I PASSED LAST SEMESTER.
SEE, IT'S NOT ALL BAD HERE. WHO KNOWS-- YOU MIGHT EVEN LEARN TO LIKE IT.

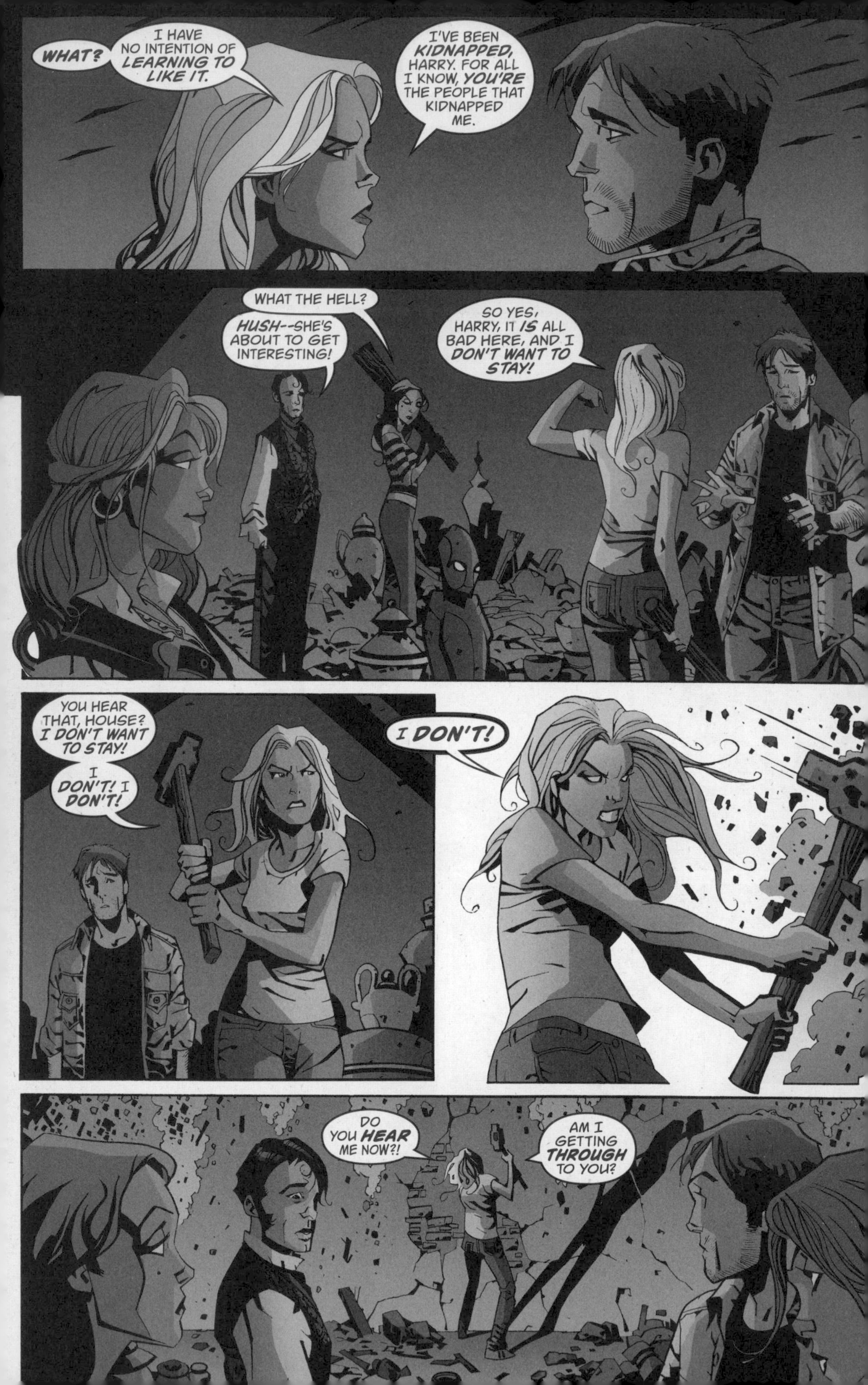
WHAT?
I HAVE NO INTENTION OF LEARNING TO LIKE IT.
I'VE BEEN KIDNAPPED, HARRY. FOR ALL I KNOW, YOU'RE THE PEOPLE THAT KIDNAPPED ME.
WHAT THE HELL?
HUSH--SHE'S ABOUT TO GET INTERESTING!
SO YES, HARRY, IT IS ALL BAD HERE, AND I DON'T WANT TO STAY!
YOU HEAR THAT, HOUSE? I DON'T WANT TO STAY!
I DON'T! I DON'T!
I DON'T!
DO YOU HEAR ME NOW?!
AM I GETTING THROUGH TO YOU?

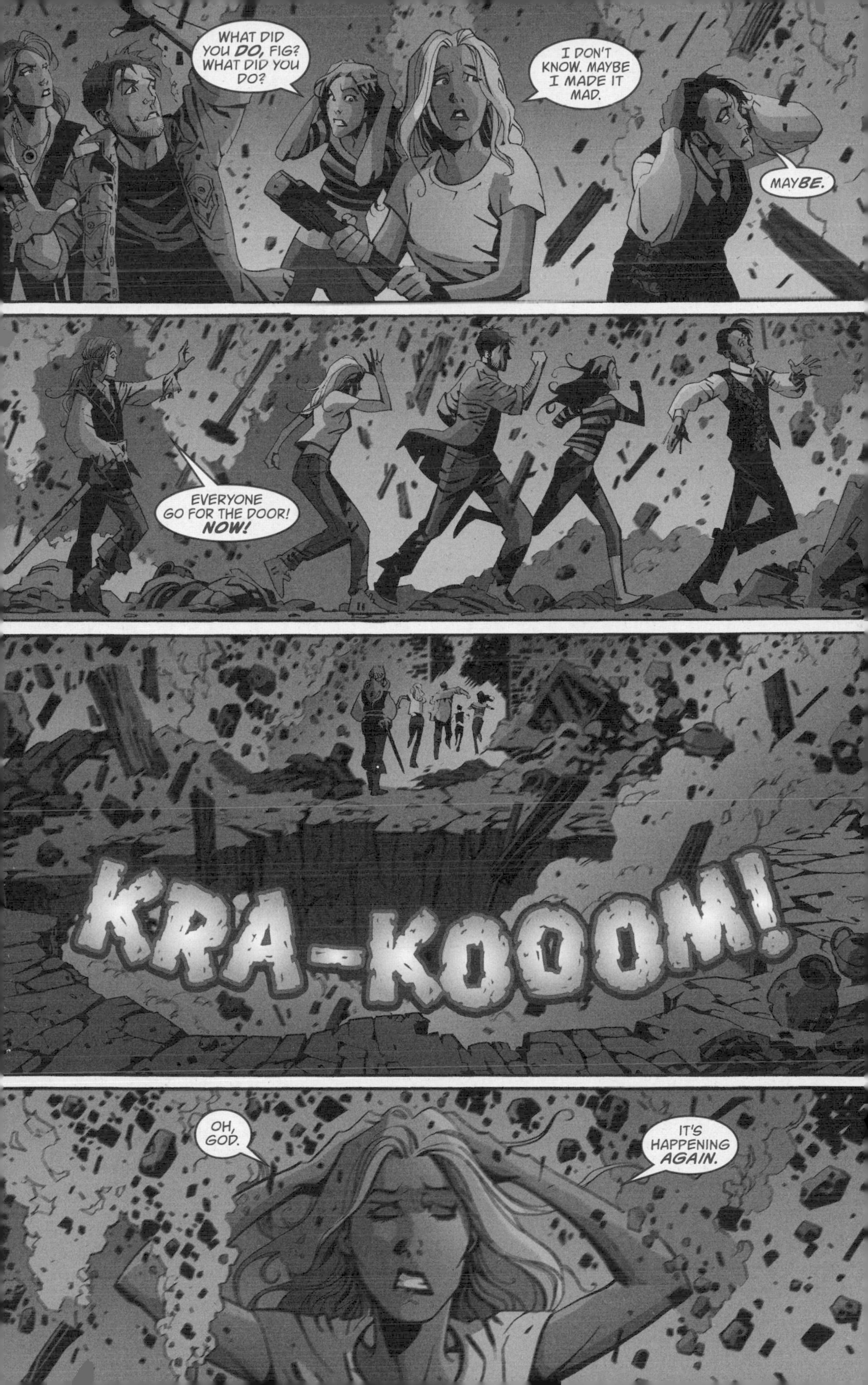
WHAT DID YOU DO, FIG? WHAT DID YOU DO?
I DON'T KNOW. MAYBE I MADE IT MAD.
MAYBE.
EVERYONE GO FOR THE DOOR! NOW!
KRA-KOOOM!
OH, GOD.
IT'S HAPPENING AGAIN.

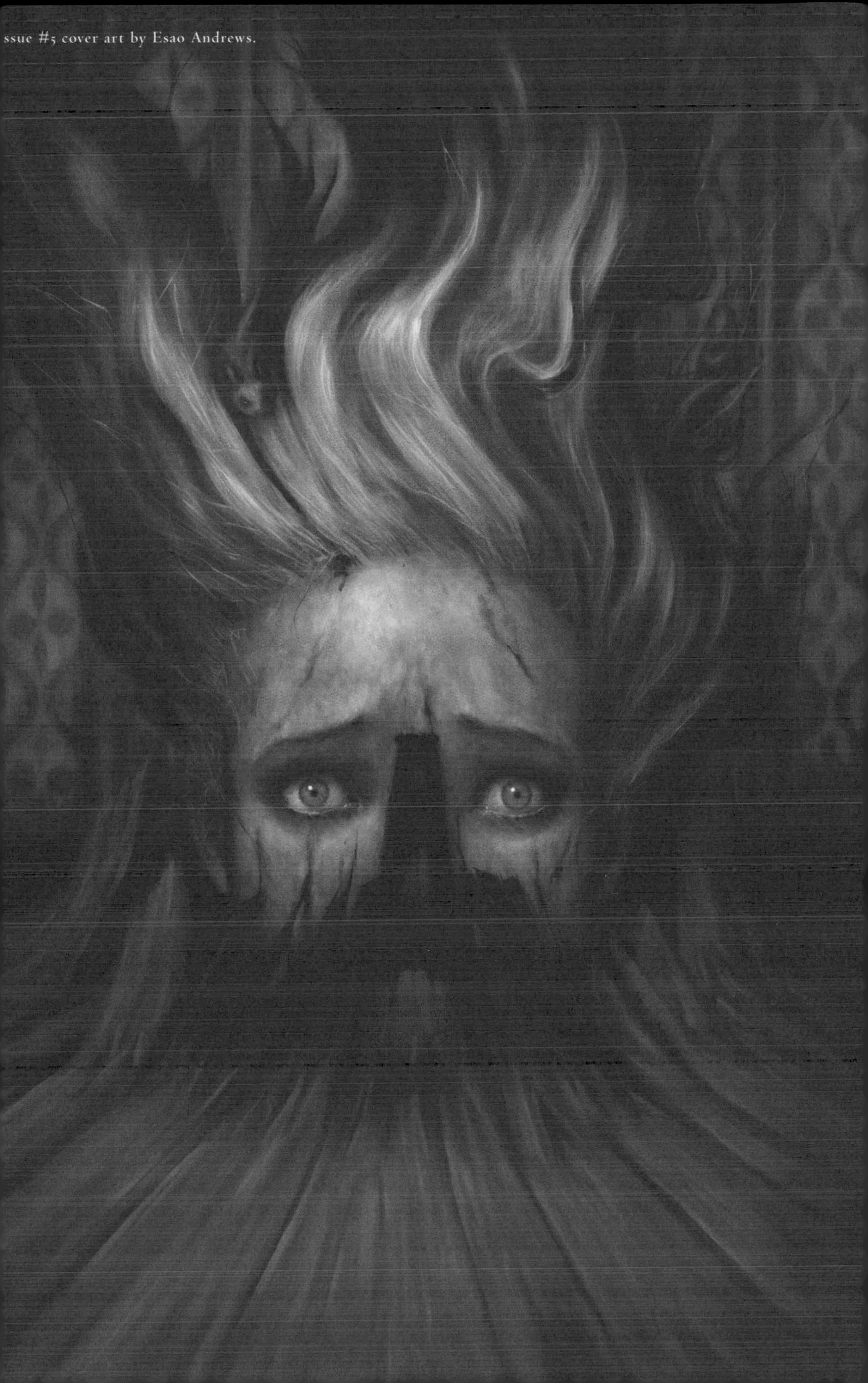

ssue #5 cover art by Esao Andrews.

When I was a little girl I used to tell my father bedtime stories.

The stories were about a little girl named Fig who went on adventures in all sorts of different worlds.

Fig was plucky and brave, and with the assistance of her faithful stuffed rabbit Walden, she encountered every peril you can imagine.

She faced down monsters and wicked stepmothers alike, saving the denizens of these worlds from danger.

All she asked in return was a bowl of vanilla ice cream with sprinkles on top.

My father was a writer, and he wrote up my stories and sold them as the *Fig's Adventure* books.

Fig's Adventure in Stuffytown

Peter and Bethany Keele

Fig's Adventure in the Cloud Castle of Puffery

Fig's Adventure in the Clown Kingdom

Fig's Adventure in Stuffytown

Fig's Adventure in the Cloud Castle of Puffery

Fig's Adventure in the Clown Kingdom

Fig's Adventure in the Cloud Castle of Puffery

Fig's Adventure in Stuffytown

The books were a little too weird to be bestsellers, but we managed to put away enough for college.

Then my parents got divorced, and Dad moved to Texas.

We had summers and Christmas together, but Fig's adventures were through.

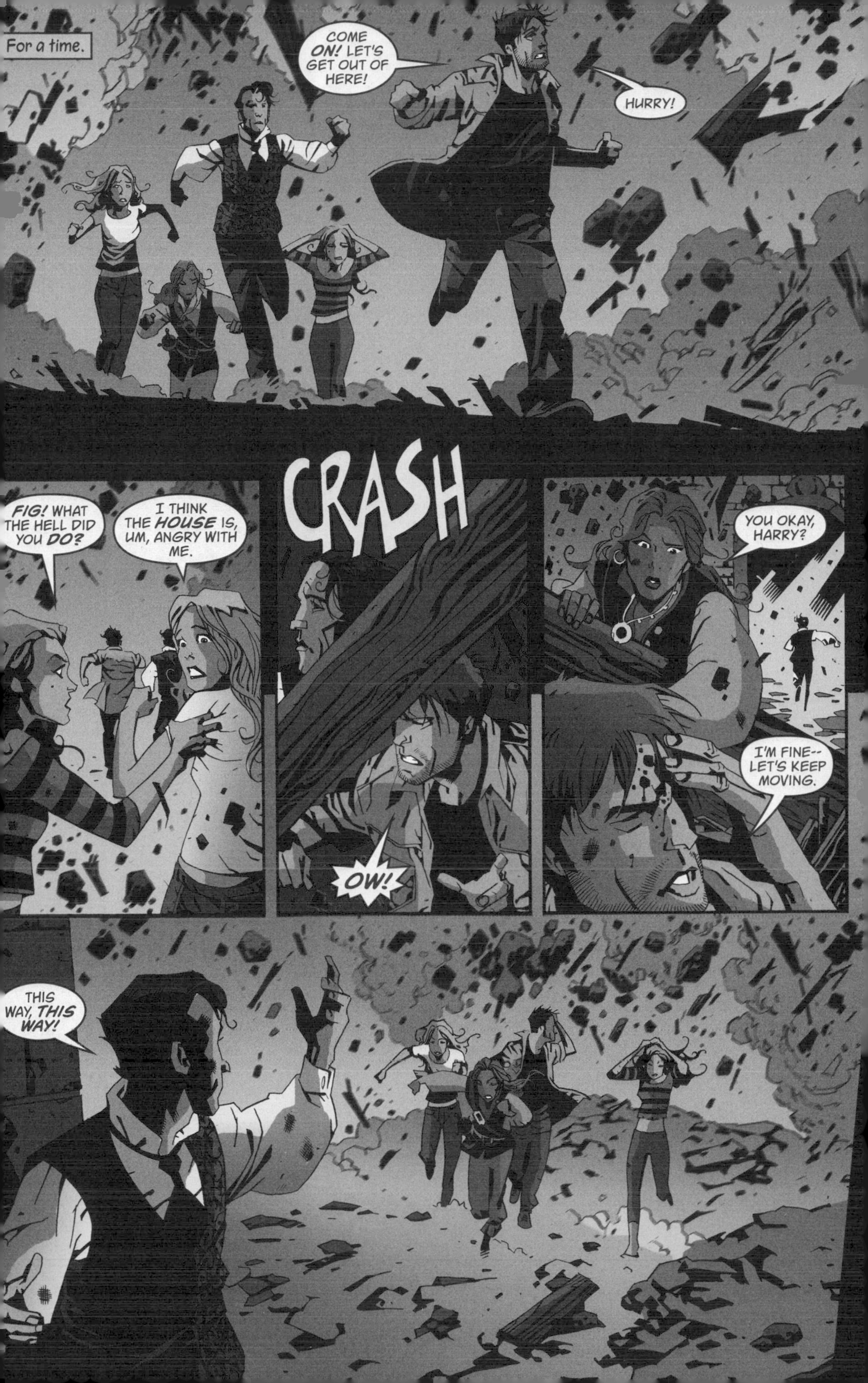
For a time.
COME ON! LET'S GET OUT OF HERE!
HURRY!
CRASH
FIG! WHAT THE HELL DID YOU DO?
I THINK THE HOUSE IS, UM, ANGRY WITH ME.
OW!
YOU OKAY, HARRY?
I'M FINE-- LET'S KEEP MOVING.
THIS WAY, THIS WAY!

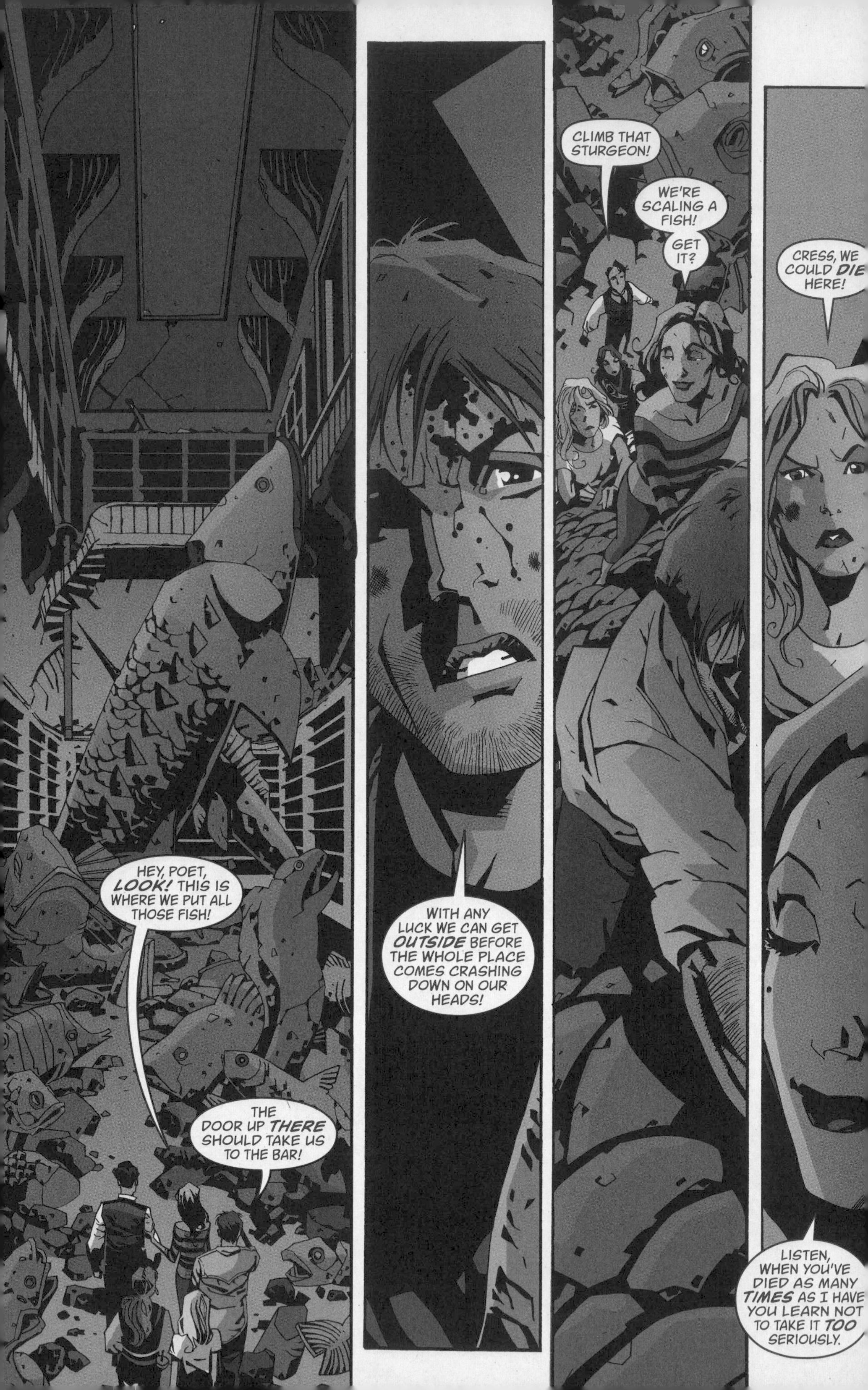
HEY, POET, LOOK! THIS IS WHERE WE PUT ALL THOSE FISH!
THE DOOR UP THERE SHOULD TAKE US TO THE BAR!
WITH ANY LUCK WE CAN GET OUTSIDE BEFORE THE WHOLE PLACE COMES CRASHING DOWN ON OUR HEADS!
CLIMB THAT STURGEON!
WE'RE SCALING A FISH!
GET IT?
CRESS, WE COULD DIE HERE!
LISTEN, WHEN YOU'VE DIED AS MANY TIMES AS I HAVE YOU LEARN NOT TO TAKE IT TOO SERIOUSLY.

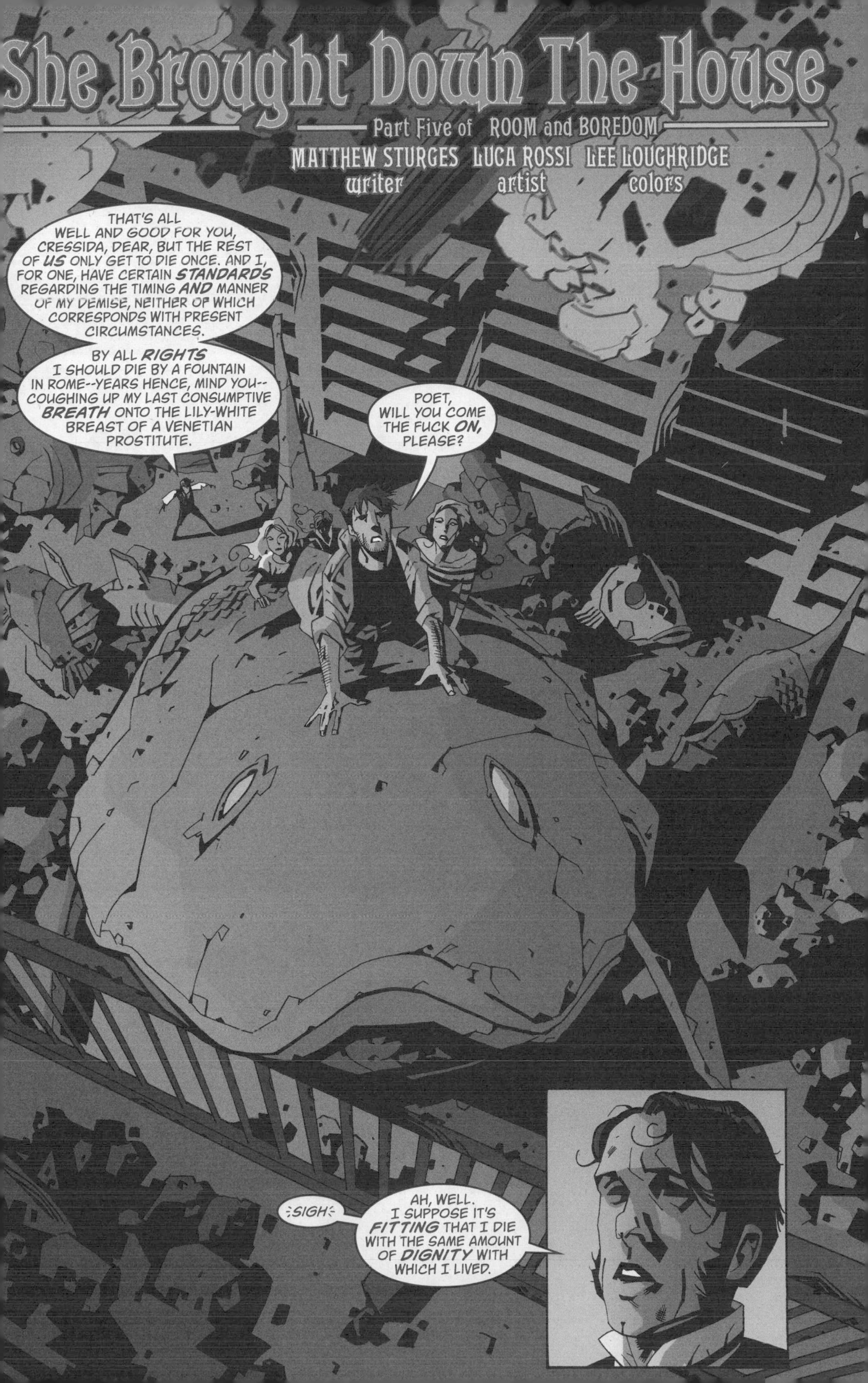
She Brought Down The House
Part Five of ROOM and BOREDOM
MATTHEW STURGES writer LUCA ROSSI artist LEE LOUGHRIDGE colors
THAT'S ALL WELL AND GOOD FOR YOU, CRESSIDA, DEAR, BUT THE REST OF US ONLY GET TO DIE ONCE. AND I, FOR ONE, HAVE CERTAIN STANDARDS REGARDING THE TIMING AND MANNER OF MY DEMISE, NEITHER OF WHICH CORRESPONDS WITH PRESENT CIRCUMSTANCES.
BY ALL RIGHTS I SHOULD DIE BY A FOUNTAIN IN ROME--YEARS HENCE, MIND YOU--COUGHING UP MY LAST CONSUMPTIVE BREATH ONTO THE LILY-WHITE BREAST OF A VENETIAN PROSTITUTE.
POET, WILL YOU COME THE FUCK ON, PLEASE?
SIGH
AH, WELL. I SUPPOSE IT'S FITTING THAT I DIE WITH THE SAME AMOUNT OF DIGNITY WITH WHICH I LIVED.

AT THAT PRECISE MOMENT...

RUMBLE RUBBLE

AWK!

OH, AH... JORDAN! WHATEVER ARE YOU *DOING* HERE THIS LATE?

I HELP OUT AROUND THE BAR. HARRY LETS ME, 'CAUSE I DON'T HAVE ANY GOOD STORIES.

WHAT ARE *YOU* DOING HERE, OVERHILL? CLOSING TIME WAS LIKE AN HOUR AGO.

OH, I FELL ASLEEP IN THE *BATHROOM* AGAIN.

IT WAS AN *ACCIDENT* THIS TIME, I PROMISE.

WHAT- EVER YOU SAY, PAL.

COME ON AND I'LL--

WHOA!

GOODNESS! WHAT'S GOING ON?!

CREEEEEAK

SCR

In the Conception there's a saying:

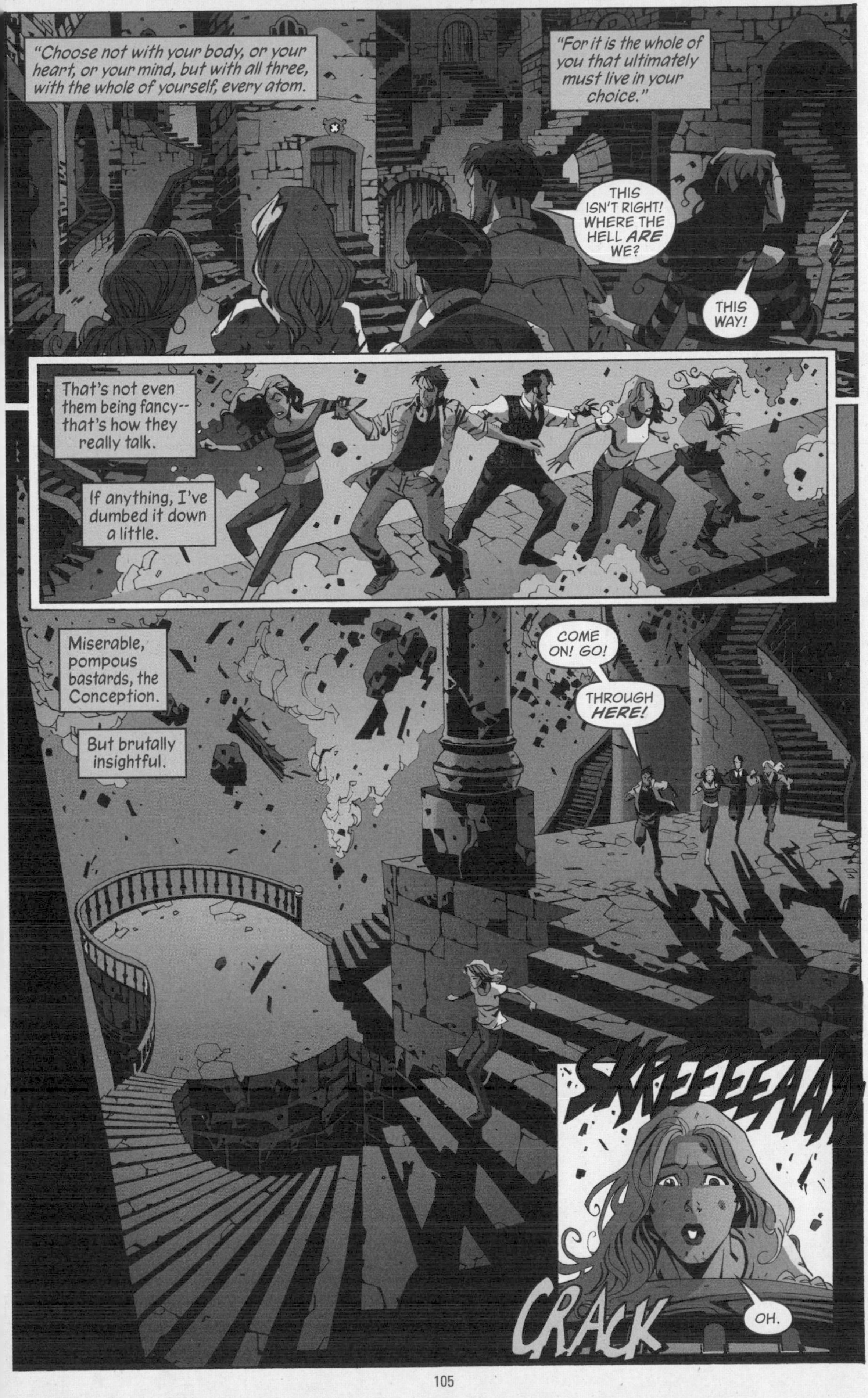
"Choose not with your body, or your heart, or your mind, but with all three, with the whole of yourself, every atom.
"For it is the whole of you that ultimately must live in your choice."
THIS ISN'T RIGHT! WHERE THE HELL ARE WE?
THIS WAY!
That's not even them being fancy--that's how they really talk.
If anything, I've dumbed it down a little.
Miserable, pompous bastards, the Conception.
But brutally insightful.
COME ON! GO!
THROUGH HERE!
SKREEEEAAAW
CRACK
OH.

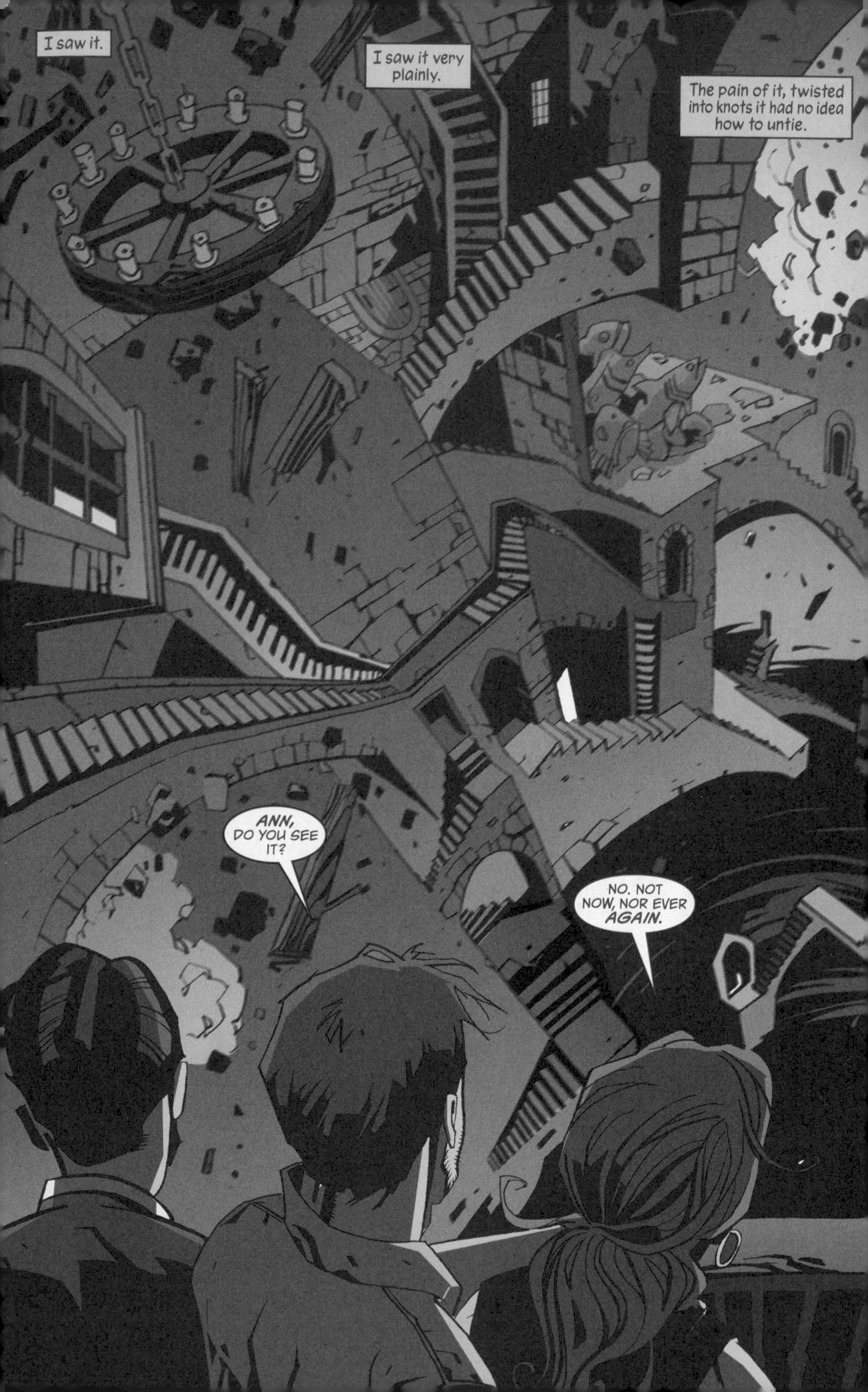
I saw it.
I saw it very plainly.
The pain of it, twisted into knots it had no idea how to untie.
ANN, DO YOU SEE IT?
NO. NOT NOW, NOR EVER AGAIN.

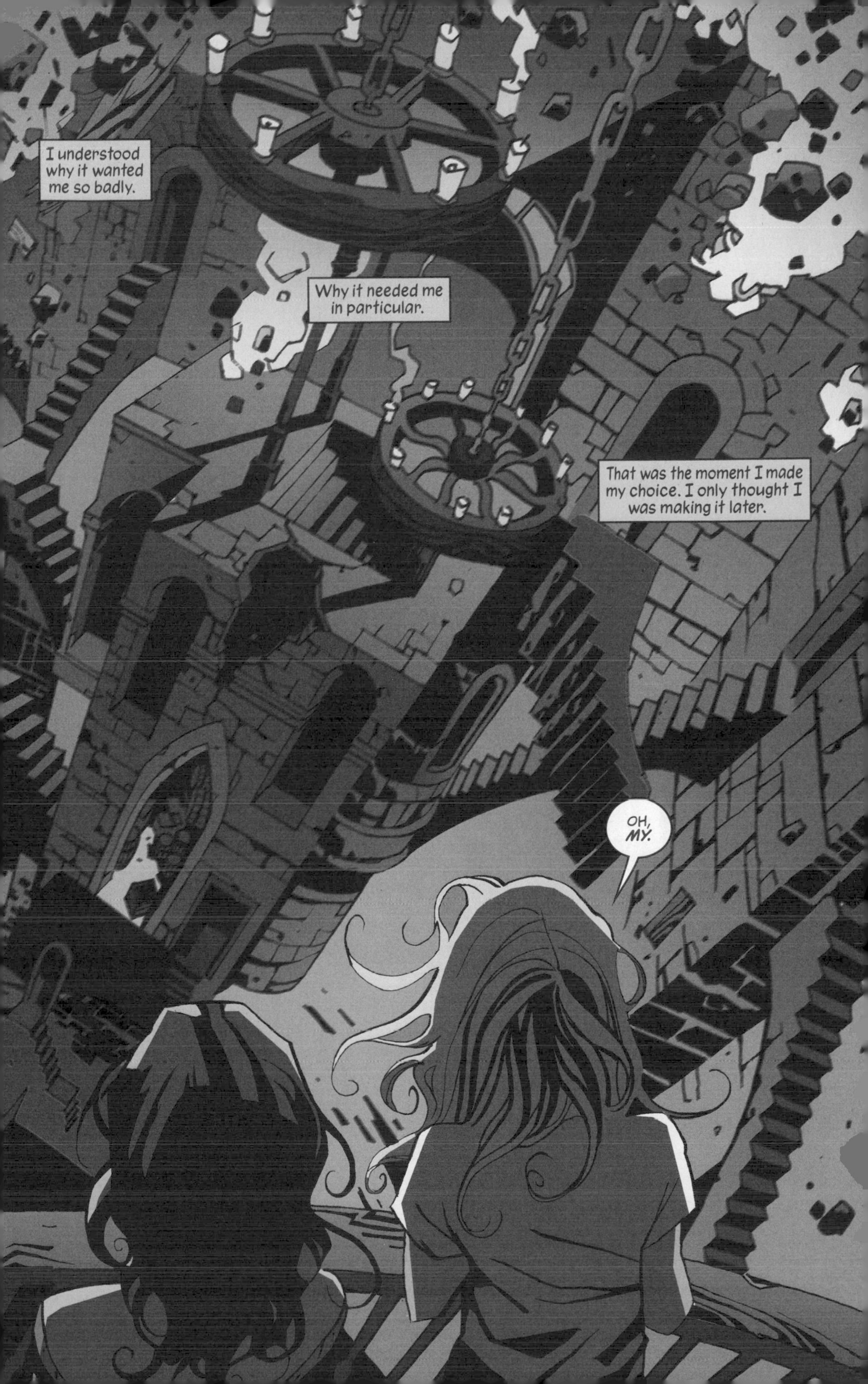
I understood why it wanted me so badly.
Why it needed me in particular.
That was the moment I made my choice. I only thought I was making it later.
OH, MY.

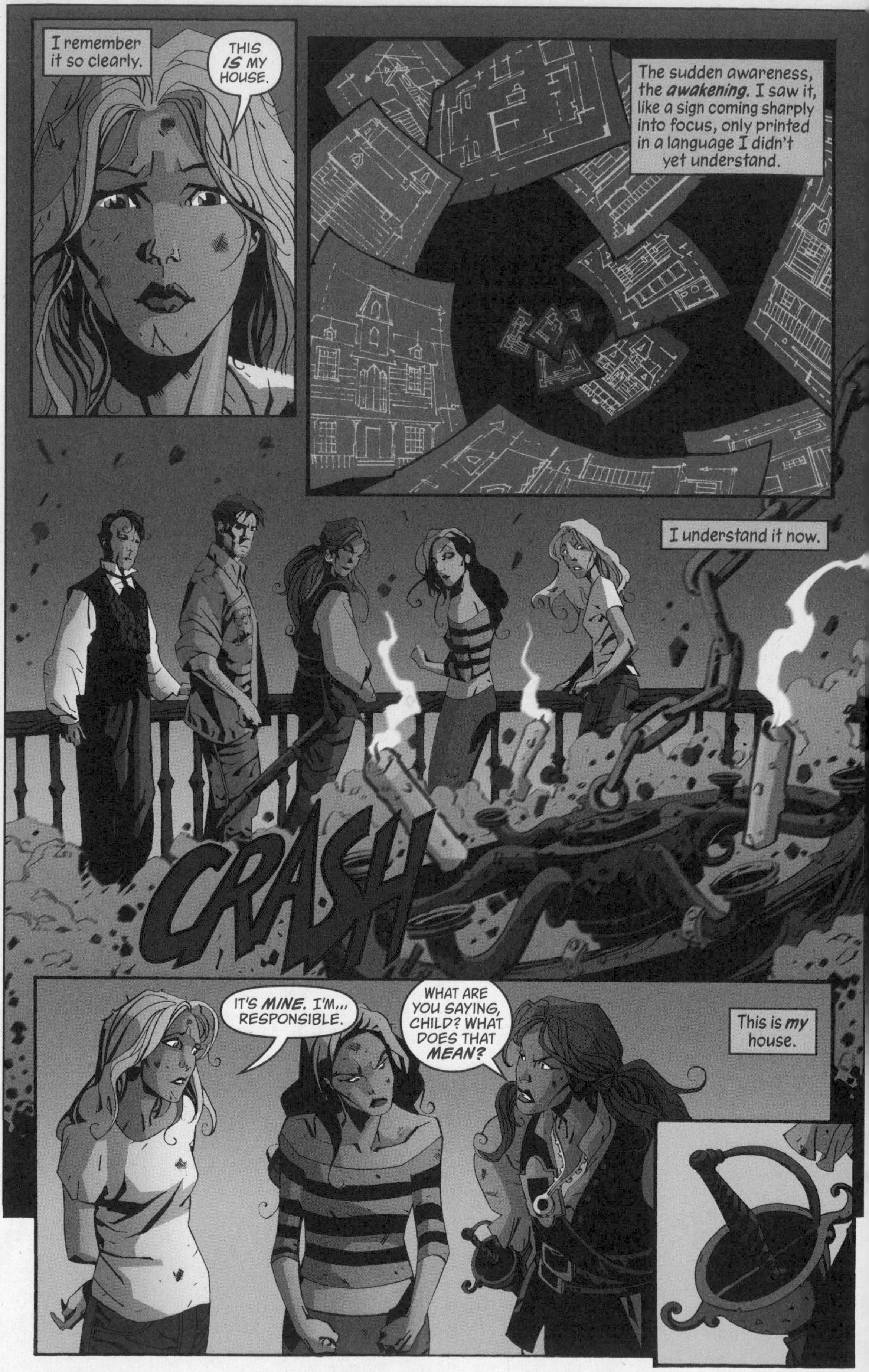
I remember it so clearly.
THIS *IS* MY HOUSE.
The sudden awareness, the *awakening.* I saw it, like a sign coming sharply into focus, only printed in a language I didn't yet understand.
I understand it now.
CRASH
IT'S *MINE.* I'M... RESPONSIBLE.
WHAT ARE YOU SAYING, CHILD? WHAT DOES THAT *MEAN?*
This is *my* house.

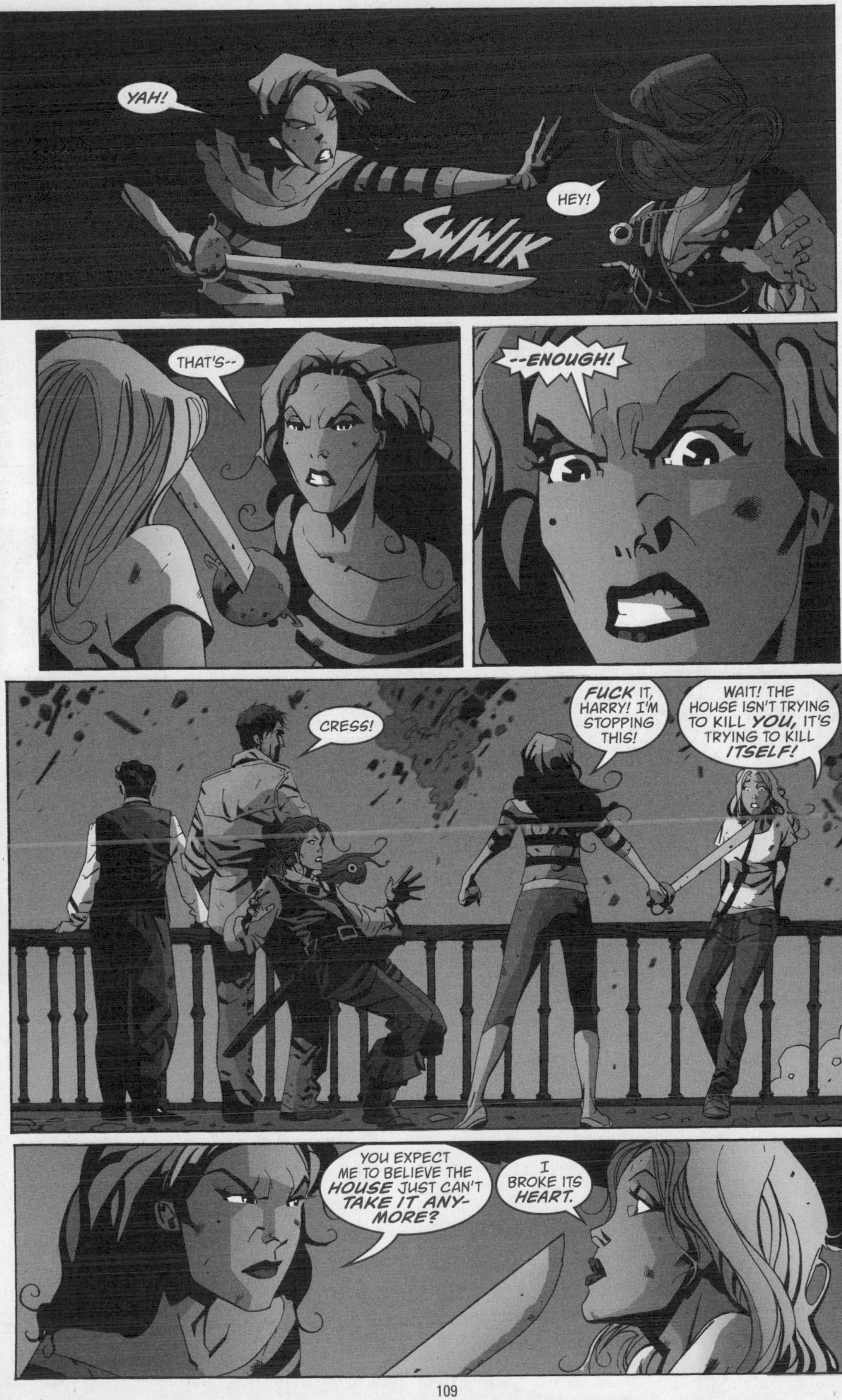
YAH!
HEY!
SWIK
THAT'S--
--ENOUGH!
CRESS!
FUCK IT, HARRY! I'M STOPPING THIS!
WAIT! THE HOUSE ISN'T TRYING TO KILL YOU, IT'S TRYING TO KILL ITSELF!
YOU EXPECT ME TO BELIEVE THE HOUSE JUST CAN'T TAKE IT ANY-MORE?
I BROKE ITS HEART.

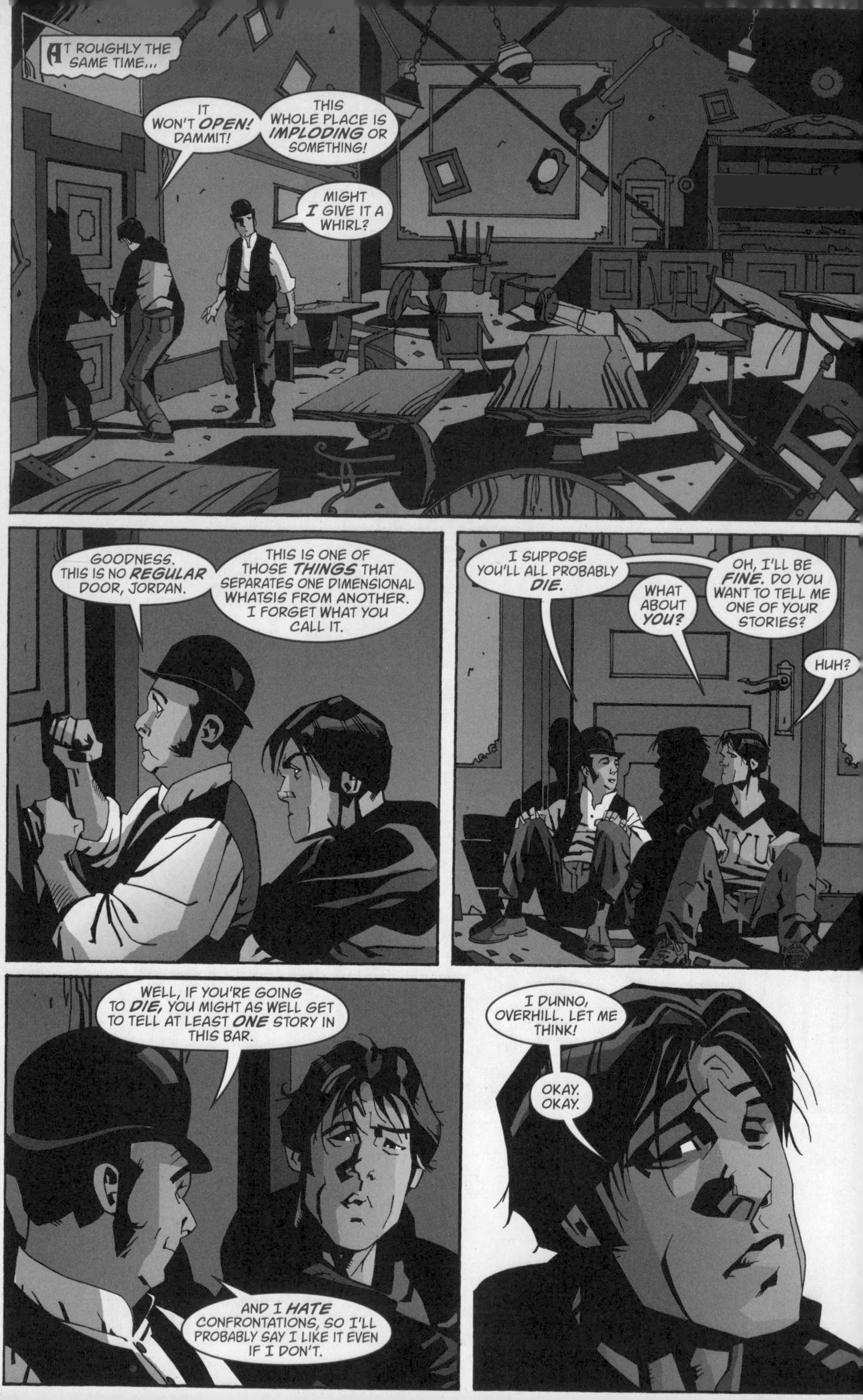
AT ROUGHLY THE SAME TIME...
IT WON'T OPEN! DAMMIT!
THIS WHOLE PLACE IS IMPLODING OR SOMETHING!
MIGHT I GIVE IT A WHIRL?
GOODNESS. THIS IS NO REGULAR DOOR, JORDAN.
THIS IS ONE OF THOSE THINGS THAT SEPARATES ONE DIMENSIONAL WHATSIS FROM ANOTHER. I FORGET WHAT YOU CALL IT.
I SUPPOSE YOU'LL ALL PROBABLY DIE.
WHAT ABOUT YOU?
OH, I'LL BE FINE. DO YOU WANT TO TELL ME ONE OF YOUR STORIES?
HUH?
NYU
WELL, IF YOU'RE GOING TO DIE, YOU MIGHT AS WELL GET TO TELL AT LEAST ONE STORY IN THIS BAR.
AND I HATE CONFRONTATIONS, SO I'LL PROBABLY SAY I LIKE IT EVEN IF I DON'T.
I DUNNO, OVERHILL. LET ME THINK!
OKAY. OKAY.

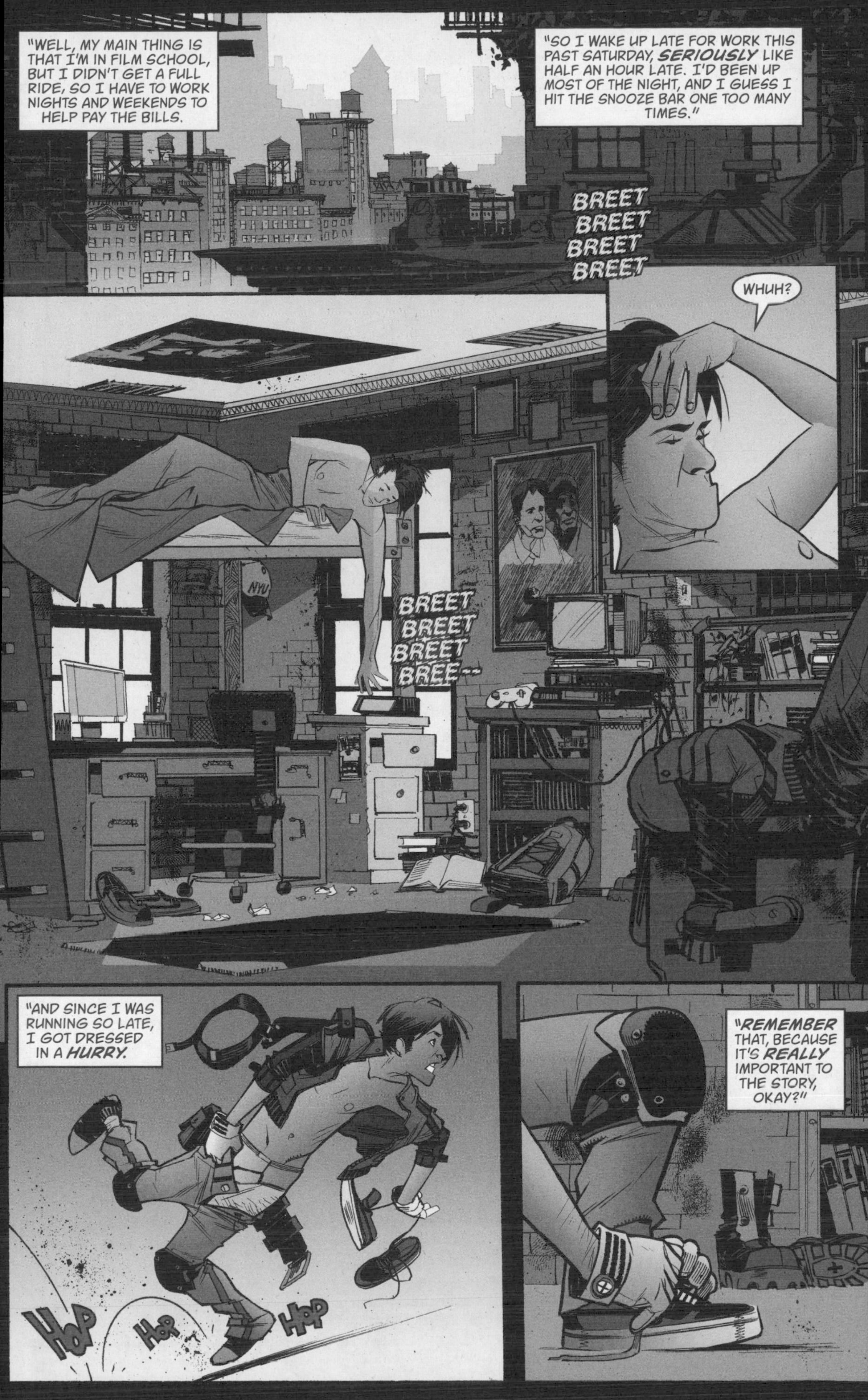
"WELL, MY MAIN THING IS THAT I'M IN FILM SCHOOL, BUT I DIDN'T GET A FULL RIDE, SO I HAVE TO WORK NIGHTS AND WEEKENDS TO HELP PAY THE BILLS.
"SO I WAKE UP LATE FOR WORK THIS PAST SATURDAY, SERIOUSLY LIKE HALF AN HOUR LATE. I'D BEEN UP MOST OF THE NIGHT, AND I GUESS I HIT THE SNOOZE BAR ONE TOO MANY TIMES."
BREET BREET BREET BREET
WHUH?
NYU
BREET BREET BREET BREE--
"AND SINCE I WAS RUNNING SO LATE, I GOT DRESSED IN A HURRY.
HOP HOP HOP
"REMEMBER THAT, BECAUSE IT'S REALLY IMPORTANT TO THE STORY, OKAY?"

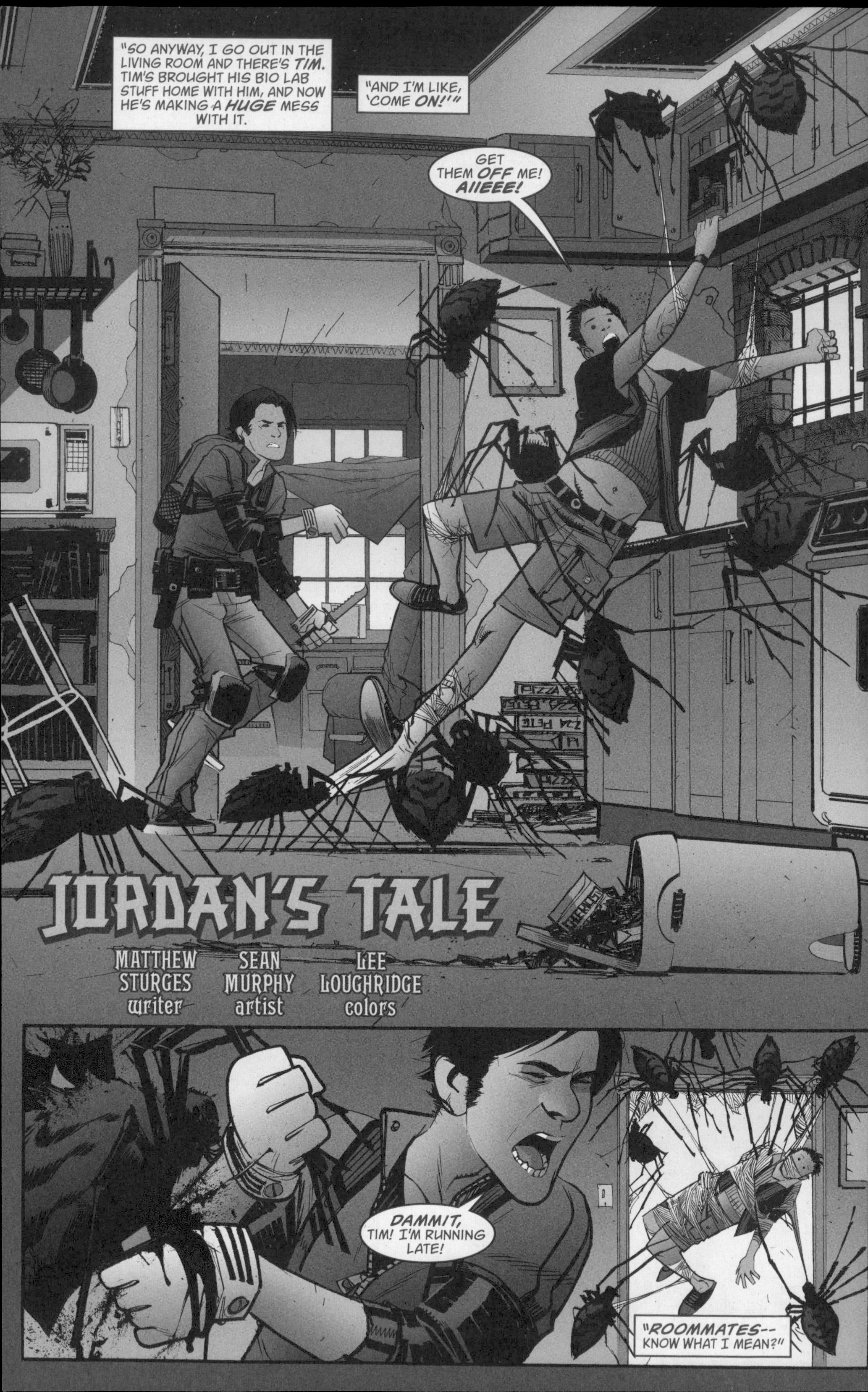
"SO ANYWAY, I GO OUT IN THE LIVING ROOM AND THERE'S TIM. TIM'S BROUGHT HIS BIO LAB STUFF HOME WITH HIM, AND NOW HE'S MAKING A HUGE MESS WITH IT.
"AND I'M LIKE, 'COME ON!'"
GET THEM OFF ME! AIIEEE!
JORDAN'S TALE
MATTHEW STURGES writer
SEAN MURPHY artist
LEE LOUGHRIDGE colors
DAMMIT, TIM! I'M RUNNING LATE!
"ROOMMATES-- KNOW WHAT I MEAN?"

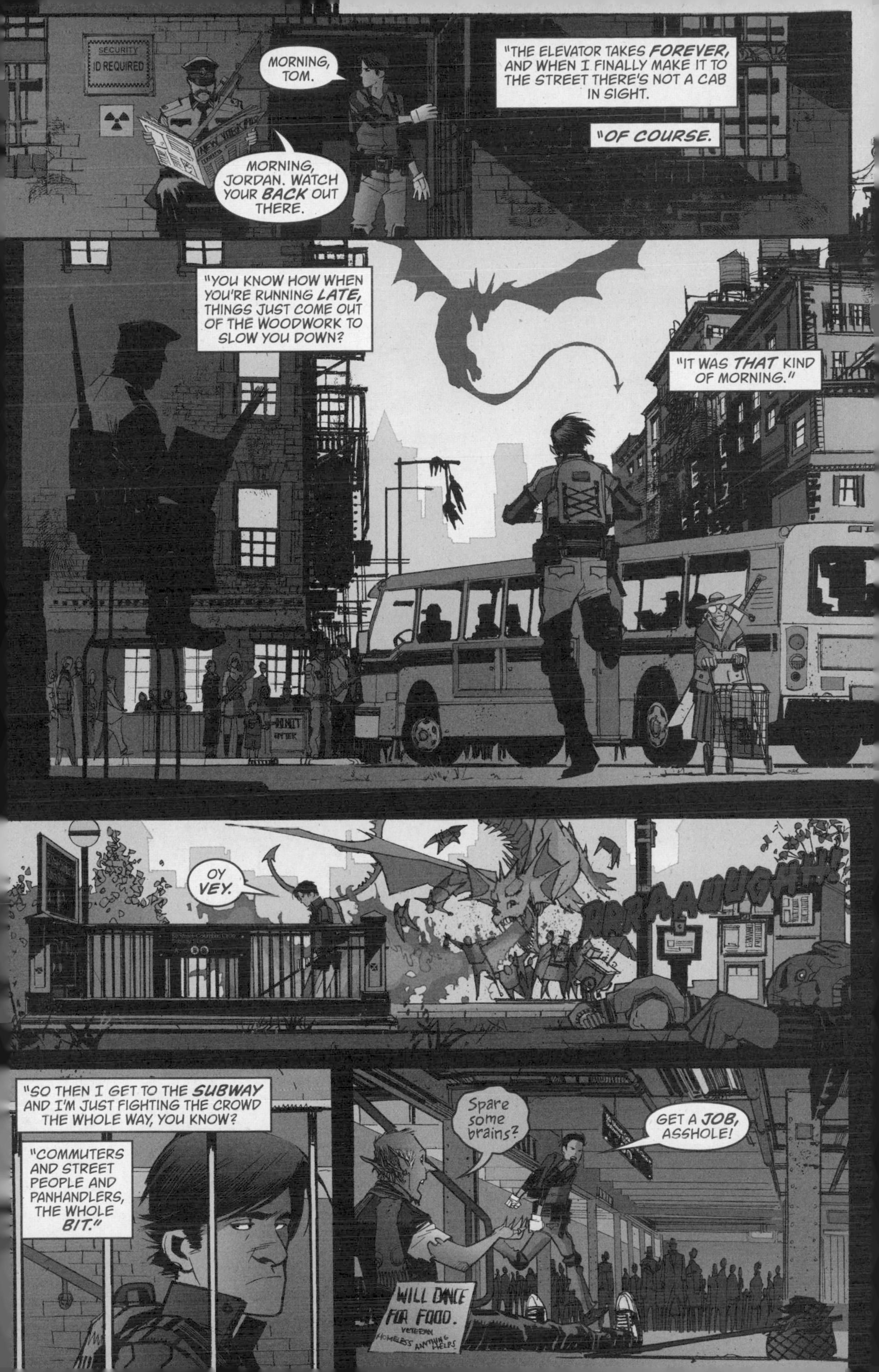

SECURITY
ID REQUIRED
MORNING, TOM.
MORNING, JORDAN. WATCH YOUR BACK OUT THERE.
"THE ELEVATOR TAKES FOREVER, AND WHEN I FINALLY MAKE IT TO THE STREET THERE'S NOT A CAB IN SIGHT.
"OF COURSE.
"YOU KNOW HOW WHEN YOU'RE RUNNING LATE, THINGS JUST COME OUT OF THE WOODWORK TO SLOW YOU DOWN?
"IT WAS THAT KIND OF MORNING."
OY VEY.
RRRAAAUGHH!
"SO THEN I GET TO THE SUBWAY AND I'M JUST FIGHTING THE CROWD THE WHOLE WAY, YOU KNOW?
"COMMUTERS AND STREET PEOPLE AND PANHANDLERS, THE WHOLE BIT."
Spare some brains?
GET A JOB, ASSHOLE!
WILL DANCE FOR FOOD.
VETERAN
HOMELESS ANYTHING HELPS

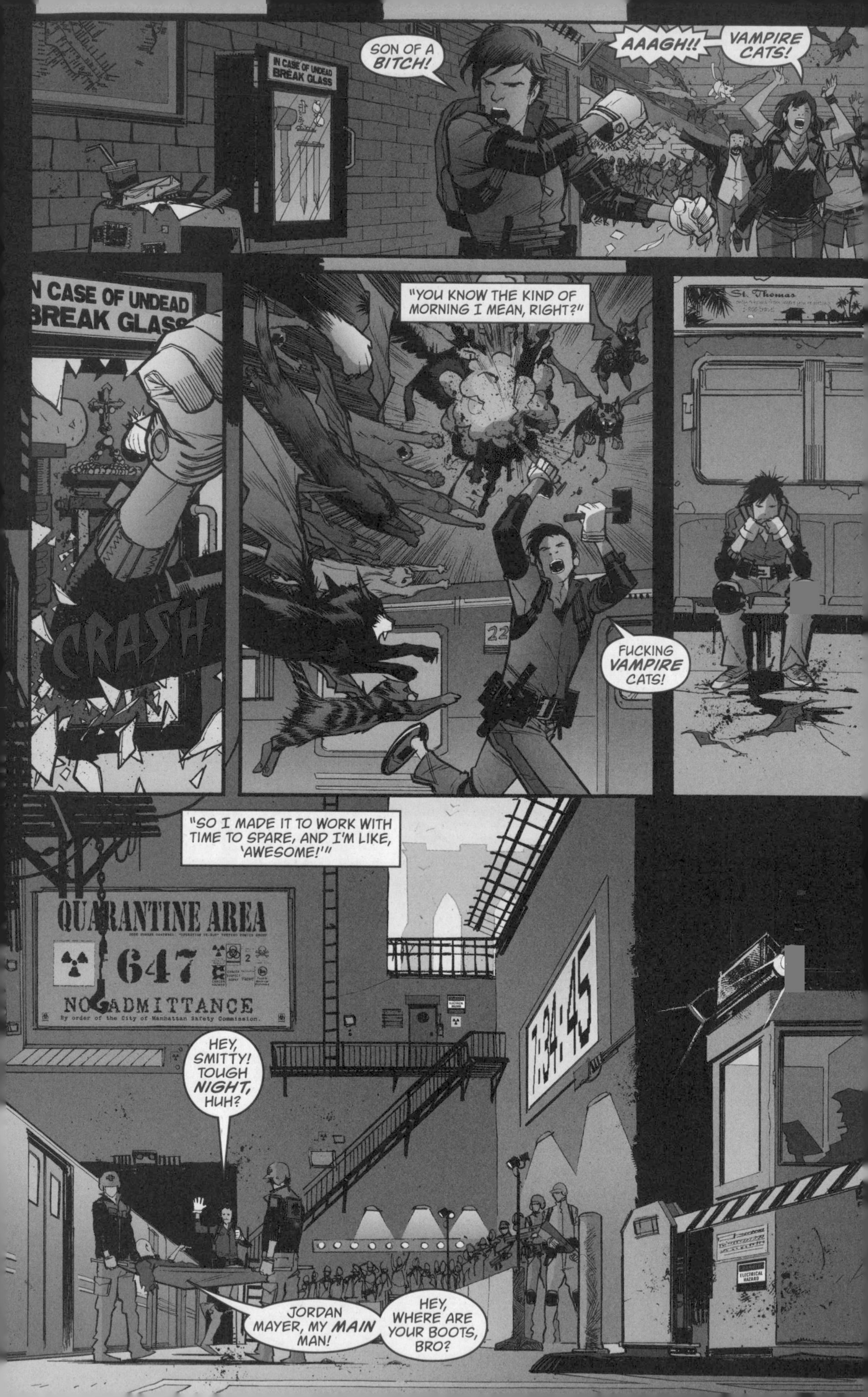

IN CASE OF UNDEAD
BREAK GLASS
SON OF A BITCH!
AAAGH!!
VAMPIRE CATS!
IN CASE OF UNDEAD
BREAK GLASS
CRASH
"YOU KNOW THE KIND OF MORNING I MEAN, RIGHT?"
22
FUCKING VAMPIRE CATS!
St. Thomas
"SO I MADE IT TO WORK WITH TIME TO SPARE, AND I'M LIKE, 'AWESOME!'"
QUARANTINE AREA
647
NO ADMITTANCE
By order of the City of Manhattan Safety Commission.
7:34:45
HEY, SMITTY! TOUGH NIGHT, HUH?
JORDAN MAYER, MY MAIN MAN!
HEY, WHERE ARE YOUR BOOTS, BRO?
ELECTRICAL HAZARD

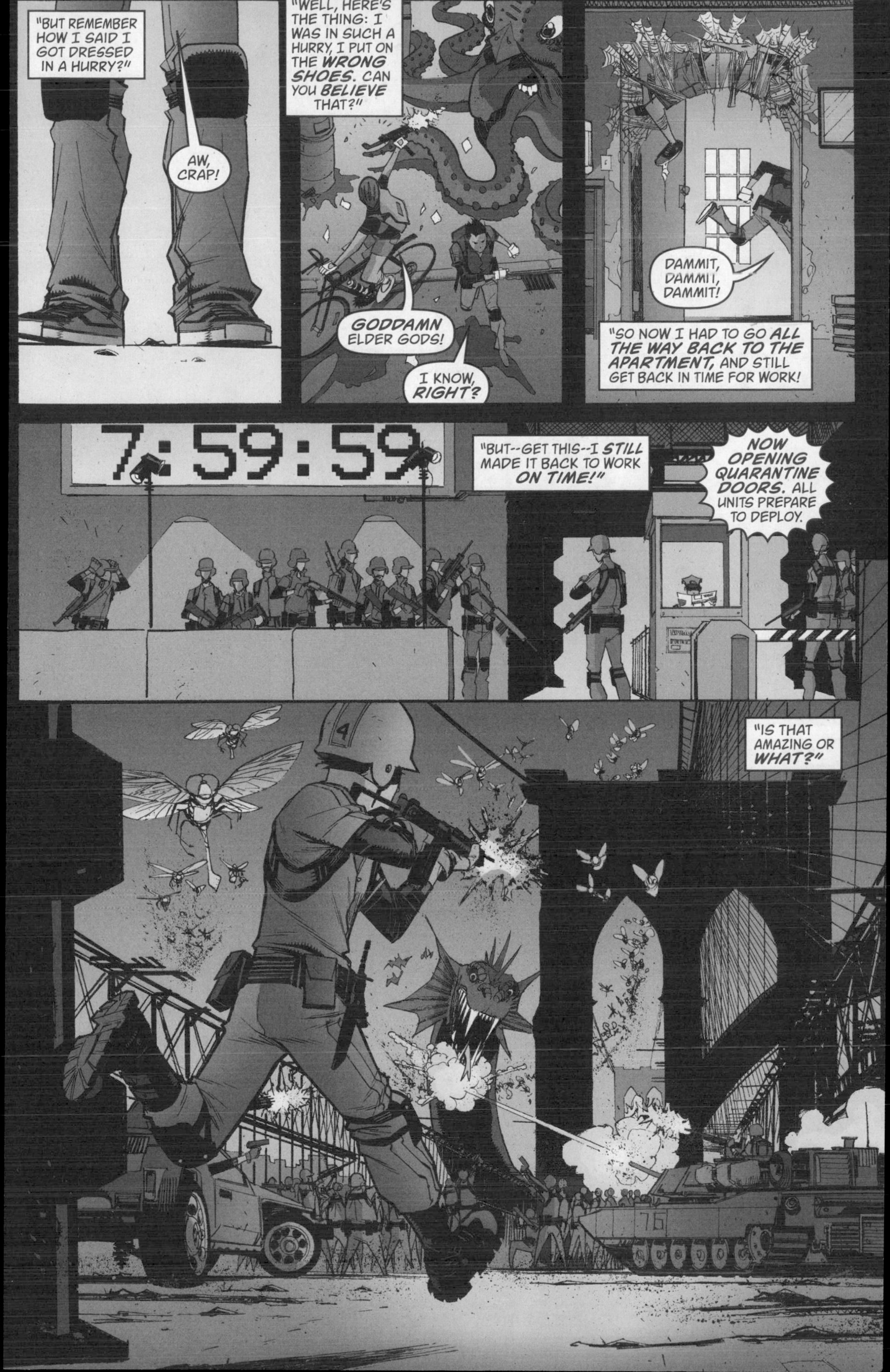
"BUT REMEMBER HOW I SAID I GOT DRESSED IN A HURRY?"
AW, CRAP!
"WELL, HERE'S THE THING: I WAS IN SUCH A HURRY, I PUT ON THE WRONG SHOES. CAN YOU BELIEVE THAT?"
GODDAMN ELDER GODS!
I KNOW, RIGHT?
DAMMIT, DAMMIT, DAMMIT!
"SO NOW I HAD TO GO ALL THE WAY BACK TO THE APARTMENT, AND STILL GET BACK IN TIME FOR WORK!
7:59:59
"BUT--GET THIS--I STILL MADE IT BACK TO WORK ON TIME!"
NOW OPENING QUARANTINE DOORS. ALL UNITS PREPARE TO DEPLOY.
"IS THAT AMAZING OR WHAT?"

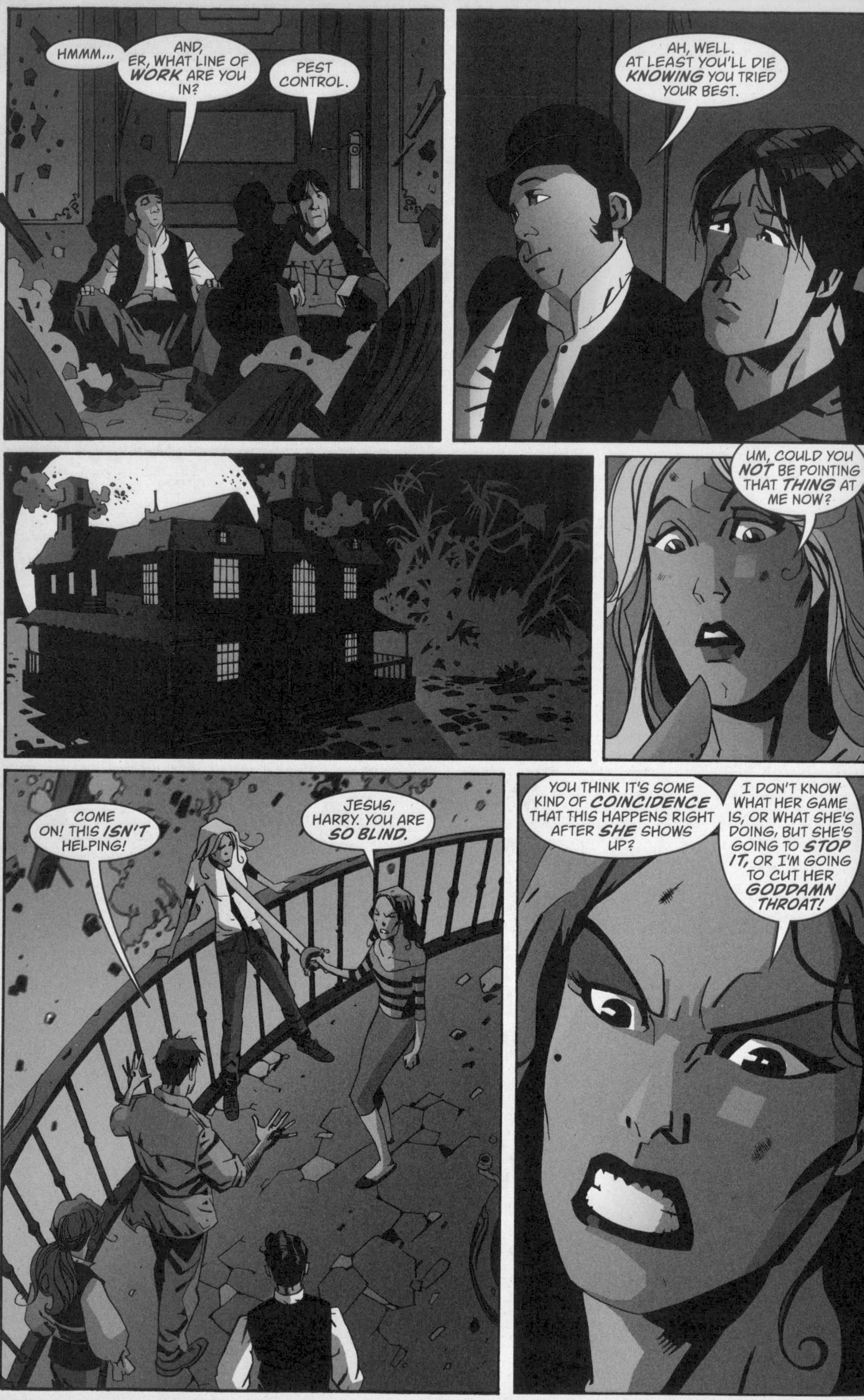
HMMM...
AND, ER, WHAT LINE OF WORK ARE YOU IN?
PEST CONTROL.
AH, WELL. AT LEAST YOU'LL DIE KNOWING YOU TRIED YOUR BEST.
UM, COULD YOU NOT BE POINTING THAT THING AT ME NOW?
COME ON! THIS ISN'T HELPING!
JESUS, HARRY. YOU ARE SO BLIND.
YOU THINK IT'S SOME KIND OF COINCIDENCE THAT THIS HAPPENS RIGHT AFTER SHE SHOWS UP?
I DON'T KNOW WHAT HER GAME IS, OR WHAT SHE'S DOING, BUT SHE'S GOING TO STOP IT, OR I'M GOING TO CUT HER GODDAMN THROAT!

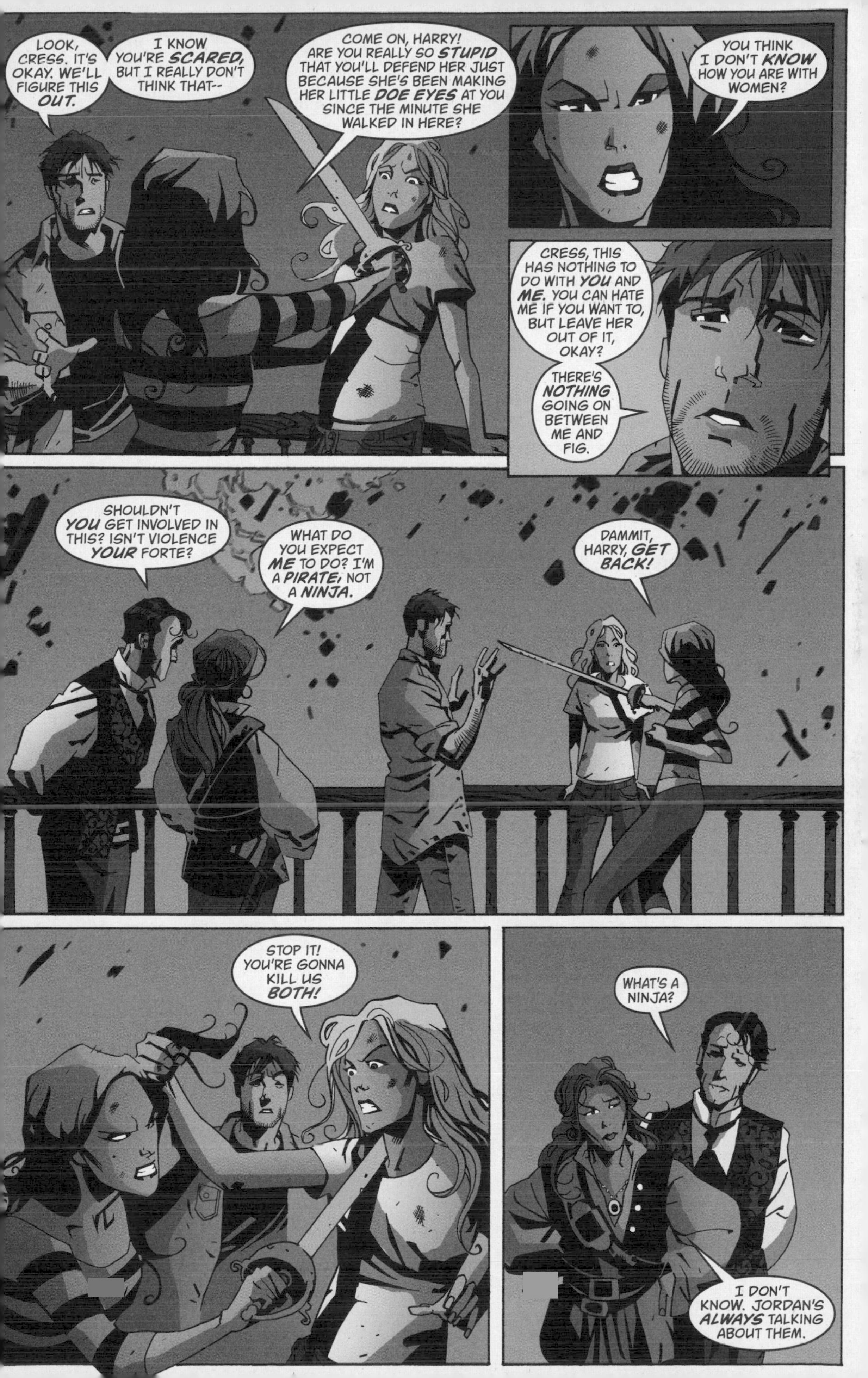
LOOK, CRESS. IT'S OKAY. WE'LL FIGURE THIS OUT.
I KNOW YOU'RE SCARED, BUT I REALLY DON'T THINK THAT--
COME ON, HARRY! ARE YOU REALLY SO STUPID THAT YOU'LL DEFEND HER JUST BECAUSE SHE'S BEEN MAKING HER LITTLE DOE EYES AT YOU SINCE THE MINUTE SHE WALKED IN HERE?
YOU THINK I DON'T KNOW HOW YOU ARE WITH WOMEN?
CRESS, THIS HAS NOTHING TO DO WITH YOU AND ME. YOU CAN HATE ME IF YOU WANT TO, BUT LEAVE HER OUT OF IT, OKAY?
THERE'S NOTHING GOING ON BETWEEN ME AND FIG.
SHOULDN'T YOU GET INVOLVED IN THIS? ISN'T VIOLENCE YOUR FORTE?
WHAT DO YOU EXPECT ME TO DO? I'M A PIRATE, NOT A NINJA.
DAMMIT, HARRY, GET BACK!
STOP IT! YOU'RE GONNA KILL US BOTH!
WHAT'S A NINJA?
I DON'T KNOW. JORDAN'S ALWAYS TALKING ABOUT THEM.

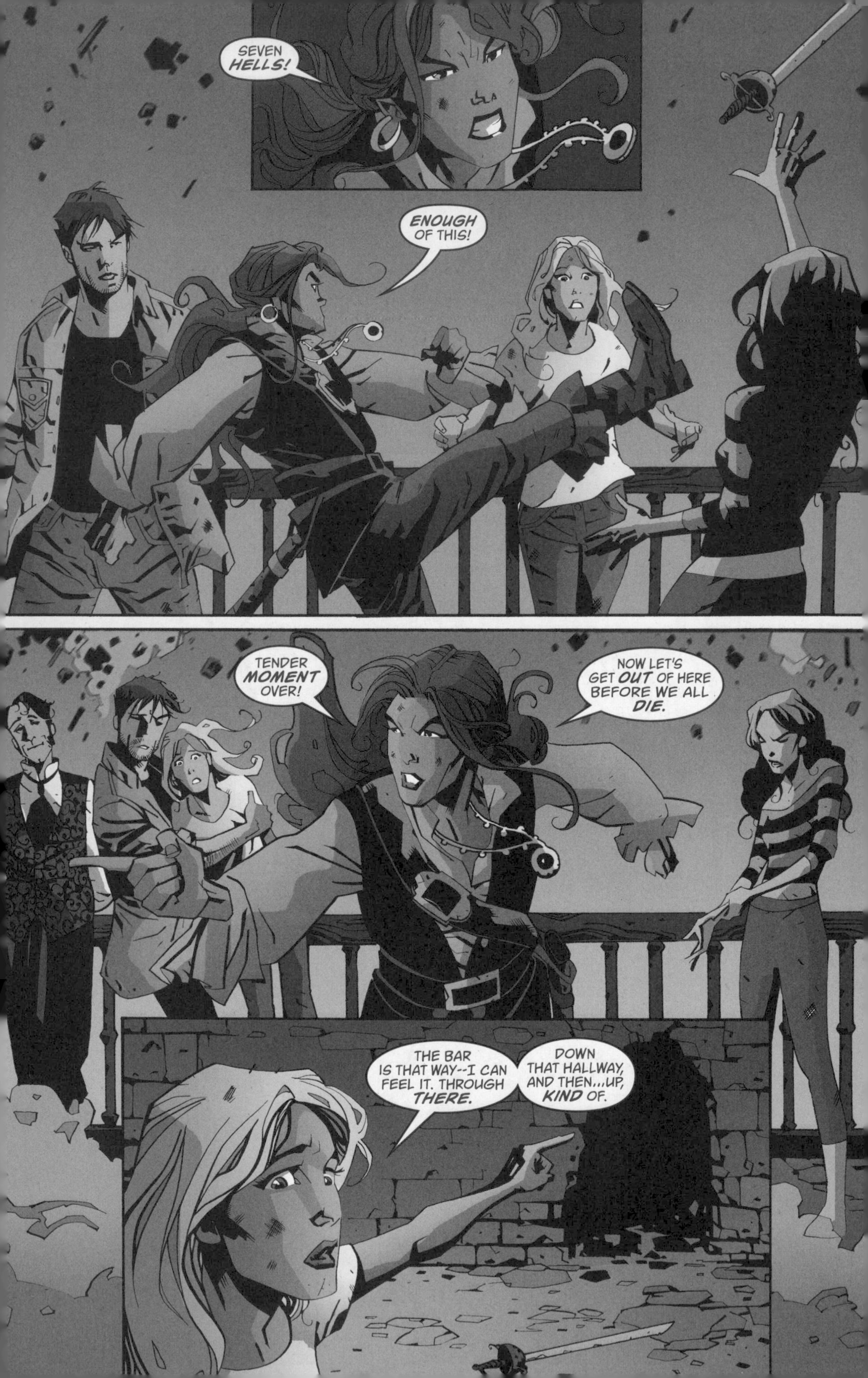
SEVEN HELLS!
ENOUGH OF THIS!
TENDER MOMENT OVER!
NOW LET'S GET OUT OF HERE BEFORE WE ALL DIE.
THE BAR IS THAT WAY--I CAN FEEL IT. THROUGH THERE.
DOWN THAT HALLWAY, AND THEN...UP, KIND OF.

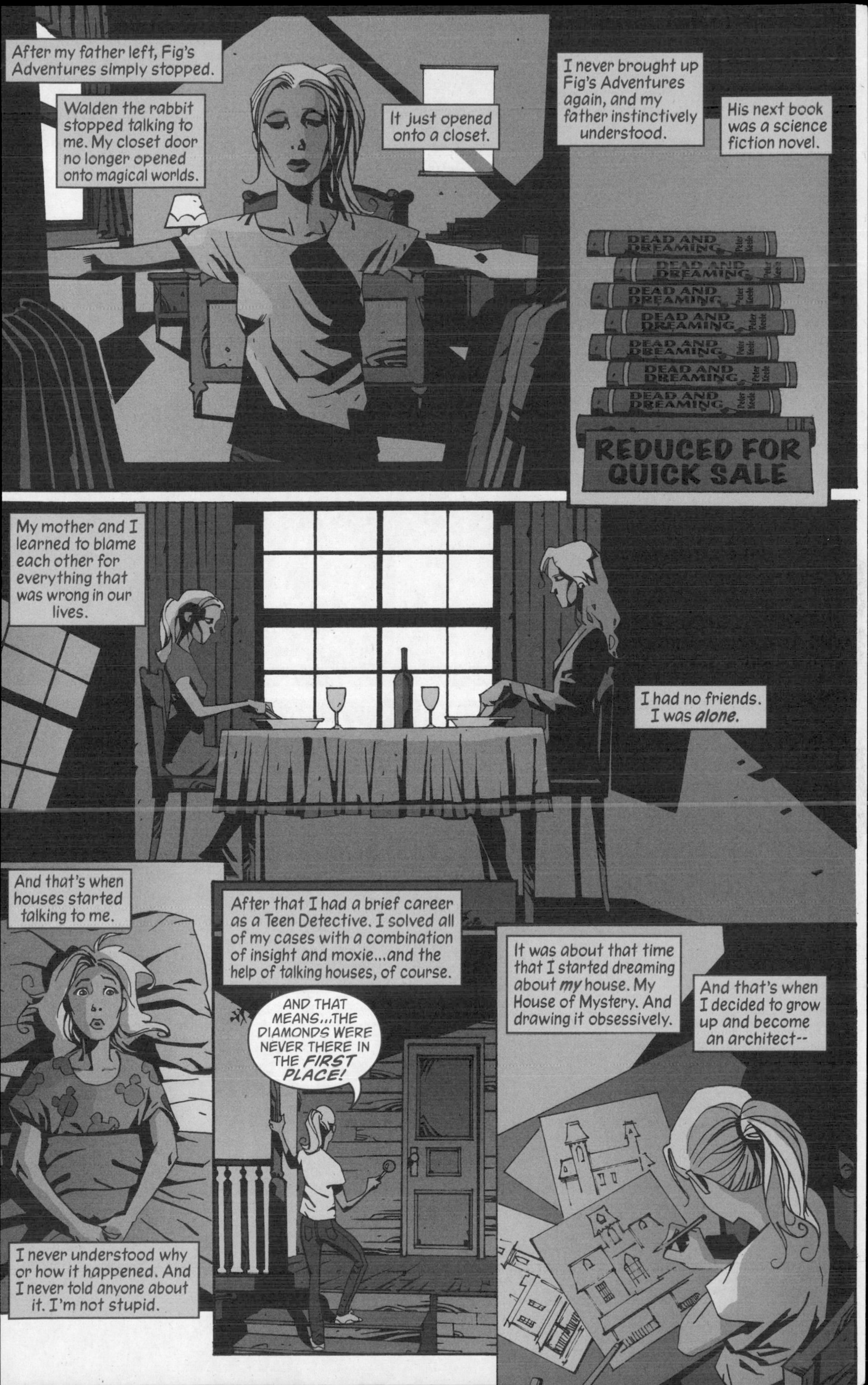
After my father left, Fig's Adventures simply stopped.
Walden the rabbit stopped talking to me. My closet door no longer opened onto magical worlds.
It just opened onto a closet.
I never brought up Fig's Adventures again, and my father instinctively understood.
His next book was a science fiction novel.
DEAD AND DREAMING Peter Keele
REDUCED FOR QUICK SALE
My mother and I learned to blame each other for everything that was wrong in our lives.
I had no friends. I was *alone*.
And that's when houses started talking to me.
I never understood why or how it happened. And I never told anyone about it. I'm not stupid.
After that I had a brief career as a Teen Detective. I solved all of my cases with a combination of insight and moxie...and the help of talking houses, of course.
AND THAT MEANS...THE DIAMONDS WERE NEVER THERE IN THE *FIRST PLACE!*
It was about that time that I started dreaming about *my* house. My House of Mystery. And drawing it obsessively.
And that's when I decided to grow up and become an architect--

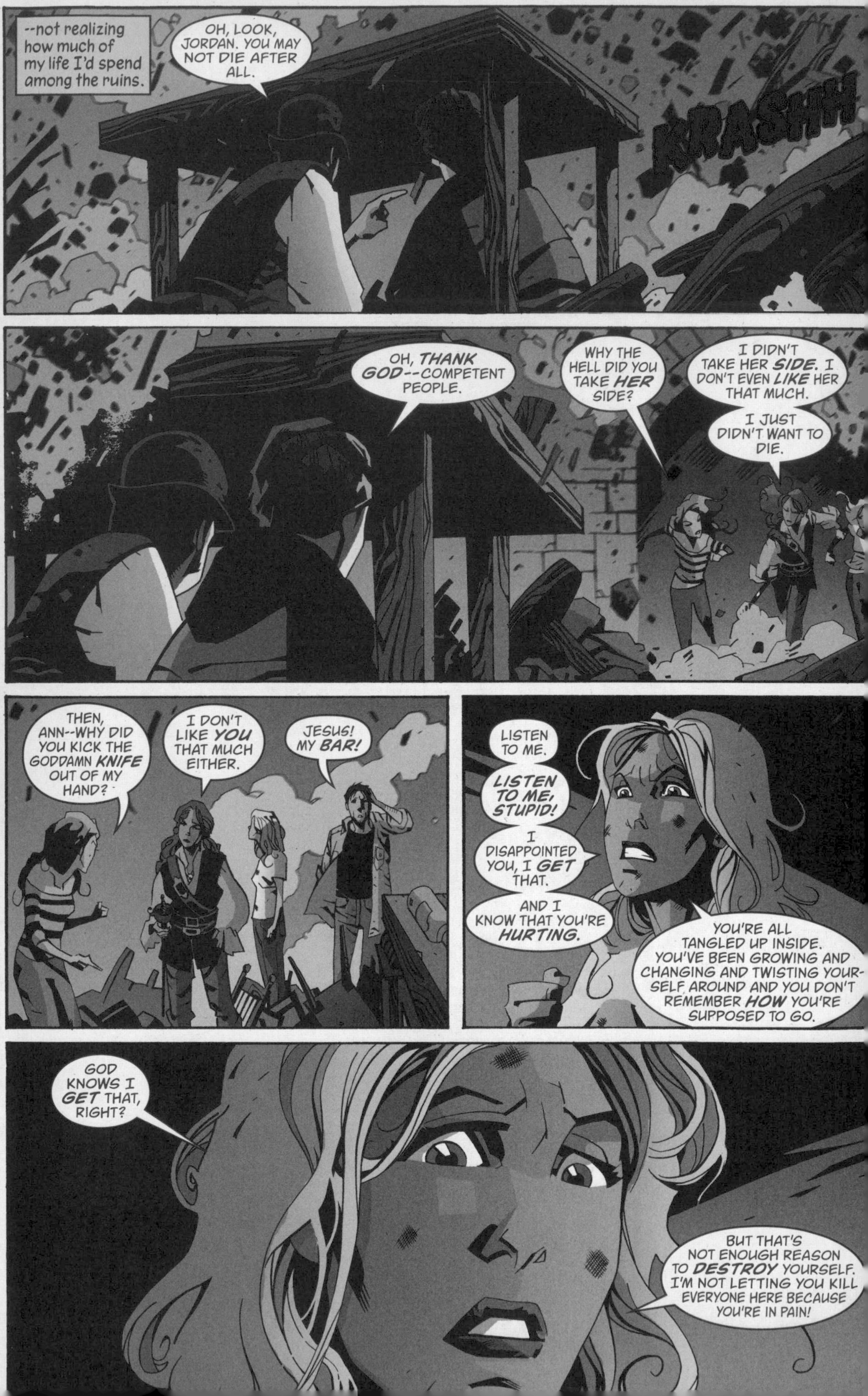
--not realizing how much of my life I'd spend among the ruins.
OH, LOOK, JORDAN. YOU MAY NOT DIE AFTER ALL.
KRASHH
OH, THANK GOD--COMPETENT PEOPLE.
WHY THE HELL DID YOU TAKE HER SIDE?
I DIDN'T TAKE HER SIDE. I DON'T EVEN LIKE HER THAT MUCH.
I JUST DIDN'T WANT TO DIE.
THEN, ANN--WHY DID YOU KICK THE GODDAMN KNIFE OUT OF MY HAND?
I DON'T LIKE YOU THAT MUCH EITHER.
JESUS! MY BAR!
LISTEN TO ME.
LISTEN TO ME, STUPID!
I DISAPPOINTED YOU, I GET THAT.
AND I KNOW THAT YOU'RE HURTING.
YOU'RE ALL TANGLED UP INSIDE. YOU'VE BEEN GROWING AND CHANGING AND TWISTING YOURSELF AROUND AND YOU DON'T REMEMBER HOW YOU'RE SUPPOSED TO GO.
GOD KNOWS I GET THAT, RIGHT?
BUT THAT'S NOT ENOUGH REASON TO DESTROY YOURSELF. I'M NOT LETTING YOU KILL EVERYONE HERE BECAUSE YOU'RE IN PAIN!

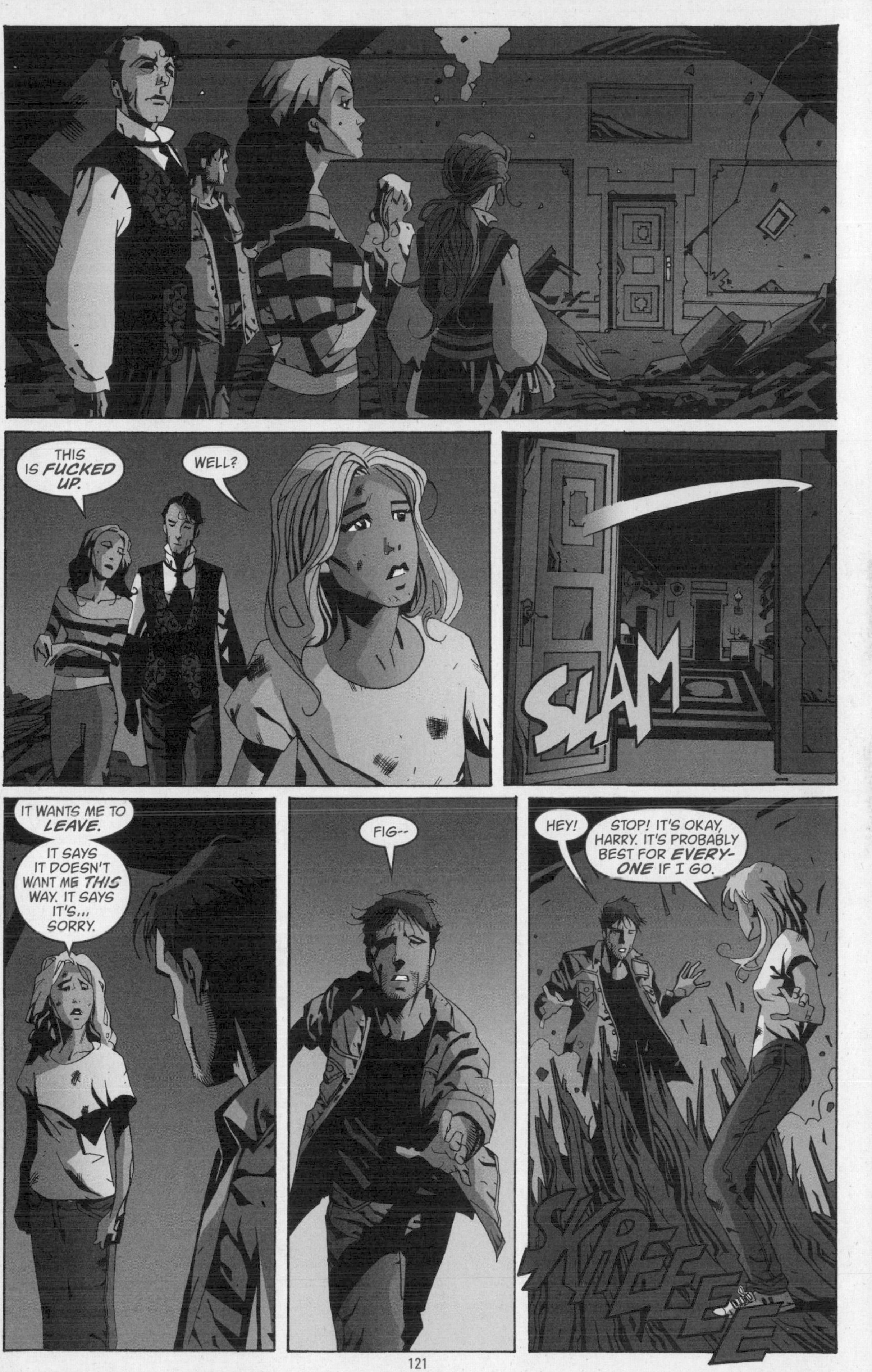
THIS IS **FUCKED UP.**
WELL?
SLAM
IT WANTS ME TO **LEAVE.**
IT SAYS IT DOESN'T WANT ME **THIS** WAY. IT SAYS IT'S... SORRY.
FIG--
HEY!
STOP! IT'S OKAY, HARRY. IT'S PROBABLY BEST FOR **EVERY-ONE** IF I GO.

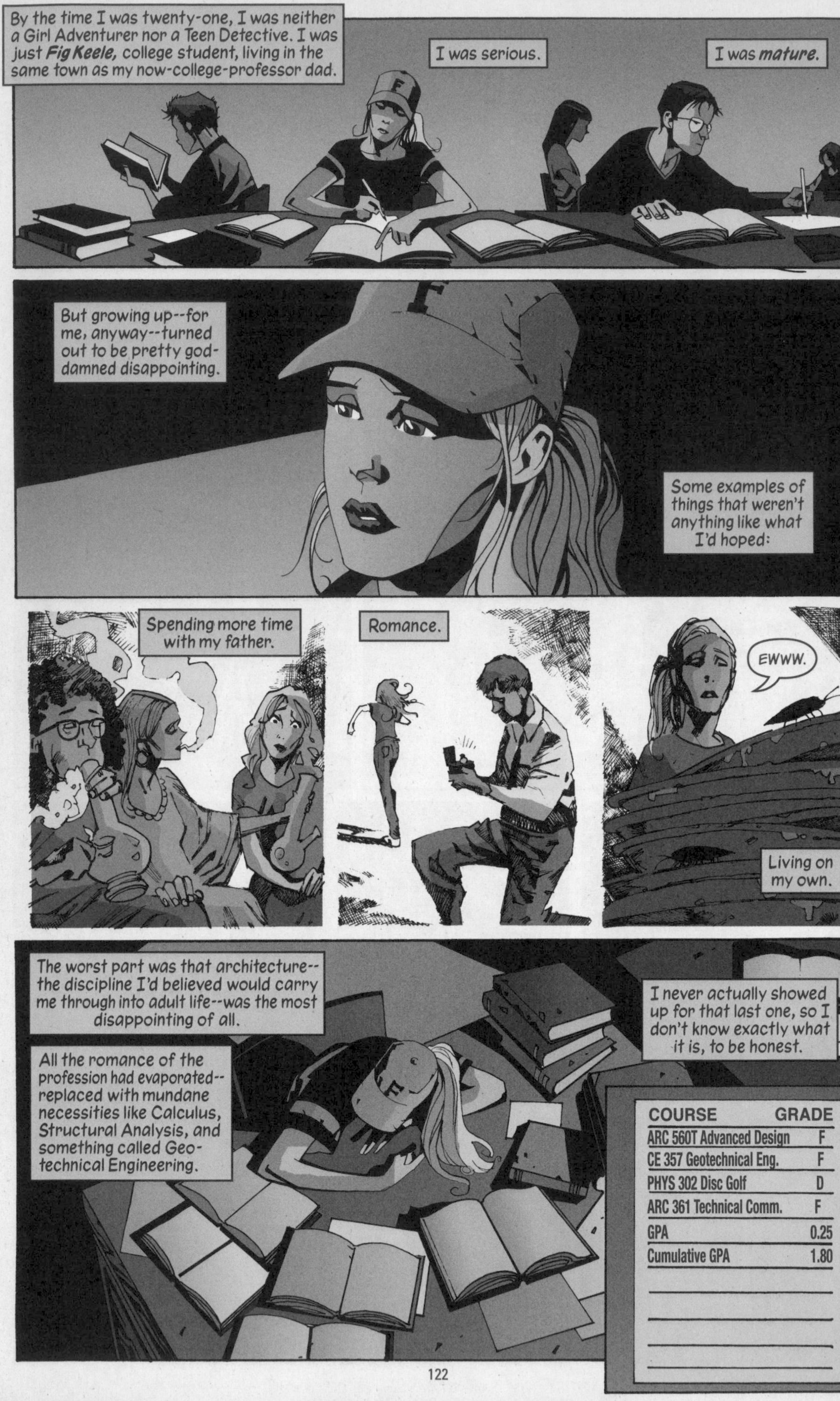
By the time I was twenty-one, I was neither a Girl Adventurer nor a Teen Detective. I was just **Fig Keele,** college student, living in the same town as my now-college-professor dad.
I was serious.
I was *mature.*
But growing up--for me, anyway--turned out to be pretty god-damned disappointing.
Some examples of things that weren't anything like what I'd hoped:
Spending more time with my father.
Romance.
EWWW.
Living on my own.
The worst part was that architecture--the discipline I'd believed would carry me through into adult life--was the most disappointing of all.
All the romance of the profession had evaporated--replaced with mundane necessities like Calculus, Structural Analysis, and something called Geo-technical Engineering.
I never actually showed up for that last one, so I don't know exactly what it is, to be honest.
COURSE GRADE
ARC 560T Advanced Design F
CE 357 Geotechnical Eng. F
PHYS 302 Disc Golf D
ARC 361 Technical Comm. F
GPA 0.25
Cumulative GPA 1.80

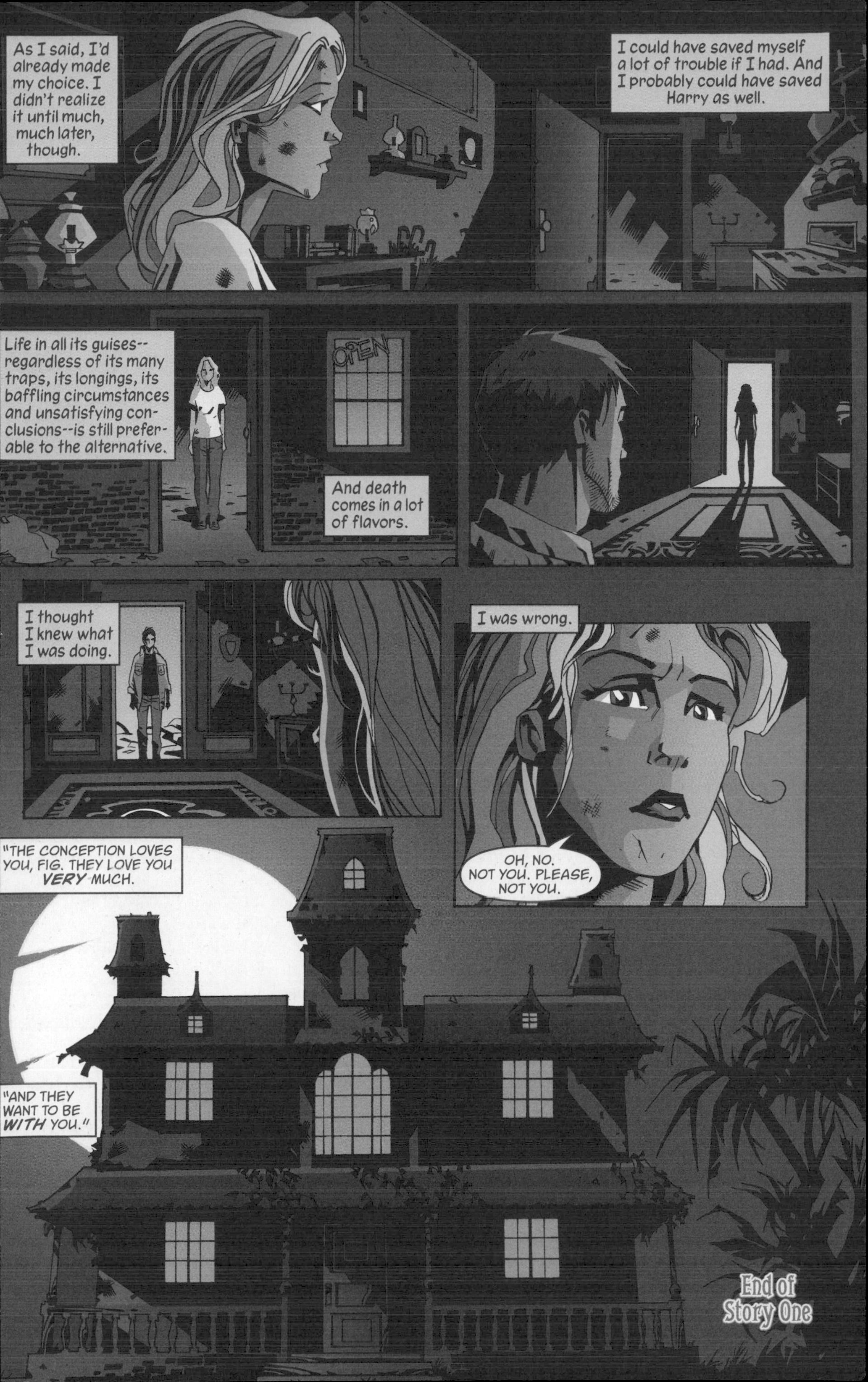
As I said, I'd already made my choice. I didn't realize it until much, much later, though.
I could have saved myself a lot of trouble if I had. And I probably could have saved Harry as well.
Life in all its guises--regardless of its many traps, its longings, its baffling circumstances and unsatisfying conclusions--is still preferable to the alternative.
OPEN
And death comes in a lot of flavors.
I thought I knew what I was doing.
I was wrong.
OH, NO. NOT YOU. PLEASE, NOT YOU.
"THE CONCEPTION LOVES YOU, FIG. THEY LOVE YOU VERY MUCH.
"AND THEY WANT TO BE WITH YOU."
End of Story One

SKIN OF SCALES, HEART OF FLAME

A Tale from the House of Mystery by Matthew Sturges

I tread carefully down the hallway on unfamiliar legs and into the bar where a thousand scents assault me. She is there, waiting, and I feel my skin flush. Her permanent scowl: what tender smiles lie beneath it, waiting to be teased out by a lover's grace?

Ann Preston. Pirate Queen. My secret love.

Does she even know my name? Not my true name, certainly, but the one I use here. Does she know it?

I took a human shape out of mere curiosity. A knight came to slay me, as they sometimes do. After I took his sword arm out of its socket, I said that I might free him if he relieved my boredom with a good story. He had a smashing one, he said; he'd heard it at a secret place, a tavern where stories act as currency.

And it *was* a good story, at that. But I ate the flesh from his bones anyway.

I was not looking for love when I stole his form. Had I been I would certainly have been more selective. So when I first came to the House of Mystery, it was in a rather plain visage. I listened to a few stories and drank a sampling of bubbling brews. Charming, yes, but nothing I hadn't seen before. I shrugged and stood to leave.

And then I saw her.

As my eyes swelled with the sight of Ann Preston, I became suddenly aware of my newfound humanness. I felt my soft skin prickle. Heat (of a kind with which I was wholly unfamiliar) raced up my neck, my ears and cheeks. With horror, I realized that human flesh is inseparable from human desire. All my life until that moment, the only things I'd piquantly desired were pure blood and a glittering hoard. But these things were now ash compared to the tender grace of Ann Preston as she bludgeoned a misbehaving patron into submission with her elegant fists.

Now, years later, I sit at the bar with a studied nonchalance. Trying not to look too hard or too long at her.

"Evening," says Harry, the bartender. He has kind eyes and a strong face. He is inescapably handsome. Had it been his visage I'd stolen, perhaps I would have found the nerve to speak to Ann long before now.

He follows my gaze. "Can I offer you some advice, friend?" he says kindly. I nod uncomfortably, feeling that I will not appreciate his advice.

"I don't think she's the one for you," he says, a look of — my God, is it *pity*? — peeking from his eyes. "Ann *is* beautiful, and she's a good person, but..." He pauses, looking for the word that will not offend. "She's... hard. Do you get what I mean?"

I can feel my human blood boiling. I could tell Harry the truth. I could tell him that my scales are harder than any diamond, that my teeth can saw through steel, that with a single breath I could reduce his entire bar to a smoking charnel house. But I do not say these things for fear of being banned. If I were never to see her again, how long before I went mad?

"I understand," I mumble, looking down into my beer. I look up at him and I say with no artifice, "But a man can dream, can't he?"

For the briefest instant, Harry recoils, seeing something in my eyes that he does not like. Let us be honest — he sees something that *terrifies* him. He sees through these soft, moist human eyes into the soul behind and he shudders.

I don't think he understands what he's seen. The moment ends and he regains his composure admirably.

"Seriously," says Harry. "You seem like a nice guy. A girl like Ann would eat you alive."

He reaches over the bar and pats me on the shoulder, sliding another beer in front of me. "On the house," he says.

Perhaps someday this charade will become too much for me. Perhaps I will summon every shred of magic in my fiery being and take Ann by force, tearing her by sheer will from the confines of this place. I will bring her back to my den and I will make her love me. I will pull her skin against my glowing scales and she will fear me, at least. I could do it. If I had to, I could.

Perhaps someday, but not today. I finish my drink, wave to Harry, and head for the exit. When I reach the door, she is standing there, so close! My heart leaps in my chest — if I reached out my hand I could touch her, tangle my fingers in her hair.

"Good night, Ann," I say, tipping my hat. She glares at me, glares *past* me, and grunts. The sound, surely, of angels in their heavenly bowers.

Then she looks away abruptly and I can sense that I am gone from her thoughts in an instant.

Perhaps someday. But not today, my love.

Discuss HOUSE OF MYSTERY online at the official site of Matthew Sturges and Bill Willingham: www.clockworkstorybook.net

FIG

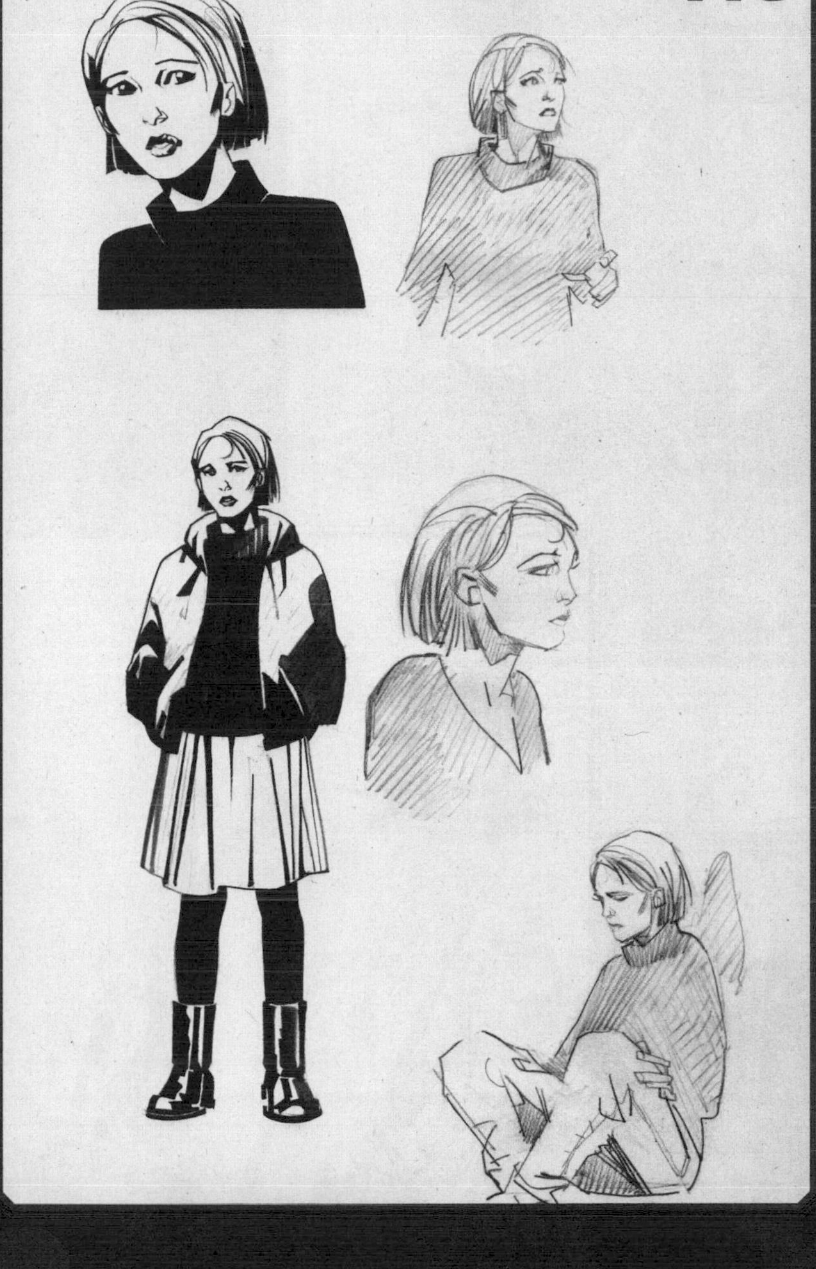

BUILDING THE HOUSE OF MYSTERY

Character Designs by Luca Rossi

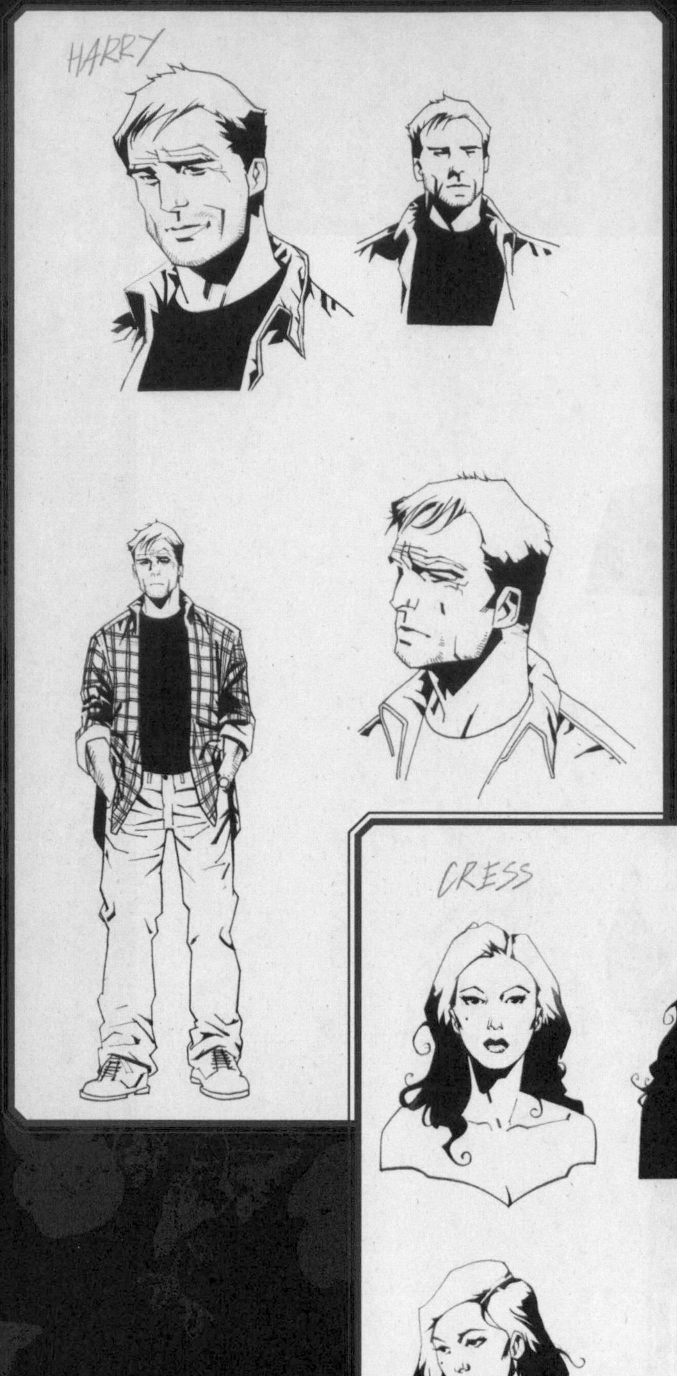
HARRY

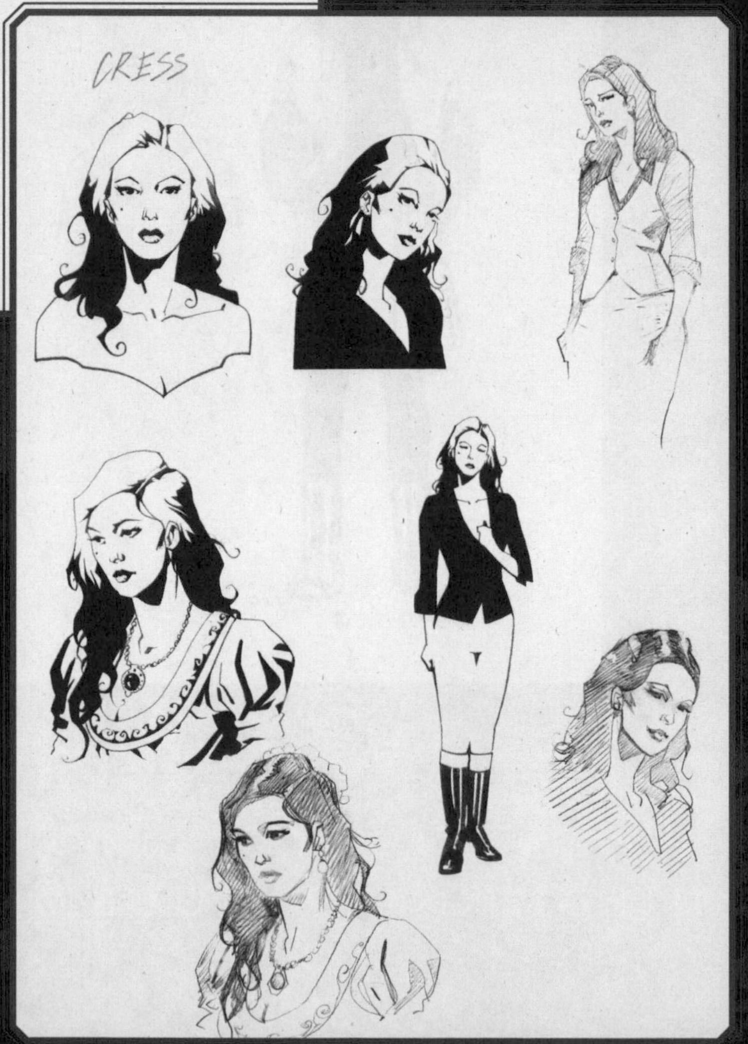
CRESS